PERSPECTIVES ON COMPUTER SCIENCE

PERSPECTIVES
ON COMPUTER SCIENCE

From the 10th Anniversary Symposium
at the Computer Science Department,
Carnegie-Mellon University

Edited by

ANITA K. JONES

Department of Computer Science
Carnegie-Mellon University
Schenley Park
Pittsburgh, Pennsylvania

ACADEMIC PRESS   New York   San Francisco   London   1977

A Subsidiary of Harcourt Brace Jovanovich, Publishers

ACADEMIC PRESS, INC.
111 Fifth Avenue, New York, New York 10003

United Kingdom Edition published by
ACADEMIC PRESS, INC. (LONDON) LTD.
24/28 Oval Road, London NW1

Library of Congress Cataloging in Publication Data

Main entry under title:

Perspectives on computer science.

(ACM monograph series)
Held Oct. 6–8, 1975.
Includes bibliographies.
1.   Electronic data processing—Congresses.
2.   Electronic digital computers—Programming—
Congress.   3.   Programming languages (Electronic
computers)—Congresses.   I.   Jones, Anita K.
II.   Carnegie-Mellon University.   Computer Science
Dept.   III.   Series: Association for Computing
Machinery.   ACM monograph series.
QA75.5.P47   001.6'4   77-8319
ISBN 0–12–389450–6

Contents

Some Thoughts on the Next Generation
of Programming Languages

WILLIAM A. WULF

List of Contributors

Numbers in parentheses indicate the pages on which the authors' contributions begin.

C. GORDON BELL (7), Digital Equipment Corporation, Maynard, Massachusetts and Department of Computer Science, Carnegie-Mellon University, Pittsburgh, Pennsylvania

HANS BERLINER (39), Department of Computer Science, Carnegie-Mellon University, Pittsburgh, Pennsylvania

RICHARD E. FIKES* (63), Artificial Intelligence Center, Stanford Research Institute, Menlo Park, California

A. N. HABERMANN (77), Department of Computer Science, Carnegie-Mellon University, Pittsburgh, Pennsylvania

RENATO ITURRIAGA (91), Coordinor General del Sistema Nacional de Informacion, Palacio Nacional, Mexico City, Mexico

ZOHAR MANNA† (103), Applied Mathematics Department, The Weizmann Institute of Science, Rehovot, Israel

ALBERT R. MEYER (125), Laboratory for Computer Science, Massachusetts Institute of Technology, Cambridge, Massachusetts

ALLEN NEWELL (147, 183), Computer Science Department, Carnegie-Mellon University, Pittsburgh, Pennsylvania

ALAN PERLIS (1), Deparement of Computer Science, Yale University, New Haven, Connecticut

R. REDDY (183), Department of Computer Science, Carnegie-Mellon University, Pittsburgh, Pennsylvania

GEORGE ROBERTSON (147), Computer Science Department, Carnegie-Mellon University, Pittsburgh, Pennsylvania

ADI SHAMIR‡ (103), Applied Mathematics Department, The Weizmann Institute of Science, Rehovot, Israel

MICHAEL IAN SHAMOS (125), Department of Computer Science, Carnegie-Mellon University, Pittsburgh, Pennsylvania

*Present address: Xerox Corporation, Palo Alto Research Center, Palo Alto, California
†Present address: Artificial Intelligence Laboratory, Stanford University, Stanford, California.
‡ Present address: Computer Science Department, University of Warwick, Coventry, England.

HERBERT A. SIMON (199), Departments of Computer Science and Psychology, Carnegie-Mellon University, Pittsburgh, Pennsylvania

WILLIAM A. WULF (217), Department of Computer Science, Carnegie-Mellon University, Pittsburgh, Pennsylvania

Preface

This volume is a record of the Carnegie-Mellon University computer science department's 10th Anniversary Symposium, held October 6–8, 1975 in Pittsburgh, Pennsylvania. The symposium was a celebration of the 10 years of research and education of the computer science department. Founded in the summer of 1965, it was a natural outgrowth of an interdisciplinary systems and communication sciences program. Throughout its life the department has had a major commitment to research. So it seemed appropriate that any celebration of its 10th anniversary should be a vehicle for continuing to do science, a medium through which researchers could communicate their current concerns and ideas.

We wished to have the symposium at the site of the department, but physical facilities limited the number of people we could accommodate. So we decided to invite all those who have been members of the department "family" to participate. This included students, faculty members, research associates, relatively long-term visitors (i.e., here at CMU for a month or more), and some friends and benefactors of the department.

The technical program consisted of invited papers, panel discussions, contributed talks, and demonstrations of some ongoing research at CMU. It is mainly the invited papers that are reproduced here, although we have tried to chronicle the flavor of the whole symposium by listing the demonstrations and contributed talks and including excerpts from the panel discussions.

One of the invited talks is the "riverboat speech" delivered at the symposium banquet held aboard the riverboat, the Gateway Clipper Showboat, while it plied the waters around Pittsburgh. The speaker was Alan Perlis, the first head of the computer science department.

The symposium focused on diverse topics, and is a reflection of the interests that have remained strong at CMU during the past 10 and more years. Many of the papers provide perspectives. Gordon Bell looks back on the experiences of the design and production of the PDP-11 family of machines. Raj Reddy and Allen Newell look ahead, seeking multiplicative speedup in programs performing AI tasks; Bill Wulf considers the next generation of programming languages. The symposium also provided an opportunity to analyze our own day-to-day experience and inquire after the methods of doing computer science research here at CMU. In particular, Allen Newell's paper and the related "little engines" panel provided a forum for discussing the experiences of a number of research groups that have had different interests and goals, but that cooperate and interact as they share the use of the C.mmp hardware.

We used this volume itself as an excuse to further develop our department's facilities for document production. With only two exceptions, the papers in this book were delivered to us in digitized form. A set of existing document formatting programs was augmented and new ones developed, mainly by Brian Reid, so that we could build the command string to drive a photocomposing system to "typeset" text. That is how this volume was produced. The troubles attendant on automating a portion of the book production process has made the symposium volume disappointingly late in being published. Now, of course, we know how to produce such a book right!

In a lighter vein the symposium was an excuse to sponsor a contest to find a department logo that would graphically represent our interests and activities. The winning logo, designed by Peter Hibbard, appears on the dust jacket of this volume (as well as on scores of T-shirts, following a well-established local custom). In the *Science* article which Alan Perlis mentions in his riverboat speech, computer science is described as the study of the phenomena surrounding computers. Perhaps the logo bears this attitude out. One of the few things we all have in common is the computing engine. Our logo has a one-core memory, threaded on the read, write, and sense wires, and surrounded on four sides by the initials "CMU".

This record of the symposium is a commemorative volume as well as a scientific source. It conveys the directions and the flavor of the department's collective research interests. It reflects our basically pragmatic goal-oriented bias and our bent toward system development as a vehicle to do science. But mainly it is a product of and a testimonial to those who find "fun" in computer science.

I would like to thank the many members of the department who contributed to the success of the symposium in one way or another, particularly George Robertson and Guy Almes. My grateful thanks also to Brian Reid and to David Jefferson, who contributed greatly to the production of this book. The Academic Press production staff were ever patient and helpful, especially with the confusing foibles of computerland.

Foreword

EDUCATION AND RESEARCH AT CMU

When did computer science start at CMU?

Was it in 1956 when Herb Simon told his class in the Graduate School of Industrial Administration that over the Christmas holidays he and Allen Newell had invented a thinking machine? That was the very same year Alan Perlis arrived to start a computing center. Or was it in 1961 when Newell, Perlis, and Simon, along with Abe Lavi of EE and Bert Green and Lee Gregg of Psychology, started an interdisciplinary graduate program in Systems and Communication Sciences? Perhaps it was in 1965 with the founding of the Computer Science Department. That is certainly the founding date we used in computing our 10th anniversary. The precise date is not important, except for purposes of celebration. What does matter is that from the beginning a serious and continuing commitment was made here to excellence in computer science.

In some ways today's department is very different from the department in 1965. With several very significant exceptions the faculty is new. Yet the tradition of leadership in computer science teaching and research continues. I could cite statistics: publications, honors, research contracts, indicators of student quality, and positions held by our graduates. But these can be found in our annual Computer Science Research Review. Here I prefer to list some of the unique aspects which we have evolved and of which I am particularly proud:

(1) The Immigration Course, a six-week acculturation in computer science which gives our entering graduate students a common foundation.

(2) The total integration of research and teaching: From the time they leave the Immigration Course, students spend at least half their time on research. Of course, as the students enter "thesis mode," this becomes essentially full-time.

(3) The "Black Friday" Review: This semiannual evaluation by the entire faculty of every student in the department permits us to monitor

progress and apply appropriate forcing functions while allowing students great individual freedom.

It is almost mandatory at an anniversary to consider the future. I will confine myself to two issues, one concerning the field and the other the department.

In many ways this has been a relatively easy decade for computer science. We have been the bright new science with many more good research problems than people to solve them and many more good positions than people to fill them. That is changing rapidly as the discipline matures and takes its place as one of the major sciences. I welcome that maturity even though I realize that in many ways our lives will be harder. An important issue for the maturing discipline is to maintain the vigor and excitement which first drew us to the field.

I'll turn to what I regard as a central issue for the department. Human institutions ranging from baseball teams to empires first achieve and then lose excellence. How can the department maintain and even strengthen its excellence over a long period of time? I believe this can be done only by continuing to select faculty who are broad and able to move with and, indeed, to lead the field. We must continually look at the brightest people and bring at least some of them here; and we must do this over a long period of time. This is particularly crucial in a field which gives every sign of continuing to evolve rapidly. It seems to me that the answer is to continue to grow but slowly, always exercising the highest standards. This is almost a cliche and yet it is the key to continued excellence. I want the department in 20 years to still enjoy some of the flexibility in bringing in new people that we have today.

Finally, a word about this symposium. I have never been prouder of the department than during the days we were preparing for it and during the symposium itself. Anita Jones showed herself to be one of our typical faculty members, seizing all possible resources (faculty, staff, students) as the time of the symposium approached and putting it all together.

The technical quality of the symposium is reflected in these pages—the reader can judge for himself.

J. F. TRAUB

The Keynote Speech

Alan Perlis

Department of Computer Science
Yale University
New Haven, Connecticut

An after dinner speaker is usually classified as someone who is not otherwise gainfully employed, because it is really a full-time occupation to say something that will be interesting and not be buried in the occasion itself. And this is a very interesting and important occasion. I find that I am quite shocked and pleased at the large size of the turnout and the interest that so many of the alumni have shown in coming back to Carnegie.

I don't know why Carnegie is—if, indeed it is—different from other departments of computer science, though I suspect that Carnegie's role in shaping computer science is much stronger than anyone would guess from the size of the department, or the size of the school, or its location in Pittsburgh. I have no answer. I'll just lay out one suggestion. I think it's because the environment at Carnegie was not then, and I think is still not, rigidly stratified or organized into small cells of individually honed views of computer science. The department never consisted, and I don't think it does now, of a set of independent fiefdoms, where each professor rules supreme over his own piece of the computer science pie. Instead, there was always a large amount of communication and friction between people who held quite different views about what computer science was and ought to become. That difference existed then, and still does in the whole world, let alone Carnegie. It has had a lot to do with the freedom with which the graduate students, unencumbered by dogma when they left Carnegie, were able to maneuver in a new field. I hope that always remains true of computer science. A lot of other sciences have suffered badly from the fact that their feet became encased in cement much too soon.

I guess as an after dinner speaker it is important that I give an overview of computer science. I can't. Indeed, I think that most of the views that we get today are what I would call "underviews". I can think of very few blights that have befallen our field more disturbing than that called

1

"structured programming". It has substituted preoccupation with style for concern with content. It has cast a pall on so much of what remains to be done. But it will wear itself out in time. Complexity theory is the latest entry in the mathematical sweepstakes. Refugees from automata theory and formal languages, cast out from their own countries have found a new grazing ground. However, they will soon denude it and computer science will go on its merry way again.

One of the great things about this field is its "robustness", to use a famous word of Edsger Dijkstra. It's very robust, and the reason it's robust is the computer. We keep finding new things to do with it, new groups of people who want to play with it, who bring new problems to it, and who turn to us for help. And each time they do that the field is revived. It takes off in another direction. Only an idiot, which I don't think I am, would say, "This that we do today is computer science, and will always be computer science."

Some years back in the publication that I hope my name will be bound most closely to, Herb Simon, Al Newell, and I submitted a letter to *Science Magazine* in which we said what computer science was. And in our confessed ignorance, we said it had to be the study of the phenomena arising around computers. We were right then, we're right today, and I think we'll be right twenty years from now. The computer should make us all humble because it is not possible for any of us, no matter how bright we are, or what our experience, to predict what it is going to be used for. It may ultimately disappear and be hidden under all kinds of gadgets and never be seen again, like the electric motor, and our only memories of the computer will be abstractions—things we talk about, things we draw, music we play, who knows? But to say that computer science is artificial intelligence, or complexity theory, or programming languages, or operating systems, or what-not, is ridiculous.

This makes our science, if we can call it that—and I think we should because it deals with phenomena—an extremely vital one. Departments that treat the subject that way flourish best. Both the faculty and the students approach each day open-eyed, open-minded, wondering what the day will bring in the way of new problems or new views. In a way this is also bad for many of us because it prevents us from digging very, very deeply. We don't generally tend in this field to dig very deep mines from which we disappear and are never heard from again. Those mines happen to be extremely attractive places in which to train people. Formal symbolic disciplines seem to be the ideal training grounds for students because you can train so many of them on a square foot of data.

Fortunately, this department, I think, has held to a course in which this has not been the *modus operandi*. Instead, there has been this very important open-eyed, young kid's view of the computer science world, which is constantly causing new things to be done and new points of view to be made. Certainly this is the way I've always viewed computer science and I think it's the way the faculty here has always viewed it. None of us are bright enough or wise enough to predict what this science is going to become. Anyone can predict what mathematics is going to become—more of the same. Physics—they're on a trail that will never end, searching for the ultimate. There's an aphorism of mine that says that "ultimate solutions immobilize". "The best is the enemy of the good", as Wittgenstein said. Be pragmatic. There is no such thing as truth in this field. There's only fun, the privilege to explore, to understand man.

I say the last thing very openly and without shame. I think it's extraordinarily important that we in computer science keep fun in computing. When it started out, it was an awful lot of fun. Of course, the paying customers got shafted every now and then, and after a while we began to take their complaints seriously. We began to feel as though we really were responsible for the successful, error-free, perfect use of these machines. I don't think we are. I think we're responsible for stretching them, setting them off in new directions, and keeping fun in the house. Fun comes in many ways. Fun comes in making a discovery, proving a theorem, writing a program, breaking a code. Whatever form or sense it comes in I hope the field of computer science, and this department in particular, never loses its sense of fun. Above all, I hope we don't become, or you don't—because it's bad enough when someone my age becomes one—and it's a disease of the 50s—I hope we don't become missionaries. Don't feel as if you're Bible salesmen. The world has too many of those already. What you know about computing other people will learn. Don't feel as though the key to successful computing is only in your hands. What's in your hands, I think and hope, is intelligence: the ability to see the machine as more than when you were first led up to it, that you can make it more.

Since I left Carnegie in 1971 and went to Yale I've been much concerned with how I can give students fun on the computer. What constitutes fun? When I say "fun", I don't mean playing Star Trek or chess. Those are other people's games. I mean solving puzzles, inventing algorithms, or becoming fluent in a language so that in a sense you know it through your entire body down to your fingertips. That's what I mean by fun. I've come to some interesting conclusions that may also be interesting to some of you. One is that ALGOL is a blight. You can't have fun with ALGOL. ALGOL is a code that now belongs in a plumber's union. It helps you design correct structures that don't collapse, but it doesn't have any fun in it. There are no pleasures in writing ALGOL programs. It's a labor of necessity, a preoccupation with the details of tedium.

LISP, I've found, does give a measure of fun, and the people who program in LISP really enjoy it. They have fun. The only other language that I know of that has this property is APL. And I have become a real APL nut. I find it is the first language that has anything remotely approaching the beauty of English, a language in which you can actually phrase things elegantly and 100 people will say things in 100 different ways, a language that converts the mind when you use it. So you begin to think in terms of patterns, idioms and phrases, and no longer pick up a trowel and some cement and lay things down brick by brick. The Great Wall, standing for centuries, is a monument. But building it must have been a bore.

When I participated in the creation of ALGOL, I felt very good. All of us did, because it was an awful lot better than FORTRAN. As the years have gone on though, I have come to realize—and I'm probably a voice in the wilderness here—that ALGOL really is a blight. In a sense, it is a language that belongs in the union, not on the playing fields of Eton. And as England learned over several centuries, all the important things were done on the playing fields of Eton and not on the scaffolds that went up around its buildings of state. I think the same thing is true of our field of work too. I like to think that if Shakespeare were alive today, he'd be a programmer and he'd be programming in APL.

Our country has lots of problems. One of them is BASIC. BASIC fits the minds of the people who run our secondary schools—simple, tidy, relatively cheap. And teachers find it is no more difficult to teach than anything else they teach. So it seems to fit into our secondary schools and kids are now coming to college already suffering from a disease that I don't think we'll ever be able to excise. When they come into my course, and I ask them to start programming in APL, I find they can't. They're crippled already. Their minds are already deranged. The first thing they do is set I equal to 1. The natural first step out of the womb is to set I equal to 1. Then you cast around for some place to use it. Let's use it in X, so you have $X(I)$. And you manipulate it for a while and then you increment I, and then you test and you jump, and that's programming. That's life.

When I tell these people that that's not the way to do things at all, but that they should look for a pattern and do things in parallel, to erect the whole structure at once, they can't. Then they come to me after a while and they say, "APL is unstructured. There's no *while* in it." I say, "It's got nothing but wiles", which pun they don't get. "There's no *for* statement; there's no *if–then–else*." I say, "It doesn't need them". I say, "What we do have in APL, what we have in English, what we have in all good natural languages, is a distribution of control through every part of the language, so that when one speaks or writes one weaves mosaics in which the context determines our meanings". That's what makes natural language good for people to use, and that's what been so sadly missing in programming languages. I try to tell these students something, things of that sort, and I'm afraid it's a long, lost battle, because they already know what programming is: *I* gets equal to 1.

However, fortunately, today three quarters or more of the students in high school don't learn programming, and they come to the university and they search around their schedule for an easy course, and we suck them in. These nonmathematically oriented people, people who are going to major in English, history, music, political science, etc., learn APL. For them it's not too difficult. After a couple of months when we show them FORTRAN or BASIC or ALGOL, they come back to us and say, "Why would anyone want to program in a language like that?" This is almost universally their attitude.

As a teacher, I am still interested in not digging deep holes, in teaching people fun. As I meet with graduate students in our department, I find that they have very serious questions to ask about our science. One of the things that bothers them is whether computer science is fenced in by some rather important natural barriers. I've given these natural barriers some rather fancy names. One, many of you know already—I call it the Turing Tarpit. The Turing Tarpit is a morass in which one, in a sense, finds that everything is possible and nothing is easy. One attempts to go from abstract models to real situations and finds that one cannot.

There's a second one that has recently come into being, and this is recognition that we are surrounded by mountains that are really unbelievably difficult or even impossible to scale. Indeed, the mountains are so bad that at the moment one of the greatest games around is to show that they are impossible to scale. All we're able to show is that one mountain is as bad as another one. These are tasks that are not impossible but exponentially time and space consuming. Everything of interest is outside of our reach. This bothers people—it bothers me I know—until I find out that the vast majority of the tasks that we do not yet know how to do are not in those categories.

There's one last "natural barrier", which is the most insidious of all. I call this the "semantic gulf". It's a large, placid body of water on which so many voyage. This gulf stretches out in every direction, and when we are upon it as a Columbus, we find that every time we reach a piece of land the continent we seek is farther away than it was before. Every time we learn something, we find that we knew less about what we were looking for than we thought we did. Every problem that we solve opens up a hundred new ones, each of which is more critical to solve than the one we just solved. This is not to say that we shouldn't voyage on this gulf, because I don't think we have any choice. It's in our nature that we take this voyage, but we must be aware of the fact that it's probably a voyage that we're unlikely to ever satisfactorily complete, hence a fantastic voyage, a fun voyage.

Nevertheless, I don't think all this makes our science weak; it makes it human. We have big goals in this science. Probably goals that are as big as any science, bigger than any science other than physics, or possibly molecular biology. Our goal is the complete and total understanding of the human mind. And we really believe that the computer will lead us to that goal. Well, when we get wise enough and humble enough we realize that we're probably not any closer to it now than we were when we started years ago. But it's been fun riding on the semantic gulf. It's a boat ride that's far more pleasurable than this one. You certainly don't have to listen to any after dinner speeches on it.

Well, I think I've said about all that I wanted to say. It's such a great pleasure to be back here. I think there are only a few faces that I didn't recognize and I can be forgiven because they've since become changed by growth. And I find the same spirit of fun, enjoyment in our work, that was in the department when I was here. Carnegie is still a great place for corrupting the sober and the serious, for turning them into human beings, not just automatons. So, in your next ten years, I wish you nothing but the best, and those of us outside of the department expect you to provide us with a new set of glorious, unbelievable, and useless inventions that will titillate our lives in the years to come. So let me wish you all "Bon Voyage" in the next so many years, and a good career to you all. Thank you.

What Have We Learned from the PDP-11?

C. Gordon Bell

Digital Equipment Corporation
Maynard, Massachusetts
and
Department of Computer Science
Carnegie-Mellon University
Pittsburgh, Pennsylvania

In the six years that the PDP–11 has been on the market, more than 20,000 units in 10 different models have been sold. Although one of the original system design goals was a broad range of models, the actual range of 500 to 1 (in cost and memory size) has exceeded the design goals.

The PDP–11 was designed to be a small computer, yet its design has been successfully extended to high-performance models. This paper recollects the experience of designing the PDP–11, commenting on its success from the point of view of its goals, its use of technology, and on the people who designed, built and marketed it.

1. INTRODUCTION

A computer is not solely determined by its architecture; it reflects the technological, economic, and human aspects of the environment in which it was designed and built. Most of the non-architectural design factors lie outside the control of the designer: the availability and price of the basic electronic technology, the various government and industry rules and standards, the current and future market conditions. The finished computer is a product of the total design environment.

In this chapter, we reflect on the PDP–11: its goals, its architecture, its various implementations, and the people who designed it. We examine the design, beginning with the architectural specifications, and observe how it was affected by technology, by the development organization, the sales, application, and manufacturing organizations, and the nature of the final users. Figure 1 shows the various factors affecting the design of a computer. The lines indicate the primary flow of information for product behavior and specifications. The physical flow of materials is along nearly

8

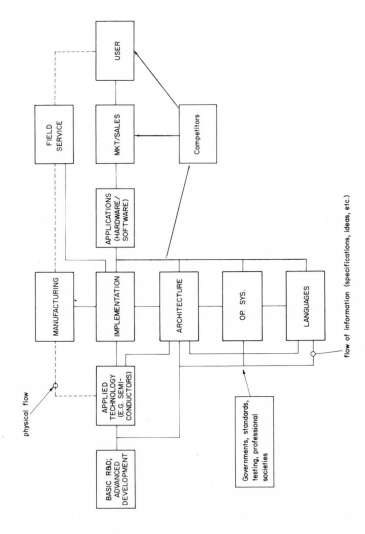

Fig. 1. Structure of organization affecting a computer design.

the same lines, but more direct: beginning with the applied technology manufacturers, material moves through computer manufacturing and then to service personnel before delivery to the end user.

2. BACKGROUND: THOUGHTS BEHIND THE DESIGN

It is the nature of computer engineering to be goal-oriented, with pressure to produce deliverable products. It is therefore difficult to plan for an extensive lifetime. Nevertheless, the PDP-11 evolved rapidly, and over a much wider range than we expected. This rapid evolution would have placed unusual stress even on a carefully planned system. The PDP-11 was not extremely well planned or controlled; rather it evolved under pressure from implementation and marketing groups.

Because of the many pressures on the design, the planning was asynchronous and diffuse; development was distributed throughout the company. This sort of decentralized design organization provides a system of checks and balances, but often at the expense of perfect hardware compatibility. This compatibility can hopefully be provided in the software, and at lower cost to the user.

Despite its evolutionary planning, the PDP-11 has been quite successful in the marketplace: over 20,000 have been sold in the six years that it has been on the market (1970–1975). It is not clear how rigorous a test (aside from the marketplace) we have given the design, since a large and aggressive marketing organization, armed with software to correct architectural inconsistencies and omissions, can save almost any design.

It has been interesting to watch as ideas from the PDP-11 migrate to other computers in newer designs. Although some of the features of the PDP-11 are patented, machines have been made with similar bus and ISP structures. One company has manufactured a machine said to be "plug compatible" with a PDP-11/40. Many designers have adopted the UNIBUS as their fundamental architectural component. Many microprocessor designs incorporate the UNIBUS notion of mapping I/O and control registers into the memory address space, eliminating the need for I/O instructions without complicating the I/O control logic. When the LSI-11 was being designed, no alternative to the UNIBUS-style architecture was even considered.

An earlier paper [Bell *et al.* 70] described the design goals and constraints for the PDP-11, beginning with a discussion of the weaknesses frequently found in minicomputers. The designers of the PDP-11 faced each of these known minicomputer weaknesses, and our goals included a solution to each one. In this section we shall review the original design goals and constraints, commenting on the success or failure of the PDP–11 at meeting each of them.

The first weakness of minicomputers was their limited addressing capability. The biggest (and most common) mistake that can be made in a computer design is that of not providing enough address bits for memory addressing and management. The PDP–11 followed this hallowed tradition of skimping on address bits, but it was saved by the principle that a good design can evolve through at least one major change.

For the PDP–11, the limited-address problem was solved for the short run, but not with enough finesse to support a large family of minicomputers. That was indeed a costly oversight, resulting in both redundant development and lost sales. It is extremely embarassing that the PDP–11 had to be redesigned with memory management only two years after writing the paper that outlined the goal of providing increased address space. All predecessor DEC designs have suffered the same problem, and only the PDP–10 evolved over a long period (ten years) before a change was needed to increase its address space. In retrospect, it is clear that since memory prices decline 26 to 41% yearly, and users tend to buy "constant-dollar" systems, then every two or three years another address bit will be required.

A second weakness of minicomputers was their tendency not to have enough registers. This was corrected for the PDP–11 by providing eight 16-bit registers. Later, six 32-bit registers were added for floating-point arithmetic. This number seems to be adequate: there are enough registers to allocate two or three (beyond those already dedicated to program counter and stack pointer) for program global purposes and still have registers for local statement computation. More registers would increase the multiprogramming context switch time and confuse the user.

A third weakness of minicomputers was their lack of hardware stack capability. In the PDP–11, this was solved with the autoincrement/autodecrement addressing mechanism. This solution is unique to the PDP–11 and has proven to be exceptionally useful. (In fact, it has been copied by other designers.)

A fourth weakness, limited interrupt capability and slow context switching, was essentially solved with the device of UNIBUS interrupt vectors, which direct device interrupts. Implementations could go further by providing automatic context saving in memory or in special registers. This detail was not specified in the architecture, nor has it evolved from any of the implementations to date. The basic mechanism is very fast, requiring only four memory cycles from the time an interrupt request is issued until the first instruction of the interrupt routine begins execution.

A fifth weakness of prior minicomputers, inadequate character-handling capability, was met in the PDP–11 by providing direct byte addressing capability. Although string instructions are not yet provided in the hardware, the common string operations (move, compare, concatenate) can be programmed with very short loops. Benchmarks have shown that systems which depend on this string-handling mechanism do not suffer for it.

A sixth weakness, the inability to use read-only memories, was avoided in the PDP-11. Most code written for the PDP-11 tends to be pure and reentrant without special effort by the programmer, allowing a read-only memory (ROM) to be used directly. ROMs are used extensively for bootstrap loaders, program debuggers, and for normal simple functions. Because large ROMs were not available at the time of the original design, there are no architectural components designed specifically with large ROMs in mind.

A seventh weakness, one common to many minicomputers, was primitive I/O capabilities. The PDP-11 answers this to a certain extent with its improved interrupt structure, but the more general solution of I/O processors has not yet been implemented. The I/O-processor concept is used extensively in the GT4X display series, and for signal processing. Having a single machine instruction that would transmit a block of data at the interrupt level would decrease the CPU overhead per character by a factor of three, and perhaps should have been added to the PDP-11 instruction set.

Another common minicomputer weakness was the lack of system range. If a user had a system running on a minicomputer and wanted to expand it or produce a cheaper turnkey version, he frequently had no recourse, since there were often no larger and smaller models with the same architecture. The problem of range and how it is handled in the PDP-11 is discussed extensively in a later section.

A ninth weakness of minicomputers was the high cost of programming them. Many users program in assembly language, without the comfortable environment of editors, file systems, and debuggers available on bigger systems. The PDP-11 does not seem to have overcome this weakness, although it appears that more complex systems are being built successfully with the PDP-11 than with its predecessors, the PDP-8 and PDP-15. Some systems programming is done using higher-level languages; the optimizing compiler for BLISS-11, however, runs only on the PDP-10.

One design constraint that turned out to be expensive, but probably worth it in the long run, was that the word length had to be a multiple of eight bits. Previous DEC designs were oriented toward 6-bit characters, and DEC has a large investment in 12-, 18-, and 36-bit systems. The notion of word length is somewhat meaningless in machines like the PDP-11 and the IBM System/360, because data types are of varying length, and instructions tend to be multiples of 16 bits.

Microprogrammability was not an explicit design goal, partially since the large ROMs which make it feasible were not available at the time of the original Model 20 implementation. All subsequent machines have been microprogrammed, but with some difficulty and expense.

Understandability as a design goal seems to have been minimized. The PDP–11 was initially a hard machine to understand, and was marketable only to those who really understood computers. Most of the first machines were sold to knowledgeable users in universities and research laboratories. The first programmers' handbook was not very helpful, and the second, arriving in 1972, helped only to a limited extent. It is still not clear whether a user with no previous computer experience can figure out how to use the machine from the information in the handbooks. Fortunately, several computer science textbooks [Gear 74, Eckhouse 75, and Stone and Siewiorek 75] have been written based on the PDP–11; their existence should assist the learning process.

We do not have a very good understanding of the style of programming our users have adopted. Since the machine can be used so many ways, there have been many programming styles. Former PDP–8 users adopt a one-accumulator convention; novices use the two-address form; some compilers use it as a stack machine; probably most of the time it is used as a memory-to-register machine with a stack for procedure calling.

Structural flexibility (modularity) was an important goal. This succeeded beyond expectations, and is discussed extensively in the UNIBUS section.

3. TECHNOLOGY: COMPONENTS OF THE DESIGN

The nature of the computers that we build is strongly influenced by the basic electronic technology of their components. The influence is so strong, in fact, that the four generations of computers have been named after the technology of their components: vacuum-tube, single semiconductors (transistors), integrated circuits (multiple transistors packaged together), and LSI (large-scale integration). The technology of an implementation is the major determinant of its cost and performance, and therefore of its product life. In this section, we shall examine the relationship of computer design to its supporting technology.

3.1. Designing with Improved Technologies

Every electronic technology has its own set of characteristics, all of which the designer must balance in his choice of a technology. They have different cost, speed, heat dissipation, packing density, reliability, etc. These factors combine to limit the applicability of any one technology; typically, we use one until we reach some such limit, then convert to another. Often the reasons for the existence of a newer technology will lie outside the computer industry: integrated circuits, for example, were developed to meet aerospace requirements.

When an improved basic technology becomes available to a computer designer, there are three paths he can take to incorporate that technology in a design: use the newer technology to build a cheaper system with the same performance, hold the price constant and use the technological improvement to get a slight increase in performance, or push the design to the limits of the new technology, thereby increasing both performance and price.

If we hold the cost constant and use the improved technology to get better performance, we will get the best increase in total-system cost effectiveness. This approach provides a growth in quality at a constant price and is probably the best for the majority of existing users.

If we hold the performance constant and use the improved technology to lower the cost, we will build machines that make new applications possible. The minicomputer (for *mini*mal *computer*) has traditionally been the vehicle for entering new applications, since it has been the smallest computer that could be constructed with a given technology. Each year, as the price of the minimal computer continues to decline, new applications become economically feasible. The microprocessor, or processor-on-a-chip, is a new yet evolutionary technology that again provides alternatives to solve new problems.

If we use the new technology to build the most powerful machine possible, then our designs advance the state of the art. We can build completely new designs that can solve problems previously not considered feasible. There are usually two motivations for operating ahead of the state of the art: preliminary research motivated by the knowledge that the technology will catch up, and national defense, where an essentially infinite amount of money is available because the benefit—avoiding annihilation—is infinite.

3.2.　Specific Improvements in Technology

The evolution of a computer system design is shaped by the technology of its constituent parts. Machines of varying sizes will often be based on different technologies, and will therefore evolve differently as the component evolutions differ.

The evolutionary rate of computers has been determined almost exclusively by the technology of magnetic storage and semiconductor logic. Memory is the most basic component of a computer, and it is used throughout the design. Besides the obvious uses as "main" program memory and file storage devices (disks and tapes), we find memory inside the processor in the form of registers and indicators, memory as a cache between the processor and the program memory, and memory in I/O devices as buffers and staging areas. Memory can be substituted for nearly all logic, by substituting table-lookup for computation. We are therefore deeply interested in all forms of memory used throughout a computer system.

Disk technology has evolved in a different style than the primary memory devices. The price of a physical structure, such as a disk pack with 10 platters, actually increases somewhat in time, but the storage density per square inch increases dramatically. IBM's disk packs with 10 platters (beginning with the 1311) have increased in capacity at the rate of 42% per year, and the price per bit has decreased at 38% per year. For disks, there has been an economy of scale; the number of bits for larger disk units increases more rapidly than cost, giving a decreased cost per bit. The overhead of motors, power supply, and packaging increases less rapidly with size. Also, more effort is placed to increasing the recording density of larger disks. The technology developed for the large disks shows up on smaller designs after several years.

The price of a chip of semiconductor memory is essentially independent of its size. A given design is available for one or two years at a high price (about $10 per chip) while people buy in to evaluate the component. Within a year, enough have been sold that the price drops sharply, sometimes by more than a factor of two. The density of state-of-the-art laboratory semiconductor memory has doubled every year since 1962. The relative growth of different semiconductor technologies is shown in Table I; the density of MOS read/write is used as a reference.

Keeping in mind this simple model for the growth of specific semiconductor technologies, we find the situation shown in Table II.

The various technology improvement rates per year for other major components are 30% for magnetic cores, 25% for terminals, 23% for magnetic tape density, 29% for magnetic tape performance, and –3% for packaging and power. The total effect of all component technologies on minicomputers has been an average price decline of about 31% per year

TABLE I

Bipolar read/write	Lags by 2 years
Bipolar read-only	Lags by 1 year
MOS read/write	(Reference year)
MOS read-only	Leads by 1 year
Production volumes	Lags by 1 or 2 years

TABLE II

Technology	Bits	Production availability
Bipolar read/write	16	1969–1970
	64	1971–1972
	1024	1975–1976
MOS read/write	16,384	1977–1978
Bipolar read-only	256	1971–1972
	1024	1974–1975
	2048	1975–1976

[Bell and Newell 71]. In 1972 an 8-bit 1-chip microprocessor was introduced; the price of these machines is declining at a rate comparable to the 12- and 16-bit minicomputers. In summary, if we look at the price/performance behavior of computers over time, the computer performance simply tracks memory performance.

3.3. PDP-11 Evolution through Memory Technologies

The design of the PDP–11 series began in 1969 with the Model 20. Subsequently, three models were introduced as minimum-cost, best cost/performance, and maximum-performance machines. The memory technology of 1969 imposed several constraints. First, core memory was cost effective for the primary (program) memory, but a clear trend toward semiconductor primary memory was visible. Second, since the largest high-speed read/write memories available were 16 words, then the number of processor registers should be kept small. Third, there were no large high-speed read-only memories that would have permitted a microprogrammed approach to the processor design.

These constraints established four design attitudes toward the PDP–11's architecture. First, it should be asynchronous, and thereby capable of accepting different configurations of memory that operate at different speeds. Second, it should be expandable to take eventual advantage of a larger number of registers, both user registers for new data types and internal registers for improved context switching, memory mapping and protected multiprogramming. Third, it could be relatively complex, so that a microcode approach could eventually be used to advantage: new data types could be added to the instruction set to increase performance, even though they might add complexity. Fourth, the UNIBUS width should be relatively large, to get as much performance as possible, since the amount of computation possible per memory cycle is relatively small.

As semiconductor memory of varying price and performance became available, it was used to trade cost for performance across a reasonably wide range of models. Different techniques were used on different models to provide the range. These techniques include microprogramming to enhance performance (for example, faster floating point), use of faster program memories for brute-force speed improvements, use of fast caches to optimize program memory references, and expanded use of fast registers inside the processor.

3.3.1. MICROPROGRAMMING

Microprogramming is the technique by which the conventional logic of a sequential machine is replaced by an encoded representation of the logic and circuitry to decode that microprogram. Microprograms are stored in conventional random-access memories, though often in read-only versions.

Computer designers use microprogramming because it permits relatively complex control sequences to be generated without proportionately complex logic. It is therefore possible to build more complex processors without the attendant problems of making such large sequential circuits. Additionally, it is much easier to include self-diagnosis and maintenance features in microprogrammed logic. Microprogramming depends on the existence of fast memories to store the microprograms. The memory speed is determined by the task at hand: whether it be for an electric typewriter or a disk controller, the microprogram memory must be fast enough to keep up with the application. Typically, processors and fast disks present the most difficult control problems.

Microprogramming a fast, complex processor often presents a dilemma, since the technology used for the microprogram memory is often used for the main program memory. But a microprogram needs to run 5 to 10 times as fast as the primary memory if all components are to be fully utilized. To be cost effective, microprogramming depends on the microstore memories being cheaper than conventional combinatorial logic. Some circuits may be cheaper and faster built out of conventional sequential components, while others will be cheaper or faster if microprogrammed. It depends on the number of logic states, inputs, and outputs.

3.3.2. SEMICONDUCTORS FOR PROGRAM MEMORY

We naturally expect that semiconductor memory will ultimately replace core for primary program memories, given their relative rates of price decline (60–100% per year versus 30% per year). The crossover time, determined by a function of the basic costs for different producer–consumer pairs, is complex. It includes consideration of whether there is an adequate supply of production people in the labor-intensive core assembly process, as well as the reliability and service costs. For IBM, with both core and semiconductor memory technology in-house, the cost crossover occurred in 1971; IBM offered semiconductor memory (actually bipolar) on System/370 (Model 145) and System/7 computers. Within DEC, which has cores and core stacks manufacturing, the crossover point has not yet occurred for large memories. It occurred for small memories (less than 16K) in 1975. In 1969 IBM first delivered the 360 Model 85, which used a mixture of 80-nsec bipolar and 1800-nsec core. This general structure, called a *cache* has been used in the PDP–11/70. The effect on core memories has been to prod their development to achieve lower costs. Recent research has shown that it is possible to hold several states (4 to 16) in a single core. A development of this type, in effect, may mean up to three years additional life in core memory systems.

3.3.3. PROGRAM MEMORY CACHING

A cache memory is a small fast associative memory located between the central processor *Pc* and the primary memory *Mp*. Typically, the cache is implemented in bipolar technology while *Mp* is implemented in MOS or magnetic core technology. The cache contains address/data pairs consisting of an *Mp* address and a copy of the contents of that address. When the *Pc* references *Mp*, the address is compared against the addresses stored in the cache. If there is a match, then *Mp* is not accessed, rather the datum is retrieved directly from the cache. If there is no match, then *Mp* is accessed as usual. Generally, when an address is not found in the cache, it is placed there by the "not found" circuitry, thereby bumping some other address that was in the cache. Since programs frequently cluster their memory references locally, even small caches provide a large improvement over the basic speed of *Mp*.

A significant advantage of a cache is that it is totally transparent to all programs; no software changes need be made to take advantage of it. The PDP–11/70 uses a cache to improve on memory speed.

4. PEOPLE: BUILDERS OF THE DESIGN

Any design project, whether for computers or washing machines, is shaped by the skill, style, and habit of its designers. In this section, we shall outline the evolutionary process of the PDP–11 design, describing how the flavor of the designs was subtly determined by the style of the designers.

A barely minimal computer, i.e., one that has a program counter and a few instructions and that can theoretically be programmed to compute any computable function, can be built trivially. From this minimal point, performance increases. Eventually the size increases and the design becomes unbuildable or nearly unprogrammable, and therefore not marketable. The designer's job is to find a point on the cost/performance curve representing a reasonable and marketable design, and produce the machine corresponding to that point. There is a nearly universal tendency of designers to $n + 1$ their systems: incrementally improve the design forever. No design is so perfect that a redesign cannot improve it.

The problems faced by computer designers can usually be attributed to one of two causes: inexperience or second-systemitis. *Inexperience* is just a problem of resources: Are there designers available? What are their backgrounds? Can a small group work effectively on architectural specifications? Perhaps most important is the principle that no matter who the architect might be, the design must be clearly understood by at least one person. As long as there is one person who clearly understands the total design, a project can usually succeed with many inexperienced designers. *Second-systemitis* is the tendency of many designers to specify a system that solves all of the problems faced by prior systems—and borders on the unbuildable.

We can see the results of second-systemitis in the history of the PDP–8 implementation designs: alternate designs were bigger, then cheaper. The big designs solved the performance problems of the smaller ones; then smaller ones solved the cost problems of the bigger ones.

4.1. The System Architecture

Some of the initial work on the architecture of the PDP–11 was done at Carnegie-Mellon University by Harold McFarland and Gordon Bell. Two of the useful ideas, the UNIBUS and the generalized use of the program registers (such as for stack pointers and program counters), came out of earlier work by Gordon Bell and were described in Bell and Newell [71]. The detailed design specification was the work of Harold McFarland and Roger Cady.

The PDP–11/20 was the first model designed. Its design and implementation took place more or less in parallel, but with far less interaction between architect and builder than for previous DEC designs, where the first architect was the implementor. As a result, some of the architectural specifications caused problems in subsequent designs, especially in the area of microprogramming.

As there began to appear other models besides the original Model 20, strong architectural controls disappeared; there was no one person responsible for the family-wide design. A similar loss of control occurred in the design of the peripherals after the basic design.

4.2. A Chronology of the Design

The internal organization of DEC design groups has through the years oscillated between market orientation and product orientation. Since the company has been growing at a rate of 30 to 40% a year, there has been a constant need for reorganization. At any given time, one third of the staff has been with the company less than a year.

At the time of the PDP–11 design, the company was structured along product lines. The design talent in the company was organized into tight groups: the PDP–10 group, the PDP–15 (an 18-bit machine) group, the PDP–8 group, an ad hoc PDP–8/S subgroup, and the LINC–8 group. Each group included marketing and engineering people responsible for designing a product, software and hardware. As a result of this organization, architectural experience was diffused among the groups, and there was little understanding of the notion of a range of products.

The PDP–10 group was the strongest group in the company. They built large, powerful time-shared machines. It was essentially a separate division of the company, with little or no interaction with the other groups. Although the PDP–10 group as a whole had the best understanding of system architectural controls, they had no notion of system range, and were only interested in building higher-performance computers.

The PDP–15 group was relatively strong, and was an obvious choice to build the new mid-range 16-bit PDP–11. The PDP–15 series was a constant-cost series that tended to be optimized for cost performance. However, the PDP–11 represented direct competition with their existing line. Further, the engineering leadership of that group changed from one implementation to the next, and thus there was little notion of architectural continuity or range.

The PDP–8 group was a close-knit group who did not communicate very much with the rest of the company. They had a fair understanding of architecture, and were oriented toward producing minimal-cost designs with an occasional high-performance model. The PDP–8/S "group" was actually one person, someone outside the regular PDP–8 group. The PDP–8/S was an attempt to build a much lower-cost version of the PDP–8 and show the group engineers how it should be done. The 8/S worked, but it was not terribly successful because it sacrificed too much performance in the interests of economy.

The LINC–8 group produced machines aimed at the biomedical and laboratory market, and had the greatest engineering strength outside the PDP–10 group. The LINC–8 people were really the most systems oriented. The LINC design came originally from MIT's Lincoln Laboratory, and there was dissent in the company as to whether DEC should continue to build it or to switch software to the PDP–8.

The first design work for a 16-bit computer was carried out under the eye of the PDP-15 manager, a marketing person with engineering background. This first design was called PDP-X, and included specification for a range of machines. As a range architecture, it was better designed than the later PDP-11, but was not otherwise particularly innovative. Unfortunately, this group managed to convince management that their design was potentially as complex as the PDP-10 (which it was not), and thus ensured its demise, since no one wanted another large computer unrelated to the company's main large computer. In retrospect, the people involved in designing PDP-X were apparently working simultaneously on the design of Data General.

As the PDP-X project folded, the DCM (Desk Calculator Machine, a code name chosen for security) was started. Design and planning were in disarray, as Data General had been formed and was competing with the PDP-8, using a very small 16-bit computer. Work on the DCM progressed for several months, culminating in a design review at Carnegie-Mellon University in late 1969. The DCM review took only a few minutes; the general feeling was that the machine was dull and would be hard to program. Although its benchmark results were good, we now believe that it had been tuned to the benchmarks and would not have fared well on other sorts of problems.

One of the DCM designers, Harold McFarland, brought along the kernel of an alternative design, which ultimately grew into the PDP-11. Several people worked on the design all weekend, and ended by recommending a switch to the new design. The machine soon entered the design-review cycle, each step being an $n + 1$ of the previous one. As part of the design cycle, it was necessary to ensure that the design could achieve a wide cost/performance range. The only safe way to design a range is to simultaneously do both the high- and low-end designs. The 11/40 design was started right after the 11/20, although it was the last to come on the market. The low and high ends had higher priority to get into production, as they extended the market.

Meanwhile an implementation was underway, led by Jim O'Laughlin. The logic design was conventional, and the design was hampered by the holdover of ideas and circuit boards from the DCM. As ideas were tested on the implementation model, various design changes were proposed; for example, the opcodes were adjusted and the UNIBUS width was increased with an extra set of address lines.

With the introduction of large read-only memories, various follow-on designs to the Model 20 were possible. Figure 2 sketches the cost of various models over time, showing lines of constant performance. The graphs show clearly the differing design styles used in the different models.

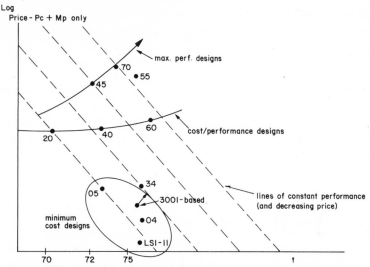

Fig. 2. PDP-11 models price versus time with lines of constant performance.

The 11/40 and 11/45 design groups went through extensive "buy-in" processes, as they each came to the PDP-11 by first proposing alternative designs. The people who ultimately formed the 11/45 group had started by proposing a PDP-11-like 18-bit machine with roots in the PDP-15. Later a totally different design was proposed, with roots in the LINC group, that was instruction subset-compatible at the source program level. As the groups considered the impact of their changes on software needs, they rapidly joined the mainstream of the PDP-11 design.

Note from Fig. 2 that the minimum-cost group had two successors to their original design, one cheaper with slightly improved performance, the other the same price with greatly improved performance and flexibility.

5. THE PDP-11: AN EVALUATION

The end product of the PDP-11 design is the computer itself, and in the evolution of the architecture we can see images of the evolution of ideas. In this section, we outline the architectural evolution, with a special emphasis on the UNIBUS.

In general, the UNIBUS has behaved beyond all expectations. Several hundred types of memories and peripherals have been interfaced to it; it has become a standard architectural component of systems in the $3K to $100K price range (1975). The UNIBUS is a price and performance equalizer: it limits the performance of the fastest machines and penalizes the lower-performance machines with a higher cost. For larger systems, supplementary buses were added for *Pc–Mp* and *Mp–Ms* traffic. For very small systems like the LSI–11, a narrower bus (called a Q-bus) was designed.

The UNIBUS, as a standard, has provided an architectural component for easily configuring systems. Any company, not just DEC, can easily build components that interface to the bus. Good buses make good engineering neighbors, since people can concentrate on structured design. Indeed, the UNIBUS has created a secondary industry providing alternative sources of supply for memories and peripherals. With the exception of the IBM 360 Multiplexor/Selector bus, the UNIBUS is the most widely used computer interconnection standard.

5.1. The Architecture and the UNIBUS

The UNIBUS is the architectural component that connects together all of the other major components. It is the vehicle over which data flow takes place. Its structure is shown in Fig. 3. Traffic between any pair of components moves along the UNIBUS. The original design anticipated the following traffic flows.

1. *Pc–Mp* for the processor's programs and data.
2. *Pc–K* for the processor to issue I/O commands to the controller *K*.
3. *K–Pc*, for the controller *K* to interrupt the *Pc*.
4. *Pc–K* for direct transmission of data from a controller to *Mp* under control of the *Pc*.
5. *K–Mp* for direct transmission of data from a controller to *Mp*; i.e., DMA data transfer.
6. *K–T–K–Ms*, for direct transmission of data from a device to secondary memory without intervening *Mp* buffering; e.g., a disk refreshing a CRT.

Experience has shown that paths 1 through 5 are used in every system that has a DMA (direct memory access) device. An additional communications path has proved useful: demons, i.e., special *Kio/Pio/Cio* com-

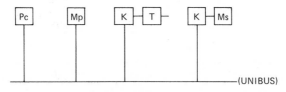

Fig. 3. UNIBUS structure.

municating with a conventional K. These demons are used for direct control of another K in order to remove the processing load from Pc.

Several examples of a demon come to mind: a K that handles all communication with a conventional subordinate Kio (e.g., an A/D converter interface or communications line); a full processor executing from Mp a program to control K; or a complete I/O computer, Cio, which has a program in its local memory and which uses Mp to communicate with Pc. Effectively, Pc and the demon act together, and the UNIBUS connects them. Demons provide a means of gracefully off-loading the Pc by adding components, and is useful for handling the trivial pre-processing found in analog communications, and process-control I/O.

5.1.1. UNEXPECTED BENEFITS FROM THE DESIGN

The UNIBUS has turned out to be invaluable as an "umbilical cord" for factory diagnostic and checkout procedures. Although such a capability was not part of the original design, the UNIBUS is almost capable of dominating the Pc, Tk's, and Mp during factory checkout and diagnostic work.

Ideally, the scheme would let all registers be accessed during full operation. This is now possible for all devices except Pc. By having all Pc registers available for reading and writing in the same way that they are now available from the console switches, a second system could fully monitor the computer in the same fashion as a human. Although the DEC factory uses a UNIBUS umbilical cord to watch systems under test, human intervention is occasionally required.

In most recent PDP-11 models, a serial communications line is connected to the console, so that a program may remotely examine or change any information that a human operator could examine or change from the front panel, even when the system is not running.

5.1.2 DIFFICULTIES WITH THE DESIGN

The UNIBUS design is not without problems. Although two of the bus bits were in the original design set aside as parity bits, they have not been widely used as such. Memory parity was implemented directly in the memory; this phenomenon is a good example of the sorts of problems encountered in engineering optimization. The trading of bus parity for memory parity exchanged higher hardware cost and decreased performance for decreased service cost and better data integrity. Since engineers are usually judged on how well they achieve production cost goals, parity transmission is an obvious choice to pare from a design, since it increases the cost and decreases the performance. As logic costs decrease and pressure to include warranty costs as part of the product design cost increases, the decision to transmit parity might be reconsidered.

Early attempts to build multiprocessor structures (by mapping the address space of one UNIBUS onto the memory of another) were beset with deadlock problems. The UNIBUS design does not allow more than one master at a time. Successful multiprocessors required much more sophisticated sharing mechanisms than this UNIBUS Window.

At the time the UNIBUS was designed, it was felt that allowing 4K bytes of the address space for I/O control registers was more than enough. However, so many different devices have been interfaced to the bus over the years that it is no longer possible to assign unique addresses to every device. The architectural group has thus been saddled with the chore of device address bookkeeping. Many solutions have been proposed, but none was soon enough; as a result, they are all so costly that it is cheaper just to live with the problem and the attendant inconvenience.

5.2. UNIBUS Cost and Performance

Although performance is always a design goal, so is low cost; the two goals conflict directly. The UNIBUS has turned out to be nearly optimum over a wide range of products. However, in the smallest system, we introduced the Q-bus, which uses about half the number of conductors. For the largest systems, we use a separate 32-bit data path between processor and memory, although the UNIBUS is still used for communication with most I/O controllers. The UNIBUS slows down the high-performance machines and increases the cost of low-performance machines; it is optimum over the middle range.

There are several attributes of a bus that affect its cost and performance. One factor affecting performance is simply the data rate of a single conductor. There is a direct tradeoff among cost, performance, and reliability. Shannon [48] gives a relationship between the fundamental signal bandwidth of a link and the error rate (signal-to-noise ratio) and data rate. The performance and cost of a bus are also affected by its length. Longer cables cost proportionately more, and the longer propagation times necessitate more complex circuitry to drive the bus.

Since a single-conductor link has a fixed data rate, the number of conductors affects the net speed of a bus. The cost of a bus is directly proportional to the number of conductors. For a given number of wires, time-domain multiplexing and data encoding can be used to trade performance and logical complexity. Since logic technology is advancing faster than wiring technology, we suspect that fewer conductors will be used in all future systems. There is also a point at which time-domain multiplexing impacts performance.

If during the original design of the UNIBUS we could have forseen the wide range of applications to which it would be applied, its design would have been different. Individual controllers might have been reduced in complexity by more central control. For the largest and smallest systems, it would have been useful to have a bus that could be contracted or expanded by multiplexing or expanding the number of conductors.

The cost-effective success of the UNIBUS is due in large part to the high correlation between memory size, number of address bits, I/O traffic, and processor speed. Amdahl's rule of thumb for IBM computers is that 1 byte of memory and 1 byte/sec of I/O are required for each instruction/sec. For DEC applications, with emphasis in the scientific and control applications, there is more computation required per memory word. Further, the PDP-11 instruction sets do not contain the complex instructions typical of IBM computers, so a larger number of instructions will be executed to accomplish the same task. Hence, we assume 1 byte of memory for each 2 instructions/sec, and that 1 byte/sec of I/O occurs for each instruction/sec.

In the PDP-11, an average instruction accesses 3–5 bytes of memory, so assuming 1 byte of I/O for each instruction/sec, there are 4–6 bytes of memory accessed on the average for each instruction/sec. Therefore, a bus that can support 2 megabyte/sec traffic permits instruction execution rates of 0.33–0.5 megainstructions/sec. This implies memory sizes of 0.16–0.25 megabytes; the maximum allowable memory is 0.064–0.256 megabytes. By using a cache memory on the processor, the effective memory processor rate can be increased to balance the system further. If fast floating point instructions were added to the instruction set, the balance would approach that used by IBM and thereby require more memory (seen in the 11/70).

5.3. Evolution of the Design

The market life of a computer is determined in part by how well the design can gracefully evolve to accommodate new technologies, innovations, and market demands. As component prices decrease, the price of the computer can be lowered, and by compatible improvements to the design (the "mid-life kicker"), the useful life can be extended. An example of a mid-life kicker is the writable control store for user microprogramming of

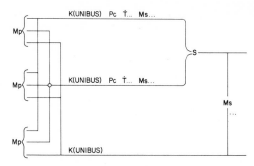

Fig. 4. Use of dual *Pc* multiprocessor system with processorless UNIBUS for I/O data transmission (from Bell *et al.* [70]).

the 11/40 [Almes *et al.* 75]. The PDP–11 designs have used the mid-life kicker technique occasionally. In retrospect, this was probably poor planning. Now that we understand the problem of extending a machine's useful life, this capability can be more easily designed in.

In the original PDP–11 paper [Bell *et al.* 70], it'was forecast that there would evolve models with increased performance, and that the means to achieve this increased performance would include wider data paths, multiprocessors, and separate data and control buses for I/O transfers. Nearly all of these devices have been used, though not always in the style that had been expected.

Figure 4 shows a dual-processor system as originally suggested. A number of systems of this type have been built, but without the separate I/O data and control buses, and with minimal sharing of *Mp*. The switch *S* permitting two computers to access a single UNIBUS, has been widely used in high-availability high-performance systems.

In designing higher-performance models, additional buses were added so

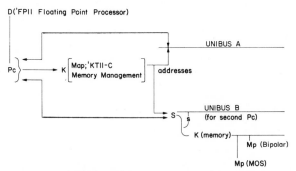

Fig. 5. PMS structure of 11/45.

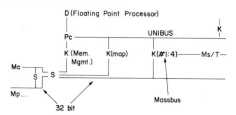

Fig. 6. PMS structure of 11/70.

that a processor could access fast local memory. The original design never anticipated the availability of large fast semiconductor memories. In the past, high-performance machines have parlayed modest gains in component technology into substantially more performance by making architectural changes based on the new component technologies. This was the case with both the PDP–11/45 (see Fig. 5) and the PDP–11/70 (see Fig. 6).

In the PDP–11/45, a separate bus was added for direct access to either

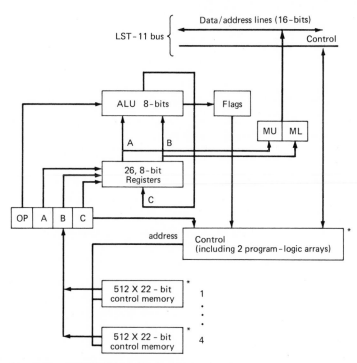

Fig. 7a. PDP – 11/03 (LSI-11) block diagram. (* indicates one LSI chip each and one for data and registers.)

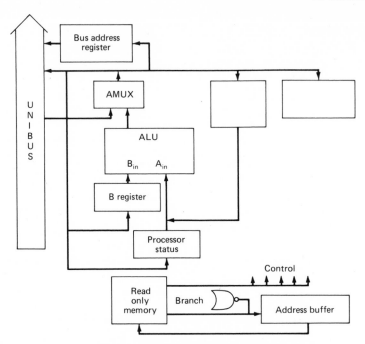

Fig. 7b. PDP-11/05 block diagram.

300-nsec bipolar or 350-nsec MOS memory. It was assumed that these memories would be small, and that the user would move the important parts of his program into the fast memory for direct execution. The 11/45 also provided a second UNIBUS for direct transmission of data to the fast memory without processor interference. The 11/45 also used a second autonomous data operation unit called a Floating Point Processor (not a true processor), which allowed integer and floating-point calculations to proceed concurrently.

The PDP–11/70 derives its speed from the cache, which allows it to take advantage of fast local memories without requiring the program to shuffle data in and out of them. The 11/70 has a memory path width of 32 bits, and has separate buses for the control and data portions of I/O transfer. The performance limitations of the UNIBUS are circumvented; the second *Mp* system permits transfers of up to 5 megabytes/sec., 2.5 times the UNIBUS limit. If direct memory access devices are placed on the UNI-BUS, their address space is mapped into a portion of the larger physical address space, thereby allowing a virtual-system user to run real devices.

Figure 7 shows the block diagrams of the LSI–11, the 11/05, and the 11/45. It includes the smallest and largest (except the 11/70) models. Note

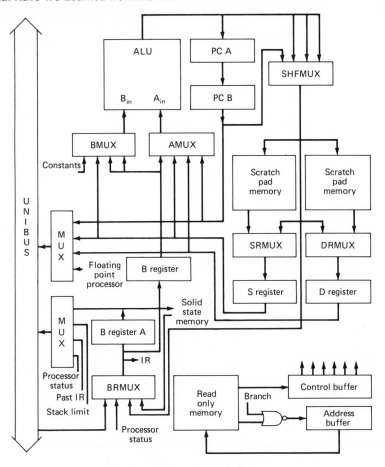

Fig. 7c. PDP-11/45 block diagram.

that the 11/45 block diagram does not include the floating-point operations, but does show the path to fast local memory. It has duplicate sets of registers, even to a separate program counter. The local *Mp.MOS* and *Mp.Bipolar* provide the greatest performance improvements by avoiding the UNIBUS protocols. When only core memory is used, the 11/45 floating-point performance is only twice that of the 11/40. Table III charts the implementation of each design and its performance and parallelism as measured by the microprogram memory width. Note that the brute-force speed of the 11/45 core is only 2 to 4 times faster than the 11/05 for simple data types, i.e., for the basic instruction set. The 11/45 has roughly twice the number of flip-flops.

TABLE III

Model	First delivery	ROM	RAM	Machine time (nsec)	Word length micromem.	No. of microwords	Relative perform.		Mp	Innovations
							Single prec. fl. pt.	Simple arith.		
03 LSI-11	6/75	1k +PLA NMOS; 150 nsec.	13W NMOS; 75 nsec	350	22	1024	3.2	1.5	MOS/core	LSI—4 chips; ODT; maint; fl. pt.
04	9/75	256, 1k; 2k; 50 nsec	4 × 16; 50 nsec	260	38	249	1.6	2.3	MOS/core	Size; maint./test; built-in ASCII console
05	6/72	256; 1k; 50 nsec	4 × 16	137,314 630	40	249	1.4	2.1	Core	Size
20	6/70	—	4 ×16	—	—	—	—	—	Core	ISP; UNIBUS
34	9/75	See 04	4 × 16	200,260	48	470	2.2	3	See 04	Size; modularity
40	1/73	See 05	4 × 16	140,200, 300	56	256	6	2.8	Core	General purpose emulation; fl. pt.
45	6/72	See 05	256 (mapping)	150	64	256	13	3.8	Core	Fastest fl. pt./mem. mgmt. Schottky–TTL
55	6/72 6/76	See 05	256 bipolar 1k bipolar	150	64	256	90	35	Bipolar	Bipolar
70	3/75	See 05	1k cache	150	64	256	85	31	Core	Cache; Systems-oriented
3001	9/75	1k bipolar	11W	170	32	512	—	—	Core	Emulation
C/D	—	—	—	?	?	—	—	—	—	Writable control store

5.4.   ISP Design

Designing the ISP level of a machine—that collection of characteristics such as instruction set, addressing modes, trap and interrupt sequences, register organization, and other features visible to a programmer of the bare machine—is an extremely difficult problem. One has to consider the performance (and price) ranges of the machine family as well as the intended applications, and there are always difficult tradeoffs. For example, a wide performance range argues for different encodings over the range. For small systems a byte-oriented approach with small addresses is optimal, whereas larger systems require more operation codes, more registers, and larger addresses. Thus, for larger machines, instruction coding efficiency can be traded for performance.

The PDP-11 was originally conceived as a small machine, but over time its range was gradually extended so that there is now a factor of 500 in price ($500 to $250,000) and memory size (8K bytes to 4 megabytes) between the smallest and largest models. This range compares favorably with the range of the 360 family (4K bytes to 4 megabytes). Needless to say, a number of problems have arisen as the basic design was extended.

For one thing, the initial design did not have enough opcode space to accommodate instructions for new data types. Ideally, the complete set of operation codes should have been specified at initial design time so that extensions would have fit. Using this approach, the uninterpreted operation codes could have been used to call the various operation functions (e.g., floating-point add). This would have avoided the proliferation of runtime support systems for the various hardware/software floating point arithmetic methods (Extended Arithmetic Element, Extended Instruction Set, Floating Instruction Set, Floating Point Processor). This technique was used in the Atlas and SDS designs, but most computer designers don't remember the techniques. By not specifying the ISP at the initial design, completeness and orthogonality have been sacrificed.

At the time the 11/45 was designed, several extension schemes were examined: an escape mode to add the floating point operations, bringing the 11 back to being a more conventional general-register machine by reducing the number of addressing modes, and finally, typing the data by adding a global mode that could be switched to select floating point instead of byte operations for the same opcodes. The FPP of the PDP-11/45 is a version of the second alternative.

It also became necessary to do something about the small address space of the processor. The UNIBUS limits the physical memory to 262,144 bytes (addressable by 18-bits). In the implementation of the 11/70, the physical address was extended to 4 megabytes by providing a UNIBUS map so that devices in a 256K UNIBUS space could transfer into the 4 megabyte space via mapping registers. While the physical address limits are acceptable for both the UNIBUS and larger systems, the address for a single program is still confined to an instantaneous space of 16 bits, the user virtual address. The main method of dealing with relatively small addresses is via process-oriented operating systems that handle many small tasks. This is a trend in operating systems, especially for process control and transaction processing. It does, however, enforce a structuring discipline in (user) program organization. The RSX series operating systems for the PDP–11 are organized this way, and the need for large addresses is minimized.

The initial memory management proposal to extend the virtual memory was predicted on dynamic, rather than static assignment of memory segment registers. In the current memory management scheme, the address registers are usually considered to be static for a task (although some operating systems provide functions to get additional segments dynamically).

With dynamic assignment, a user can address a number of segment names, via a table, and directly load the appropriate segment registers. The segment registers act to concatenate additional address bits in a base address fashion. There have been other schemes proposed that extend the addresses by extending the length of the general registers—of course, extended addresses propagate throughout the design and include double length address variables. In effect, the extended part is loaded with a base address.

With larger machines and process-oriented operating systems, the context switching time becomes an important performance factor. By providing additional registers for more processes, the time (overhead) to switch context from a process (task) to another process can be reduced. This option has not been used in the implementations of the 11's to date. Various alternatives have been suggested, and to accomplish this most effectively requires additional operators to handle the many aspects of process scheduling. This extension appears to be relatively unimportant since the range of computers coupled with networks tend to alleviate the need by increasing the real parallelism (as opposed to the apparent parallelism) by having various independent processors work on the separate processes in parallel. The extensions of the 11 for better control of I/O devices is clearly more important in terms of improved performance.

The criteria used to decide whether or not to include a particular capability in an instruction set are highly variable and border on the artistic. We ask that the machine appear elegant, where elegance is a combined quality of instruction formats relating to mnemonic significance, operator/data-type completeness and orthogonality, and addressing consistency. Having completely general facilities (e.g., registers) which are not context dependent assists in minimizing the number of instruction types, and greatly aids in increasing understandability (and usefulness). We feel the 11 provided this.

Techniques for generating code by the human and compiler vary widely and thus affect ISP design. The 11 provides more addressing modes than nearly any other computer. The 8 modes for source and destination with dyadic operators provide what amounts to 64 possible add instructions. By associating the Program Counter and Stack Pointer registers with the modes, even more data accessing methods are provided. For example, 18 varieties of the MOVE instruction can be distinguished [Bell *et al.* 70] as the machine is used in two-address, general-register and stack machine program forms. (There is a price for this generality—namely, fewer bits could have been used to encode the address modes that are actually used most of the time.)

In general, the 11 has been used mostly as a general register machine. In one case, it was observed that a user who previously used a 1-accumulator computer (e.g., PDP-8), continued to do so. Normally, the machine is used as a memory to registers machine. This provides the greatest performance, and the cost (in terms of bits) is the same as when used as a stack machine. Some compilers, particularly the early ones, are stack oriented since the code production is easier. Note, that in principle, and with much care, a fast stack machine could be constructed. However, since most stack machines use Mp for the stack, there is a loss of performance even if the top of the stack is cached. The stack machine is perhaps the most poorly understood concept in computing. While a stack is natural (and necessary) structure to interpret the nested block structure languages, it doesn't necessarily follow that the interpretation of all statements should occur in the context of the stack. In particular, the predominance of register transfer statements are of the simple 2-and 3-address forms

$$D \leftarrow S$$

and

$$D1(index\ 1) \leftarrow f(S2(index\ 2),\ S3(index\ 3)).$$

These don't require the stack organization. In effect, appropriate assignment allows a general register machine to be used as a stack machine for most cases of expression evaluation. It has the advantage of providing temporary, random access to common sub-expressions, a capability that is usually hard to exploit in stack architectures.

5.5. Multiprocessors

Although it is not surprising that multiprocessors have not been used save in highly specialized applications, it is depressing. One way to extend the range of a family is to build multiprocessors. In this section we examine some factors affecting the design and implementation of multiprocessors, and their affect on the PDP–11.

It is the nature of engineering to be conservative. Given that there are already a number of risks involved in bringing a product to the market, it is not clear why one should build a higher-risk structure that may require a new way of programming. What has resulted is a sort of deadlock situation: we cannot learn how to program multiprocessors until such machines exist, but we won't build the machine until we are sure that there will be a demand for it, i.e., that the programs will be ready.

While on the subject of demand for multiprocessors, we should note that there is little or no market pressure for them. Most users don't even know that multiprocessors exist. Even though multiprocessors are used extensively in the high-performance systems built by Burroughs, DEC (PDP–10), and Univac, the concept has not yet been blessed by IBM.

One reason that there is not a lot of demand for multiprocessors is acceptance of the philosophy that we can always build a better single-processor system. Such a processor achieves performance at the considerable expense of cost of spares, training, reliability, and flexibility. Although a multiprocessor architecture provides a measure of reliability, backup, and system tunability unreachable on a conventional system, the biggest, fastest machines are always uniprocessors.

5.5.1. MULTIPROCESSORS BASED ON THE PDP–11

Multiprocessor systems have been built out of PDP–11's. Figure 8 summarizes the design and performance of some of these machines. The topmost structure was built using 11/05 processors, but because of improper arbitration techniques in the processor, the expected performance did not materialize. Table IV shows the expected results for multiple 11/05 processors sharing a single UNIBUS:

From these results we would expect to use as many as three 11/05 processors to achieve the performance of a Model 40. More than 3 processors will increase the performance at the expense of the cost-effectiveness. This basic structure has been applied on a production basis in the GT4X series of graphics processors. In this scheme, a second *P.display* is added to the UNIBUS for display picture maintenance. A similar structure is used for connecting special signal-processing computers to the UNIBUS, although these structures are technically coupled computers rather than multiprocessors.

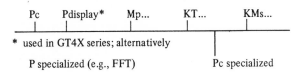

a. Multi-Pc structure using a single Unibus.

Pc   Pdisplay*   Mp...   KT...   KMs...

* used in GT4X series; alternatively

P specialized (e.g., FFT)   Pc specialized

b. Pc with P.display using a single Unibus.

Pc   KMs...   KT...   Kclock

Pc :   KMs...   KT...   Kclock

Mp...

c. Multiprocessor using multiport Mp.

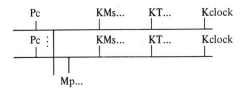

$Mp(\#0:15)$ — S[central;crosspoint; 16x16] — $Pc(\#0:15;`11/40)$ — S(Unibus) — KT... KMs...

d. C.mmp CMU multi-mini-processor computer structure.

Fig. 8. Multiprocessor computer structures implemented using PDP-11.

As an independent check on the validity of this approach, a multiprocessor system has been built, based on the Lockheed SUE [Ornstein *et al.* 72]. This machine, used as a high-speed communications processor, is a hybrid design: it has seven dual-processor computers with each pair sharing a common bus as outlined above. The seven pairs share two shared multiport memories.

TABLE IV

# Pc	Pc perf. (rel.)	Pc price	Price[a]/perf.	SYS price	Price[b]/perf.
1	1.00	1.00	1.00	3.00	1.00
2	1.85	1.23	0.66	3.23	0.58
3	2.4	1.47	0.61	3.47	0.48
40	2.25	1.35	0.60	3.35	0.49

[a] Pc cost only.
[b] Total-system cost, assuming one-third of system is Pc cost.

The second type of structure given in Fig. 8 is a conventional multi-processor using multiple-port memories. A number of these systems have been installed, and they operate quite effectively. However, they have only been used for specialized applications.

The most ambitious multiprocessor structure made from PDP–11's, C.mmp, is amply described in the literature [Wulf *et al.* 72]. As it becomes a user machine, we will gather data about its effectiveness. Hopefully, data from this and other multiprocessor efforts will establish multiprocessors as applicable and useful in a wide variety of situations.

6. FUTURE PLANS AND DIRECTIONS

The problems encountered on the PDP–11 project are not peculiar to that machine, or to any machine or style of architecture. In the course of the project, we have isolated several specific problems in computer design. We intend to explore each of them further.

6.1. The Bus Specification Problem

It has taken a long time to understand the UNIBUS in terms of its electrical, performance, and logical capabilities. The existing bus specifications, however inadequate, are the result of many iterations of respecification based on experience and redesign. Several description techniques have been tried: timing diagrams, threaded diagrams showing the cause and effect of signals, and partial state flowcharts showing state in master and slave components. A rigorous specification language, such as BNF, would be helpful. BNF has proven helpful in the specification of communication links, but is too clumsy for general use, and is not widely understood by engineers and programmers.

The most important use of a rigorous bus specification is the testing of faulty components rather than the exercising of good ones. A bus specification would provide a behavior standard against which to check faulty components. It is not clear how one should best attack the problem of bus behavior specification. A safe place to start would be an exhaustive set of examples.

6.2. Characterizing Computation Problems

When a user comes to us with a task needing computerization, we don't have a good way to describe the computational needs of the task. The needs are multidimensional, consisting of the procedural algorithms, the file structure, the interface transducers, reliability, cost, and development deadline. This communications difficulty exists between computer designers and operating-system designers as much as between computer designers and end users.

Even when there is a good way to specify to the system designer exactly what the user's computational needs might be, there is still a lot of work in finding an architecture to best solve that problem and finding an implementation to best build that architecture.

6.3. Operating Systems

A taxonomy and notation is needed to describe the functions of a system, especially the operating systems. There is no good methodology for talking about tradeoffs, because the functions and structures of a system are so vague.

There exist numerous operating systems for the PDP-11. One of the reasons for this situation is that there is no easy way to compare an existing system with a design for a new one. Instead, an engineering-marketing conspiracy invents a new system because it is oriented toward a particular market in some nebulous way. If we had the ability to specify operating system behavior in a uniform and comprehensible way, then a system could be analyzed before it is programmed.

6.4. Problems with Architectural Range

In a growing family of computers, the designer is constantly faced with the question of whether or not to build a certain model or provide an certain point on the price/performance curve. The decision is colored by technology, user requirements, competitor offerings, and available design staff. It is difficult to answer precisely even a question so simple as whether to build two models that are close together (as the 11/40 and 11/45), or to make a single model and expand it with a multiprocessor option.

The range problem occurs at other levels. Consider memory. The number of memory technologies available is growing constantly, and the once-clear boundaries between memory classes based on memory speed are blurring. Some of the new electronic-based technologies such as CCD and magnetic bubbles have an access time in the 100-microsecond range, and fill the gap between traditional random-access memories (.1 to 1 microsecond) and electromechanical memories like disks or drums (1 millisecond to 100 millisecond). The system designer must decide how much of which kinds of memory will be used in each implementation. It may well be that a solution to problems of this sort will be dependent on the ability to characterize the computational needs.

7. SUMMARY

In this paper we have reexamined the PDP–11 in the light of six years of experience, and have compared its successes and failures with the goals and problems of the initial ideas. With the clarity of hindsight, we now see the initial design problems. Many mistakes were made through ignorance, and many more because the design work was started too late. As we continue to evolve and improve the PDP–11 computer over the next five years, it will indeed be interesting to observe whether the PDP–11 can continue to be a significant, cost-effective minicomputer. We believe it can. The ultimate test is its use.

ACKNOWLEDGMENT

I would like to thank Brian Reid for editing and rewriting sections of this paper.

REFERENCES

Almes, G. T., Drongowski, P. J., and Fuller, S. H., Emulating the Nova on the PDP–11/40: a case study. *Proc. COMPCON, Washington, D.C., September 1975.*

Bell, C. G., Cady, R., McFarland, H., Delagi, B., O'Loughlin, J., Noonan, R., and Wulf, W., A new architecture of minicomputers— The DEC PDP–11. *Proc. SJCC* **36**, 657–675 (1970).

Bell, C. G., and Newell, A., *Computer Structures.* McGraw–Hill, New York, 1971.

Eckhouse, R. H., *Minicomputer Systems: Organization and Programming (PDP–11).* Prentice–Hall, Englewood Cliffs, New Jersey, 1975.

Gear, C. W., *Computer Organization and Programming, Second Edition.* McGraw–Hill, New York, 1974.

McWilliams, T., Sherwood, W., and Fuller, S., PDP–11 implementation using the Intel 3000 microprocessor chips. *Proc. NCC* **46**, 243–253 (1977).

O'Loughlin, J. F., Microprogramming a fixed architecture machine. *Microprogramming and Systems Architecture Infotech State of the Art Rep.* **23**, 205–224 (1975).

Ornstein, S. M., Heart, F. E., Crowther, W. R., Rising, H. K., Russell, S. B., and Michael, A., The terminal IMP for the ARPA computer network. *Proc. SJCC* **40**, 243–254 (1972).

Shannon, C. E., A mathematical theory of communication. *Bell Sys. Tech. J.* **27**, 379–423, 623–656 (1948).

Stone, H. S., and Siewiorek, D. P., *Introduction to Computer Organization and Data Structures: PDP–11 Edition.* McGraw–Hill, New York, 1975.

Wulf, W. A., and Bell, C. G., C.mmp: a multi-mini-processor. *Proc. FJCC* **41**, 765–778 (1972).

The Use of Domain-Dependent Descriptions in Tree Searching

Hans Berliner

Department of Computer Science
Carnegie-Mellon University
Pittsburgh, Pennsylvania

This paper proposes a set of new techniques for tree searching. Existing methods make use of domain-dependent[†] information only when calculating evaluation functions. The scalar value that is the result of such an evaluation is then used for all future decisions that control the search. Our technique provides a method for using domain-dependent descriptions to rule out the searching of subtrees, based upon notions such as causality, purpose, consistency, and problem invariance. Descriptions are inherently much richer than scalar quantities, and we develop a theoretical framework for this. The techniques discussed were developed using computer chess as a domain, but they appear to be widely applicable.

1. INTRODUCTION

To date there has been developed an impressive set of techniques for searching trees. These methods are intended to provide a tool for finding a path from the root of the tree to another node, and then demonstrating this path to be optimal or satisficing, according to some previously stated criterion. The methods can be applied both to trees that represent a struggle between two antagonists (as in a two-person game) and trees that can be considered to represent a struggle against nature (as in solving the 15–puzzle). In representing such a problem as a tree search, a node represents a point in the problem space (a problem state), and an arc represents an operator which maps one point in the problem space into another. The set of techniques available includes such well-known methods

---

[†]In performing a tree search, we distinguish between concepts that are domain-independent (e.g., that every node has a value, or the notion of generating successors) and domain-dependent information (e.g., the factors that go into evaluating a particular node, or the actual set of legal successors of a node).

as depth-first, breadth-first, and best-first searching, and variations of these. Formal definitions of these methods and examples can be found in Nilsson [71]. Interesting recent results can be found in Fuller *et al.* [73], Harris [73], and Knuth [75].

Before concentrating on search methods, let us examine briefly the notion of a solution and a search space in which the solution may exist. For practical problems, finding a solution in a search space involves the following:

(1)　Some effort limit that will terminate the search after a certain amount of time has been expended in the computation, or a certain number of nodes have been examined.

(2)　The notion of a "solution", which can be

(a)　A yes–no proposition, when the desired solution is of a certain magnitude or class. Examples of such searches are proving a theorem in predicate calculus or finding a checkmate in chess. Here the search must either succeed or fail regardless of the size of the search space and the amount of effort available to search it.

(b)　An optimum result, which will always be found as long as the search terminates. The value of this optimum can be associated with a node in the search tree and the path from the root to this node is considered the optimum path through the tree. For such searches, it must be possible to apply an ordering function F to all nodes that are defined to be leaf or terminal. F is usually called the terminal evaluation function. Solutions produced by such searches, instead of having a yes–no character, can have a continuous character since F may take any value over a large range.

(3)　The notion of a search space consisting of

(a)　The problem space, which is the space of all possible solutions. For interesting problems this is usually too large to explore by tractable methods.

(b)　The virtual search space, which is a subset of the problem space and which *a priori* defines the search space. Such a space may be specified by a maximum depth beyond which no nodes will be expanded, or by an arbitrary nearness to a hypothetical maximal solution which is satisfactory for search termination.

(c)　The actual search space, which is the space of solutions investigated within the virtual search space. Here, any node that would have been expanded in the problem space but is left unexpanded in the actual space is considered a leaf node.

When the method of searching guarantees finding the best solution in the virtual search space, we call it a complete method. Since complete methods are usually costly, it is possible to make the actual search space a subset of the virtual one. This means that certain branches within the virtual search space may not be investigated to termination (as defined by the virtual space). This is done because the search algorithm attempts to spend its effort on the most promising branches (thus allowing an overall deeper probing than a complete algorithm would be able to do in the same amount of time), but does this at the risk of terminating a branch that may contain the best solution. When the search fails to produce the best answer in the problem space, there are three possible causes:

(1) The virtual search space was not deep enough to be able to detect the solution.

(2) The branch on which the solution lay was not investigated to a sufficient depth to detect the solution, even though other branches were searched to that depth.

(3) The critical node representing the solution was reached; however, F failed to evaluate it correctly, or F erroneously evaluated another node as better, thus causing the search to produce an erroneous result.

We will refer to the above errors as being of type 1, 2, or 3. A fact that complicates any search is that as the search gets uniformly further away from the root the number of nodes grows exponentially as a function of the branching factor B (average number of successors of a node), and the depth D. The number of terminal nodes is approximately B^D. Since all nontrivial domains have a $B > 1.0$, this means that it becomes computationally intractable to search trees beyond a certain depth from the root. B can be reduced by having the actual search space be smaller than the virtual one; i.e., by not pursuing all branches that are pursuable. This allows the saved effort to be applied to reaching greater depth in the chosen branches. In general, interesting problems cannot be searched by complete methods, and thus it is necessary to accept at least one of the three possible types of errors.

Most theoretical effort to date has been devoted to developing techniques that produce complete solutions with minimum effort. While this is certainly worthwhile, it is becoming increasingly apparent that such techniques can only be applied effectively to a small subset of interesting problems:

(1) those that have shallow solutions (not many arcs between the root and the leaf node defining the optimum solution), or

(2) those in which the characteristics of the optimal solution are such that the search methods will quickly dismiss other alternatives and be able to concentrate all their efforts in a subtree that contains the solution.

The approach of using depth-limited searches has been used for several years now in computer chess [Greenblatt *et al.* 67]. This approach will avoid errors of type 2 in the given search space, and is thus capable of producing programs that are able to play at a rather high (human Class "C"), but nonexpert level. However, this state of affairs has existed for over eight years now, without noticeable progress as measured on the human scale. This suggests strongly that programs that are not designed to investigate deep and sparse (of necessity) search spaces will never reach human expert level performance in any complex domain. This in turn means that programs must be willing to risk errors of type 2, and should have the best possible mechanisms for assuring that the effect of such errors will be minimal. A ground-breaking discussion of some of the issues involved can be found in Newell [55].

If we are to distribute our search effort to nonuniform depths, then clearly some more sophisticated algorithm must exist for deciding when a descendant of a particular node is not to be searched. Several algorithms of this type already exist; some involve risk of type 2 errors, some do not. One risk-free algorithm is known as the Alpha–Beta algorithm [Slagle and Dixon 69, Fuller *et al.* 73, Knuth 75]. This depth-first search algorithm avoids looking at branches that could not contain the optimal mini-max solution. Other techniques that involve risk of type 2 errors use an arc selection function S (which may be quite similar to F), together with certain reference levels, to make decisions to terminate search at a node, even though it could be extended according to the rules of the virtual search space. The most common technique of this type is known as the forward prune. This involves rejecting an arc for searching, when an optimistic evaluation furnished by S fails to equal or better the best solution found so far at the parent node. Recent experience in chess programs has shown that programs using this algorithm are inferior to those that search all successors; however, it is evident that such results are very much dependent on the sensitivity of the function S, which does the arc selection.

It is important to understand the distinction between the incomplete methods and those, such as Alpha–Beta and various branch-and-bound techniques, which save searching effort while still assuring the finding of the best solution. The techniques we are discussing here involve risk decisions, which could and do result on occasion in failure to find the optimum solution.

Besides our arc selection function, S, the following reference levels are required to make the necessary decisions about termination of search:

(1)   The best value achieved by the side on-move at this node, thus far. This value includes results that have been achieved in other branches of

the tree searched earlier, and that are known to be forceable upon the opponent. One can think of this level as being the level that the side on-move would like to improve on and the side not-on-move cannot do worse than.

(2)   The best value achieved by the side not-on-move at this node, thus far.

(3)   A general expectation level, which is the best guess as to what the value of the root node really is, i.e., the value of the optimum solution.

These levels are necessary since S is trying to find a reason for stopping the search, and this must be based on the expected worth of the node at which such branch termination could occur. Terminations can occur when the current node represents a result so much worse than the best result achieved thus far that it appears very unlikely that a better result than the best thus far can be achieved by following this branch. Another reason is that the result is so much superior to the best achieved thus far that if this result can eventually be sustained, it would be a satisficing result. Therefore, there is no point in continuing the search to find out how good it really is, as long as we can be assured it is clearly better than anything else thus far. We are thus saved the effort of exploring this branch more deeply unless another competing branch turns out to have a solution of nearly equal magnitude associated with it, in which case both branches may have to be probed more deeply.

In these methods, the only domain-dependent knowledge that enters into the search is the knowledge in the functions F and S. In this chapter, we take steps toward developing a formalism for introducing domain dependent knowledge at many points in the search. We will show that the search effort can be reduced considerably in this manner. We also treat the question of the types of errors that can arise, both in terms of the older methods and the new ones. In the case of the new methods, we will show how error levels can be controlled by the search specification, and the amount of detail in the domain-dependent data.

It may be appropriate at this point to examine why it should be desirable to search deeply, when we cannot search the whole problem space and are thus forced to apply F at arbitrarily defined terminal nodes in any event. It is reasonable to question why all the successors of the root should not just be generated, and the one with the best value chosen as the optimum arc. There are several reasons for this.

First, F is by definition imperfect, else the search could be performed in this trivial way (as it can be in the game of NIM, for instance).

Second, F is usually designed to give large credits for things that have been accomplished, medium credits for things that appear likely to be accomplished, and small credits for generally favorable factors that are as yet too vague for us to hope with any degree of certainty that they will materialize into any definite accomplishment. Thus, a reasonable F will be able to measure within some margin of error the game-theoretic value (or nearness to the global optimum) of a particular node. Since F has estimated quantities in it, it is desirable to find a stable value of F for any node that is to be a terminal node. By stability, we will mean that the value of F at the node is very close to the value of F for its optimum successor. We are not concerned here with the basic goodness of the function F, but rather with when is the best time to apply it in order to get it to produce accuracy near its maximum potential. This is what we mean by the notion of quiescence. Quiescence of a node means that the various parameters that we are measuring are not in a state of high flux, and thus the measurement is likely to be a successful one. The problem of quiescence of measurement gives rise to the *horizon effect* [Berliner 73], which we will discuss in greater detail below.

Finally, the farther the search moves from the root, the more likely it is that one side or the other has achieved something permanent that can be measured by F. Thus, in the sense that nodes far removed from the root have had a greater chance to develop any potential that existed in the root, they can be measured with greater confidence as representing something of transcending value about the root, than would be the case for a node that is less far removed.

2. THE USE OF DOMAIN-DEPENDENT KNOWLEDGE

Previous attempts at reducing the branching factor by applying S to the successors of a node and forward pruning those that do not meet a certain criterion level have been found to be ineffective. This is particularly true in computer chess, where the application of a static S has been found insufficient to cope with the dynamic qualities (those that can best be found by exploring shallow sequences of moves) of many positions.

In order to penetrate deeply into any problem, B must be near 1.0, else the exponential growth rate will too soon become overwhelming. For problems that have a naturally high branching factor (which includes most interesting problems), merely having S order successors in terms of likelihood of success will not reduce B enough unless S is nearly perfect (and such S's do not exist in meaningful domains). Therefore, it is necessary to use a set of techniques to detect meaningful arcs at a node and pursue only the most highly recommended members of this select class. This will produce a search in which the maximum number of successors to a node will be a small fraction of the possible number of successors, and the average number of successors will be smaller still.

Our strategy for achieving this is to classify all arcs at a node into the following classes:

(1)   those that produce a state that will be recognizable as terminal (or much better than expected) by F;

(2)   those that are necessary to meet some discovered problem at the node;

(3)   those that are old (i.e., the state transition defined by this arc was possible before the search arrived at this node); and

(4)   those that are new (this arc was not possible before).

Further, S determines whether each arc is potentially useful. An arc is considered useful if either (1) it gets a good rating in terms of global goals (e.g., in chess, winning material) or (2) it conforms to a broadcast description of a theme or goal. An otherwise potentially useful arc may be disregarded if it is old and either is known to have failed before under similar circumstances (we discuss below how this is done) or is not considered by S to be better than it was considered in its best as-yet-unsearched incarnation. All other potentially useful arcs are ordered for searching. As the search progresses, the number of new arcs at a node will tend to decrease (since there are more arcs to compare with at earlier nodes). Also there will be more arcs that have failed previously, and more old arcs that do not appear to be better than before. Further, S is always at work rejecting unreasonable arcs and recommending those that are in accord with broadcast themes and goals. The effect of these actions working together will tend to reduce the average number of reasonable arcs as the search progresses. This greatly promotes convergence in the whole tree-searching process.

Even though none of these mechanisms is perfect (in the sense that it will guarantee correctness as a complete search would), we will show that perfection can be approximated to various degrees. Though the better the approximation the more costly it is, it is in fact possible to operate very well with low orders of approximation.

Our general strategy for the use of domain-dependent information is to make information derived from one node's processing available to other nodes that could benefit from it. This information can then be processed by logic built into the search control, and used for deciding whether or not an arc is processed and for deciding its processing order. To effect this, we construct facilities for the following:

(1)   Broadcasting descriptions forward in the tree, which are intended to describe the circumstances under which predecessor arcs were chosen. From these descriptions, it is then possible to extract criteria for partitioning the set of legal successor arcs at a node further down the branch.

Partitioning will separate arcs into those that are consistent with existent (broadcast) themes and those that are not, and those that make progress toward existing (broadcast) goals and those that do not. We use the term "goal" to mean a well-defined class of nodes, and the term "consistent with a theme" to mean a class of arcs that has a well-defined relation with the theme description.

(2) Backing-up descriptions of things that happened during the search of a given subtree. When the value of such a result does not measure up to the expectation level, the description is examined by the *causality facility* to determine whether or not the arc immediately leading to the subtree caused the events described. Then:

> (a) If the arc did not permit the events described (i.e., the basis for this failure already existed at the node), we use the description for finding a (domain-dependent) remedy. This is done by partitioning the set of legal arcs into those that are capable of blocking the events in the description and those that are not.

> (b) If the arc did permit the events, then we abstract from the description a set of conditions describing the circumstances under which the failure occurred, so as to be able to detect when this arc might fail again in the same way under similar circumstances. The machinery necessary to do these manipulations will be called the *invariance facility*. A set of abstracted failure-describing conditions is called an *invariance*, and is filed in a global data base.

We make the following assumptions in our discussions, in order to avoid confounding the problems we are dealing with:

(1) We are not concerned with whether the major search control algorithm is depth-first, breadth-first, or best-first, but only with providing information for making risk decisions that may result in terminating a branch that might otherwise be extended.

(2) We accept the values of F as being correct. We understand that in practice this is nearly impossible. However, this does not bear on the primary topic at hand. Since a value must be returned from any leaf node, we choose to trust F. Later we will discuss how domain-dependent information can be used to overcome one of the chief deficiencies of F: the negative horizon effect.

Let us consider what portions of a search tree, with respect to an arbitrary node N, could possess information that may be of use to a decision making process. The path from the root of the tree to N contains historical information that could conceivably be used to bring about a consistency of action in the subtree of N if this branch is to be a candidate for the optimum solution. Likewise, the subtree of N should have some interesting information having to do with the success or failure of the arc that was invoked to produce N. We will now show how this information should be formulated and used by *domain-independent* mechanisms in order to promote good decision making.

3. NECESSARY PROPERTIES OF DOMAIN-DEPENDENT DESCRIPTIONS

In order for descriptions to be of use in guiding a tree search and making risk decisions that terminate branches, they must be at a useful level of precision. This is because it will be necessary to operate on these descriptions in order to achieve anything. Thus, the notion of optimum solution is very precise, but does not allow the making of any risk decisions. On the other hand, statements in natural language are at the present state of the art too imprecise to provide useful input. We have thus chosen to focus on an in-between level, at which the descriptions that can be generated are precise but can also be used to do meaningful reasoning in the domain.

Domain-dependent descriptions must have primitives that allow the unique specification of any arc or node in the domain. It should also be possible to describe classes of arcs and nodes by specifying the common properties of the class.

We intend to have description elements that span the domain, and yet allow the building up of very complex descriptions. In general, one would like to form describable classes, such that all members of the class will be subjected to like actions. However, the actions can be of various grains. So there is a trade-off: the more precise the description, the smaller the class of things it can describe and the more fine grained the action must be; while the less precise the description, the larger the class of things it can describe and the coarser the grain of the action can be. A sensible trade-off point is one where the number of necessary actions across all classes is reasonable, while the precision of the actions is adequate. What is reasonable and adequate will probably change as a function of the competence of the program.

Thus, it would not be very useful to have knowledge about a particular problem state if the chances of encountering this state again were small. Apparently, human beings are very good at finding node-classes and arc-classes of the right size. For instance, in chess the number of possible problem states (positions) is 10^{43} [De Groot 66], the number of possible operators (moves) is about 8000, while the number of operators that are applicable in the average problem state is about 35 [Slater 50]. Yet studies indicate that the strongest players in the world can probably not recognize more than one million different node-classes, while beginning players may recognize only a few hundred node-classes [Chase and Simon 73].

The difference between 10^{43} possible nodes and the 10^6 node classes recognized by masters is drastic. However, according to De Groot [66], only one in 10^{30} legal chess positions could be arrived at in master play. Therefore there are 10^{13} chess positions that a master has to catalog into about 10^6 node classes. This yields an average of 10^7 nodes per class. Since the number of classes is correlated with the strength of the player, apparently the adequacy of an action does in fact decide what a class's membership should be; i.e., when an action associated with a class fails to be adequate, the class is subdivided and new actions are found to associate with the new classes. Thus, the hallmark of the stronger player is more (adequate) node classes, and presumably more descriptive apparatus.

Studies by De Groot [65] indicate that expert chess players are seldom aware of the actual number of legal arcs at a node, but rather concentrate on one to three possibilities. This is a reduction of 12 to 35 over the average number of legal moves in a position. This kind of selectivity could conceivably be achieved by having S very sensitive to the node-class it is dealing with. A step in this direction is to classify all arcs into categories as was suggested in Section 2. This is an attention-focusing device intended to produce few meaningful successors to a node, and thus drive the branching factor down toward the 1.0 necessary for search convergence.

The lowest level of elements from which descriptions can be built is domain-dependent. This level includes descriptions of nodes, arcs, node-classes and arc-classes. Out of these elements it will then be possible to build more complex descriptions. Among these are goal-descriptions (which describe a class of desirable nodes), theme-descriptions (which describe a class of desirable arcs), consequence-descriptions (which describe a sequence of arcs from a given subtree together with the consequence encountered when this sequence occurred), and invariances (which describe a node-class at which a particular arc is likely to fail). We now define the following descriptions:

(1) An *arc-description* is an n-tuple (where n depends on the domain) that uniquely specifies an arc in the domain. For instance, an arc in the game of tic-tac-toe can be uniquely specified by selecting one element from each set of the following $(\{X, O\}, \{1, 2, \ldots, 9\})$.

(2) A *node-description* is an n-tuple (where n depends on the domain) that uniquely specifies a node in the domain. For instance, in tic-tac-toe a node can be described by two sets of integers, drawn from the population 1 through 9, having no elements identical to both sets, and with the cardinality of the sets not differing by more than one.

(3)   An *arc-history (A, B)* is a list of all the arc-descriptions on the branch between node A and node B, where A is closer to the root than B.

(4)   A *node-history (A, B)* is a list of all the node-descriptions on the branch between node A and node B, where A is closer to the root than B.

(5)   A *consequence-description(N)* is an arc-history rooted at node N, which describes the optimum branch (by whatever method is being used to define optimum) in the subtree rooted at N, together with a reason (which also implies a value) why the branch was terminated. The reasons can be:

(a)   that there are no legal successors to the terminal node; i.e., the game is over; or

(b)   The contents of F as applied at the terminal node; i.e., the reason for terminating and the value of the terminal node. Since the search could theoretically go on, F must be able to define why it did not.

We will refer to a consequence-description(N), which has a value that fails to satisfy the side that produced the arc leading to N, as a *refutation-description(N)*.

(6)   A class description specifies what the descriptions of its members have in common. Thus an *(arc-class)-description* is a description of a set of arc-descriptions. A *(node-class)-description* is a description of a set of node-descriptions. Classes are denoted by specifying the minimum conditions that all class members must meet for inclusion; e.g., all arcs that were legal at node N, or all arcs that change a certain element in a particular (node-class)-description.

(7)   A *theme-description(N)* is a list of arc-classes accumulated across the node-history (Root, N). When S selects an arc for searching, it is possible to indicate classes of arcs that would be good follow-up arcs. These can then be broadcast forward as theme descriptions to guide the further progress of the analysis. The notion of theme was proposed in Berliner [74] and is expanded here.

(8)   A *goal-description(N)* is a list of node-classes accumulated across the node-history (Root, N). When S selects an arc for searching, it is possible to indicate node-classes that are intended to be achieved. This can then help F later on to find nodes that represent the achievement of the intent of one or more of the arcs in the current arc-history.

(9)   An *invariance(A)* is an arc-description of A together with a set of refutation-descriptions, together with a (node-class)-description. An invariance describes a class of nodes at which A will fail in the manner described by the consequence-descriptions. The notion of using descriptions to capture the features of a situation that are essential for a particular arc, which has just failed in a search, to fail again in the same manner was put forward in Berliner [74] under the name of "lemma". Here we considerably

sharpen the concept and extend it so it can also be used to describe successes as well. A program that discovers predefined invariances in bridge problems is described in Berlekamp [63].

There is one final refinement to our scheme that greatly increases its power. We will call a description a 0th-order description if it merely describes things as specified above. An nth-order description is a description of all entities of the class described that could be attained if (in a two-person game) the side for whom the description is being compiled were able to execute n arcs (moves) consecutively, before compiling the description with moves, then alternating.

Thus, a 0th-order description is a description of something immediate; a 1st-order description is one that is one arc removed from immediacy; an nth-order description is n arcs removed from immediacy. From a practical point of view, 0th-order, 1st-order, and 2nd-order descriptions appear to be useful in conceptualizing such things as the immediacy of an impending action or threat. Higher order descriptions can best be thought of as goals and strategies and are probably best handled as class descriptions. nth-order effects have been proposed in Adelson-Velskiy *et al.* [75] and Atkin [75].

From each description it is possible to deduce a set of effects that either:

(1) happened,
(2) were intended to happen, or
(3) represent conditions that are necessary for something to happen or not happen.

It is the ability to construct descriptions and make deductions from them that provides the power of our scheme.

4. DOMAIN-DEPENDENT DESCRIPTIONS FOR COMPUTER CHESS

Let us now consider of what use all these descriptions can be. In any domain there is a set of necessary conditions in order for an arc described by an arc-description to be a legal arc at an arbitrary node. Thus, it is possible to examine a description of a presently legal arc and determine what would be necessary to change its status to illegal. Likewise it is possible to examine descriptions of arcs that are presently not legal, and decide what must be changed to make the arc legal in the future. Operations also exist for making a legal, but ineffective arc into an effective one, and *vice versa*. Similar operations exist with respect to node descriptions. Thus, descriptions are a way of providing very general inputs to a continuing means–ends analysis. The nature of the means–ends analysis may depend somewhat on the domain; however, the method of generating descriptions appears to be general.

Descriptions can also be used to hold information in a very general way that might have been difficult to specify *a priori*. For instance, descriptions can hold information about a set of meaningful goals or a set of thematic continuation arcs that were proposed by *S* when an arc was selected. In a more complicated vein, descriptions can hold information about an undesirable set of events that happened in a subtree immediately below a particular arc. From this it is possible to determine whether the played arc created the conditions for its own failure, or whether it only failed to respond to some necessity that already existed at its parent node. This causal analysis can then lead either to finding the proper arc (in case the tried arc was not at fault) or positing an invariance about the arc (in case it created the problem). The invariance names the arc, how it failed, and the necessary conditions for it to fail again in the same manner. An invariance can be of use to avoid trying an arc when the necessary conditions for its failure are still present.

We now define a set of descriptions for the domain of chess, based partly on an implementation in our chess program CAPS [Berliner 74]. We will then illustrate the use of descriptions in computer chess with a set of examples.

Since chess is a geometric game, the descriptions will be couched in the geometry of the chess board (see Botwinnik [70] for a good discussion of this) and the operations needed to describe legal arcs and nodes. The basic elements from which these descriptions are formed are:

(1) The set of squares of the chessboard SQ, each of which has a name. For convenience in describing sets of moves, we include in SQ the null square and the universal square. To illustrate the use of the latter, it is easiest to portray the moving away of a piece as the set of moves from its origin square to the universal square.

(2) The types of pieces PC, where we distinguish between white pieces and black of the same type but not between different pieces of the same color and type. The null piece and the universal piece are also in this set.

(3) The names of the pieces NA, where each piece has a unique name.

(4) TURN, a binary variable that is true for a node when it is White's turn to move, and false otherwise.

(5) FILE, an integer associated with a node description, which has the value 0 if the last move was not a 2-square pawn advance, and has the value of the file of the advance otherwise.

(6) CASLRTS, which is a set of 4 binary flags, each of which is true if

castling for a certain side in a certain direction is still legal, and false otherwise.

In terms of the above primitives, an arc-description ARC(MOVER, ORIG, DEST, OCCUP) can be uniquely specified, where

MOVER is a member of PC (excluding the null and universal pieces) and specifies the type of the moving piece,
ORIG is a member of SQ (excluding the null and universal squares) and specifies the square of origin of the move,
DEST is a member of SQ (excluding the null and universal squares) and specifies the destination square,
OCCUP is a member of PC and specifies the occupant of DEST (including the null piece but not the universal piece).

Such a specification will uniquely describe any and all moves. An *en passant* pawn capture is uniquely specified by the fact that the move is a capture and the value of OCCUP is the null piece, and castling by specifying the movement of the king only, since it can only move a distance of two squares when castling.

A node-description NODE(LOCATS, TURN, FILE, CASLRTS) will uniquely define a chess position. Here LOCATS is a set of pairs (PC, SQ) and the other parameters are as defined above.

The necessary conditions for a move to be legal are:

(1)　MOVER must be on square ORIG.
(2)　OCCUP must be on square DEST.
(3)　All *path* squares for a move must be free of any pieces. By a path square we mean one that is between the origin and destination for sliding pieces, and the destination square (and any passed over) in case of a pawn advance or castling.

In addition,

(4)　The king of the moving side cannot be in check after the move.
(5)　Some other conditions associated with castling and *en passant* moves must be met.

To change the status of a move from legal to nonlegal, we note the following possibilities:

(1)　Capture the occupant of ORIG.
(2)　Block any path square of the moving piece.
(3)　If OCCUP is not the null piece, then move the occupant of DEST away.
(4)　Pin the occupant of ORIG to its king.

Further, the following actions could result in the move still being legal but no longer effective:

(5) Move a piece not presently defending DEST to a position where it is.

(6) Pin the occupant of ORIG to another piece.

For a 0th-order description, any of these actions must be taken, on the very next move, if they are to be effective. For nth-order descriptions, it is possible to project an n-move sequence to accomplish the task. However, when there are several nth-order descriptions that must be met, only moves that meet all of them collectively can be effective.

These are methods of making a move ineffective directly. It is also possible to defend indirectly against a move, by moving a piece so that it will be able to move through a square vacated by a moving piece, or in other ways also. However, these are advanced uses, which we will not treat in this paper. There are also methods of trying to make a currently illegal move into a legal one, and of trying to make a node that currently does not conform to a node-class description into one that does. Some of these are treated in the examples below.

To summarize: consequence-descriptions, refutation-descriptions, class-descriptions, theme-descriptions, goal-descriptions, histories, and invariances can be made out of the entities defined above in the way described in Section 3. We are now ready for the examples of how descriptions can be used in computer chess.

5. EXAMPLES

5.1. The Use of a History Description

In Fig. 1 it is White to play. It is very likely that the move 1. R–K1 will be investigated in the analysis. In this case Black may respond K–B1, whereupon White may consider the further alternatives (among others) of 2. R–K5 and 2. R–QB1. The program will find that 2. R–K5, R–Q1, does not accomplish much and then most likely spend much time examining the merits of 2. R–QB1. However, this move is not consistent with the previous 1. R–K1, and should not be investigated at all. The reason is that moving the rook to QB1 was possible earlier in the history of the current position and does not appear to be any better now than it was earlier. Therefore, if the move is to be investigated it should be at an earlier point, which in this case is the root position.

The above logic is formalized as follows: The node history of the current position (at depth 3, after 1. R–K1, K–B1) contains descriptions of all the

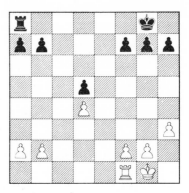

Fig. 1. White to play.

positions between the root and itself. Before a move is tried, a check is made to see whether a move with the same MOVER, DEST, and OCCUP was possible at an earlier node with the same side to play. If so, then if S applied to the present move is not better than the best evaluation S gave any similar untried move in the node-history, the move should not be investigated. This puts a certain onus on S, since if it fails to detect favorable changes in the environment that make a move better in the new environment, the move will be ignored to the detriment of the analysis. However, S gets some help from the invariance facility (discussed in Example 5). If the move in question was possible in the history of the node and was actually searched, then it must have failed to produce an outstanding result (otherwise the search would be terminated successfully). Therefore, there must be an invariance describing why the move failed to be successful, and it is possible to compare the current environment to the one in which the invariance was posited to determine whether the necessary conditions for lack of success are still present.

5.2. Causality

Consider the position in Fig. 2. Here, it is conceivable that the move P–KR3 by Black will be the first one analyzed. If this were so, then the resulting variation would be 1. P–KR3, 2. R–B8ch, K–R2, 3. R × B. A 0th-order description of the consequences will only include all the moves that were actually played in the above sequence. Thus when examining the 0th-order consequences of 1. P–KR3, the conclusion would be drawn that this leads to the loss of the black bishop. Therefore the goals of moving the bishop, defending it, blocking the path squares of the two rook moves, and guarding the destination square QB8 will be created. This would in fact produce many moves, only one of which is the solution.

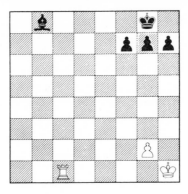

Fig. 2. Black to play.

The use of a 1st-order description is much more powerful. Consider the position after White has played 2.   R–B8ch, and examine the moves that lead to refutations if it were now White's turn to play (Black plays a null move). Now it becomes known that the black king is attacked. This is what is lost in the 0th-order description, because in finding the optimal move sequence, the king is moved and the bishop lost. After 2.   R–B8ch there are two 1st-order effects, 3.   R × B, and 3.   R × K. Since neither result is an acceptable consequence for Black, it is necessary to find a move that defends against *both* 1st-order effects simultaneously or else to lower the aspiration level. Thus, one set of moves tries to capture or pin the rook, move the king away, or block the path squares of the rook to the king; while the second set tries to capture or pin the rook, move the bishop away, or block the path squares of the rook to the bishop. Since the king must be moved in this position, there is no common move in the *intersection* of these two sets, so backing up continues.

On backing up to the point where Black played 1.   P–KR3, the description of the move 2.   R–B8ch is added to the 0th-order description, and nothing to the 1st-order description, since R–B8ch is the only threat. We now first try to find moves that counter the 0th-order description, for which there is only 1.   B–B2 (blocking one of the path squares of the rook). Since these are no 1st-order effects at this node, it means that all 1st-order effects are not immediate and thus Black has one extra move available to *prepare* to meet the 1st-order effects. This means that in addition to the objectives that were stated for move selection at the node resulting from White's 2.   R–B8ch, the present set of moves can include those that prepare to move the king or the bishop, or prepare to block any of the path squares. Thus, moves such as 1.   P–KN3, which prepares to move the king to a new square, would be in one of the sets. However, the only member common to both sets is 1.   B–Q3, which removes the bishop from the square on which it was captured, and also prepares to block one of the path squares of the rook to the king. This then leaves only two moves: 1. B–B2, which loses the bishop and would thus be poorly recommended by *S* and 1. B–Q3, which is the only way to save the position. This can then be tried, and the generate-and-test effort that would have been required to determine the inadequacy of the remaining moves that Black can play in the diagram position is avoided.

5.3. Descriptions for Propagating a Theme

In Fig. 3, assume an *S* that recognizes that the black pawn on QN3 is overloaded (the *S* of CAPS [Berliner 74] does); i.e., it has two defensive functions to fulfill (defending the knights on White's QB5 and QR5) and can only perform one. White therefore chooses the move 1. B × N with the expectation of gaining material. This is conceptualized in a theme associated with the overload that was detected by *S*. The theme is intended to guide the perpetrator of the action to its completion, and guide the other party in attempts to foil it. This particular theme is conceptualized by broadcasting (arc-class)-descriptions for moves of the universal piece to the White squares QB5 and QR5. This binds both sides to try captures on these squares in the analysis until it is determined whether or not the overload really exists. If this were not done, then in the actual analysis of the variation following 1. B × N, Black may play B × Bch first and only after 2. K × B face up to the problem of whether or not the bishop that took the knight can be recaptured. In an average situation there may be even more ways of postponing the basic issue. Further, it is frequently the case that the idea behind the original move will not work, as would be the case if the black bishop at QN2 were at QB2. This type of vacillating behavior can be avoided by the use of the broadcast. Of course, the theme

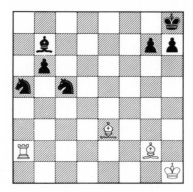

Fig. 3. White to play.

only binds the opponents in their approach to the analysis of the consequences of the move(s) that produced the theme, and does not apply to the move that will actually be selected for play. This method of operating, will cause much more rapid dismissal of unsound ideas, with the consequences that an invariance can be posited about the unsound idea, making it possible to avoid it in the future, and providing a statement that can serve as a goal for resurrecting the idea.

In the actual position, Black will thus be forced to reply 1. P × B, and White 2. R × N, after which, the idea having apparently succeeded, Black is free to try to find a less direct method of refuting it.

5.4. Positing an Invariance

Figure 4 shows a part of a possible chess position. As long as this configuration of pieces remains the same, it is very likely that whenever it is White's turn to play he will try 1. R × Pch, K × R, 2. Q–R5ch, K–N1, 3. Q–R8ch, K × Q, and then decide that this sequence does not work. In the process, a refutation-description will be backed up to the point where White originally played 1. R × Pch. Each time it will be found that the

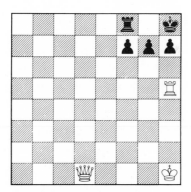

Fig. 4. White to play.

move R × Pch was responsible for the consequences, and that there is substantially nothing that White can do to make this move work. Thus, much effort will be wasted (especially if the configuration is more complex than the one in the diagram). It would be much better if, when the first time this sequence is tried and the refutation-description becomes available, an invariance were created about the move R × Pch. This is done by comparing certain elements in the refutation-description with elements in the current position. The refutation-description contains the arc-history of the refutation i.e., the list of arc-descriptions of the refutation. From this and the current position-description, it is possible to derive the following:

(1)   Type/square-name pairs of all pieces that participated in the re-futation-description for the refuting side.

(2)   All path squares, for moves of the refuting side, that are now unoccupied.

(3)   All squares to which pieces of the refuting side moved.

(4)   The names of pieces of both sides presently in a position to capture on any square named in (3).

(5)   The value and special termination reasons (if any) associated with the refutation.

The 0th-order invariance for the above position thus contains:

(1)   Type/square/name pairs: black king at KR8.

(2)   Path squares: none.

(3)   Refutation squares: KR7, KN8, KR8.

(4)   Pieces bearing on refutation squares: KR7 (white rook at KR5 and black king at KR8); KN8 (black king at KR8 and black rook at KB8); KR8 (black rook at KB8).

(5)   Value of loss: rook for pawn.

It is known that the move 1. R × Pch brought on the consequences since otherwise it would not have been possible to capture the rook on KR7. Therefore an invariance is made up to reference for future oc-currences of the move R × Pch. Now as long as the conditions mentioned in the invariance remain the same, the necessary conditions for R × Pch failing again in the same way are present. This does not mean either that R × Pch will succeed otherwise or that it could not possibly succeed as long as the above conditions remained constant. But it is very likely that it will fail again. Thus, invariances are not guaranteed and retain a heuristic aspect. This point is made in Adelson-Velskiy *et al.* [75] in discussing the "method of analogies".

As an example of a possible deficiency in an invariance consider the effect of removing Black's KNP, which is not mentioned in the invariance at all. This would allow a multitude of checks by the white queen, and R × Pch would in fact lead to a draw. Also, the role of the black rook in defending the squares KR8 and KN8 is an unnecessary artifact of the invariance. However, adding new white pieces that control any of the squares to which the refuting side moved will considerably change the power of R × Pch to the point where it may succeed. Actually, as small changes in the position take place, the move R × Pch will be tried again and every time it fails a new invariance will be derived, until a reasonably comprehensive set of conditions for the failure of R × Pch should exist. It should also be possible to get some higher-order effects into the invariance by noting conditions that keep certain moves from being effective (such as the black KNP blocking future white queen checks), and other moves from being legal (such as the white KBP blocking White checks on the diagonal QN1–KR7).

It is possible to deduce many interesting facts from an invariance. For instance, if there is no 1st-order refutation-description, then there must have been only a single thing that was wrong with the move made and anything that can be done to prevent that from happening is sufficient to describe the conditions under which it will not fail again in the same way. If there are 1st-order descriptions, then only if at least one necessary condition from each of these is no longer true, as well as the 0th-order description having some necessary condition no longer true, will the invariance not be valid. We will clarify this in Section 5.5.

The invariance about R × Pch contains all the above information. Whenever R × Pch is again proposed for searching, it is possible to search a file to determine whether there exists an invariance with respect to it. In this case, such an invariance will be found. It is now necessary to go through the process of determining whether the *necessary* conditions for R × Pch failing again in the same manner exist. The set of tests on any nth-order description of the invariance consists of the following:

(1) All the type/square-name pairs mentioned in the description must be in place in the current position.

(2) All free path squares of the refuting side that are mentioned in the description must be free in the current position.

(3) None of the squares to which the refuting side moved may now be occupied by a piece of its own side, nor may it be controlled by fewer of its own pieces than mentioned in the description, nor may any new pieces of the losing side be controlling such a square.

Basically, this set of tests consists of determining whether a previously legal move of the refuting side now is illegal, or whether anything has changed on any destination square that might make a move to it more viable for the losing side or less viable for the winning side. As long as none of these necessary conditions change, the invariance holds. However, the conditions are only necessary and not sufficient to guarantee that the move will again fail. For instance, it is possible that in the current position, a newly placed piece of the losing side could move through a square vacated in the process of executing the refutation, and thus refute it in turn. Also, it is possible that in the current position there is some new weakness that could be attacked as a result of a move that at the time the invariance was posited would have been futile. The possibilities of this happening can also be dealt with by the order-of-approximation method. Suffice it to say here that in practical situations this rarely happens. In fact, invariances can be used not only to avoid testing moves that failed previously, but also to enunciate goals for the losing side, in order to resurrect the refuted move. In such a case a theme broadcast of the idea should make it possible to tell whether the invariance is likely to be upset.

5.5. Using an Invariance to Overcome the Negative Horizon Effect

This position (Fig. 5) is taken from some earlier work of this author, which examined problems in current chess-playing programs. It is an example of the negative horizon effect [Berliner 73]. Let us assume that a search is being conducted to a depth of 3 ply, and that the terminal evaluation function F determines quiescence by examining all legal captures in any position that is a candidate leaf node. The search will find the variation 1. B–QN3, P–B5, and regardless of any move that White makes, the bishop will be lost. It will also find the variation 1. P–K5, P × P (if P × B, then P × N is satisfactory for White), 2. B–QN3. Now since the 3-ply depth has been reached and there are no captures for Black, the position is pronounced quiescent by F, and the bishop is considered safe. (It is called the negative horizon effect because a negative event was discovered during the search and the program found a way of "pushing" the event over the horizon of search. Thus it seemed to the program the problem was solved; whereas in reality it was merely postponed.)

We will avoid this kind of myopia in a general way by the use of invariances. When the variation 1. B–QN3, P–B5, winning the bishop, is backed up to the point where 1. B–QN3 was played, an invariance is posited about the move B–QN3. In the position after 1. B–QN3, P–B5, White may try some moves and eventually return to this node with the

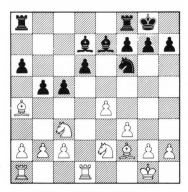

Fig. 5. White to play.

0th-order and 1st-order refutation-descriptions being identical and starting with Black's P × B. This means that this was the only threat, and the reason it succeeded was that the bishop could not get away. The *F* of our program now notes whether the bishop was pinned or merely low in mobility, and decides the latter is true. Thus, *F* provides not only the value of the loss but the reason as well, and gives the denied squares of the bishop as being QR2, QB2, QR4, and QB4. These data become part of the refutation-description as well as the usual location of refutation pieces, path squares, etc. When the search returns to the top node, an invariance is posited about the move B–QN3. This contains the names of the refutation pieces (the black QBP), path squares (White's QB4 which must be free for the pawn to advance), refutation squares (White's QB4 and QN3), pieces bearing on these squares (White's pawns at QB2 and QR2, and Black's pawn at QN4), and finally the denied squares (QR2, QB2, QR4, and QB4) and their occupants or controlling pieces. This is the invariance relating to the loss of the bishop and it is assumed that the bishop will be lost as long as this configuration remains the same.

Now when the variation 1.   P–K5, P × P, 2.   B–QN3 is examined, the invariance is available to decide that the move will not save the bishop, because all the necessary conditions of the invariance are met in the final position. Thus the negative horizon effect is overcome. In fact, analysis convinces us that this is the only way it can be overcome. It is still necessary to point out that should the variation starting with 1.   P–K5 be searched and considered correct before the invariance is found, this will not avoid the correct solution being found. Whenever an invariance is found, it is necessary to examine the current optimum line of play in order to determine whether any of the moves in it are affected by the new invariance. If so, the optimum line must be reexamined, and this will result in convergence to the correct solution.

6.   SUMMARY

In this chapter we have developed a structure for coping with the exponentiality of tree searching. Our framework makes possible formal expressions that correspond closely to the standard tools that human beings appear to have for dealing with this problem. The method allows approaching complete accuracy for any expressed quantity by orders of approximation. Low orders of approximation are considered to be quite satisfactory for emulating human performance on the complex task of chess. In this way it is possible to ignore certain branches of a tree representing a problem space, so as to be able to penetrate deeply on branches that are considered pertinent. It is also possible during a tree search to pass forward theme information for guiding the progress of the search by qualifying arcs that are thematically related to earlier arcs. Further, it is possible to discover invariances that describe conditions that are necessary for an arc to succeed or fail in a prescribed manner. We have shown several examples of our method from the domain of chess.

REFERENCES

Adelson-Velskiy, G. M., Arlazarov, V. L., and Donskoy, M. V., Some methods of controlling the tree search in chess programs. *Artificial Intelligence* **6** 4, 361–371 (1975).

Atkin, R. H., Positional play in chess by computer. In *Advances in Computer Chess 1*, (M. R. B. Clarke, ed.) Edinburgh Univ. Press, Edinburgh, 1975.

Berlekamp, E., Program for double–dummy bridge problems—a new strategy for mechanical game playing. *J. ACM* **10** 3, 357–364 (1963).

Berliner, H. J., Some necessary conditions for a master chess program. *Proc. 3rd Intern. Joint Conference Artificial Intelligence, Stanford, California, August 1973*, 77–85.

Berliner, H. J., Chess as problem solving: the development of a tactics analyzer. Ph.D. thesis, Computer Science Dept., Carnegie-Mellon Univ., Pittsburgh, Pennsylvania, 1974.

Botwinnik, M. M., *Computers, Chess and Long-Range Planning*. Springer–Verlag, Berlin, 1970.

Chase, W. G., and Simon, H. A., Perception in chess. *Cognitive Psychology* **4** 1 (January 1973).

De Groot, A. D., *Thought and Choice in Chess*. Mouton, Paris, 1965.

De Groot, A. D., Perception and memory versus thought: some old ideas and recent findings. In *Problem Solving: Research, Method and Theory* (B. Kleinmuntz, ed.). Wiley, New York, 1966.

Fuller, S. H., Gaschnig, J. H., and Gillogly, J. J., Analysis of the alpha–beta pruning algorithm. Computer Science Dept. Rep., Carnegie-Mellon University, Pittsburgh, Pennsylvania, 1973.

Greenblatt, R. D., Eastlake, D. E., and Crocker, S. D., The Greenblatt chess program. *Proc. FJCC* **31**, 801–810 (1967).

Harris, L., The bandwidth heuristic search. *Proc. 3rd Intern. Joint Conf. Artificial Intelligence, Stanford, California, August 1973*, 23–29.

Knuth, D. E. and Moore, R. E., An analysis of alpha–beta pruning. *Artificial Intelligence* **6** 4, 293–326 (1975).

Newell, A., The chess machine: an example of dealing with a complex task by adaptation. *Proc. WJCC* **7**, 101–108 (1955).

Nilsson, N. J., *Problem Solving Methods in Artificial Intelligence*. McGraw–Hill, New York, 1971.

Slagle, J. R., and Dixon, J. K., Experiments with some programs that search game trees. *J. ACM* **16** 2, 189–207 (April 1969).

Slater, E., Statistics for the chess computer and the factor of mobility. *Symp. Information Theory, Ministry of Supply, London, 1950*, 150–152.

Knowledge Representation in Automatic Planning Systems

Richard E. Fikes [†]

Artificial Intelligence Center
Stanford Research Institute
Menlo Park, California

This paper is a tutorial on automatic planning systems, with particular emphasis given to knowledge representation issues. The effectiveness of a planner depends, to a large extent, on its ability to make use of descriptions and expertise associated with particular task domains. Examples of such domain knowledge include action models, state description models, scenarios, and special purpose plan composition methods. Our discussion focuses on how such knowledge is represented in planning systems, and on how various planning strategies make use of it.

1. INTRODUCTION

A planning system is one that assists in the accomplishment of tasks by generating plans and then monitoring their execution. The active agent that actually carries out the plans might be another part of the system (e.g., a mechanical manipulator), or a human to whom the system is providing instructions. A task is usually specified to such a system by describing an initial situation and a desired (goal) situation. The system is aware of actions that the active agent can carry out, and the plan it produces is a sequence of these actions that are expected to transform the initial situation into the desired situation. Example domains for which automatic planning systems have been designed include the directing of a mobile robot doing tasks that involve pushing boxes around in several rooms [Fikes and Nilsson 71], a robot arm building towers out of multiple-shaped blocks [Fahlman 74], and humans who are repairing electromechanical equipment [Sacerdoti 75].

Taking a broader view, a planner can be thought of as being a constructor of scenarios for whatever reasons they are needed. For example,

[†]Present address: Xerox Corporation, Palo Alto Research Center, Palo Alto, California.

Minsky [74], Schank [75], and others have described the use of stored "action frames" or "scripts" as guides to a system attempting to understand a story being input in natural language. The stored scenario indicates what typically happens in the situation being described in the story (such as having dinner at a restaurant or attending a child's birthday party). It aids the system by providing a set of expectations about the sequence of events and the relationships among the characters in the story. To make effective use of stored scenarios, a system needs the capability of modifying and combining them to form new scenarios that are appropriate for understanding any particular story; that is, the system needs a planning capability.

In this paper I will examine some of the characteristics of automatic planning systems by focusing on the knowledge representation issues that arise in their design. My intention is not to survey the entire field of automatic planning, but rather to provide a feeling for the general structure of such systems and for some of the techniques that have been and are being used in their design.

2. STATE DESCRIPTION MODELS

Typically, a planner proceeds by hypothesizing sequences of actions for inclusion in a plan, and testing each hypothesis by simulating the action sequence. The simulation produces a description of the situation that would be expected to result from the actions, and that situation is examined to determine whether it satisfies the subgoals that the planner is trying to achieve. This process requires facilities for creating, updating, and querying state description models of the task domain.

Most planning systems use state description models that can be characterized as collections of relational expressions, with each expression having a truth value associated with it. The expressions are typically represented as list structures with the first element of each list being a relation name. For example, (INROOM ROBOT R1) or (STATUS (CONNECTION PUMP PLATFORM) FASTENED). The models provide the data base needed to determine for any given relationship in any given state whether the relationship is known true, known false, or unknown in that state.

Some form of retrieval mechanism is needed for this data base so that the planner can obtain information about these models. Retrieval functions rely on a basic access mechanism that in most planning systems associatively retrieves from the data base all relational expressions that match a given pattern (where a pattern is an expression containing unbound variables), and then examines the truth value of each retrieved expression with respect to the given state. For example, a retrieval using the pattern (INROOM ROBOT ←X) would be used to determine (and assign to the variable X) the name of the room the robot is in.

Usually, not all relations whose truth values are known are explicitly stored in a model. Hence, a planner needs some kind of deductive machinery for querying state description models. Most planners are designed so that a user can provide derivation functions that compute implicit truth values when they are needed. These functions may embody formal theorem-proving strategies or simply be statements of implicational rules derived from the semantics of the task domain. They serve to extend each model in the sense that, from the calling program's point of view, the derived instances of a pattern can be made to be indistingishable from instances actually found in the model.

3. ACTION MODELS

Typically, a planner has available models of the actions that can occur as steps in a plan. For example, the actions available to a mobile robot might include "Go to location (x, y)", "Turn X degrees right", etc. In order for these models to be useful to a planner, they must include certain descriptive information about the actions. In particular, the planner needs to know under what conditions an action can be carried out. These are the action's "preconditions" or "applicability conditions". They provide a source of subgoals during the planning process and allow the planner to assure that an executable plan is being produced. In addition, the planner needs a description of the transformations that execution of an action is expected to make. This information allows the planner to simulate hypothetical action sequences and thereby investigate their results. Finally, the planner needs to know what kinds of tasks or subgoals each action is useful for achieving. This information indicates to the planner which actions to consider putting into the plan being constructed.

The action models that are available to a planner as potential plan steps usually represent an entire class of actions by containing slots that must be filled by specific values. For example, a robot action for moving a box might include slots for the name of the box, the starting location of the move, and the final location of the move. Hence, the action can be used to move any box from any location to any other location. An action model will specify constraints on the values that can fill its slots such as type requirements and, for the box example, perhaps a restriction that the two locations be in the same room. A significant part of the planning activity is the determination of values for these slots that both satisfy the model's constraints and produce an instance of the model that is useful in the new plan. Hence, the planning process involves both selecting and "instantiating" a sequence of action models that will achieve the desired goal situation.

3.1. Assertional Action Models

Action models are often represented as data structures containing lists of parameters, preconditions, and effects. The parameters are the "slots" that the planner must instantiate when using the model, and they serve as the model's local variables. The preconditions are an explicit list of the relationships that must be true in a state before the action can be executed. The effects indicate the state changes that the action is expected to make. Each element of the effects list indicates a relationship and the truth value that the relationship is to have in the state produced by the action; all other relationships are assumed to remain unaffected by the action. For example, the model for a "Go to location (x, y)" robot action might have parameters x and y, preconditions that require location (x, y) to be in the same room as the robot, and an effects list that denies the old location of the robot, deletes (i.e., assigns truth value "unknown") the old orientation of the robot, and asserts (x, y) as the new location of the robot.

This type of action model representation lends itself to a means–ends analysis method for composing plans as follows. A goal state is described by a collection of relationships that must be true in the desired state. The planner proceeds by checking to see which of the goal relationships are not yet true in the current state. When such a relationship is found, a scan is made of the action models in an attempt to find one whose effects list indicates that some instance of it will assert the goal relationship. When such an action is found, it is taken to be "relevant" to achieving the goal, and the planner attempts to include it in the plan. An action can be included in a plan only if a state exists in which its preconditions are true. If they are true in the current state, then the action is simulated to produce a new current state, and the goal is reconsidered as before. If the action's preconditions are not true in the current state, then the achievement of those preconditions becomes a new goal for the planner to which the same method can be applied. Hence, the basic algorithm involves matching a goal to an action capable of achieving some portion of it, and then attempting to make that action applicable.

When more than one relevant action is found for any particular goal, or when a goal is a disjunction, then a "choice point" occurs in the algorithm. The occurrence of such choice points requires the planner to impose some form of search executive on top of the basic algorithm to decide at each step which subgoal to consider next.

3.2. Procedural Action Models

The planning algorithm described above is essentially the one used in the STRIPS system developed in 1969. One of the major ways in which the effectiveness of planning systems has been improved since then is by providing facilities for augmenting this basic algorithm by accepting planning expertise that is specific to the particular domain in which tasks are to be given. That is, in any given domain there will be planning strategies and heuristics that a planner designed specifically for that domain would employ; for example, route-finding algorithms, or tower-building strategies. To a large extent, the effectiveness of a planning system can be measured in terms of its ability to accept and utilize such expertise.

One way in which this capability has been achieved is by representing action models in a procedural form rather than as a data structure (for example, see Derksen *et al.* [72]). Such a procedure has the action's parameters as its input parameters, and begins by querying the current state description model to determine if the action's preconditions are true in that state; if they are not, then it calls the planner's executive to create a plan to achieve the preconditions. When the preconditions have been achieved, the action model then proceeds to simulate the execution of the action by creating a new state description model and making the appropriate assertions, deletions, and denials in it. Finally, the procedure adds the action that it represents to the end of the plan being constructed.

As with assertional action models, a planner using procedural action models must be able to deal with choice points that occur when multiple actions or multiple instantiations of actions are relevant. This requirement implies the need for some form of co-routine or multiprocessing facilities that allow alternative program control paths to be considered in a pseudo-parallel manner under the direction of the planner's executive.

A procedural language provides more expressive power for representing action models than do the data structures we described above. For example, a procedure can describe effects of an action that are conditional on properties of the state in which the action is executed. The most important aspect of this expressive power in terms of the effectiveness of the planning system is that procedural action models can contain strategy and heuristic information about how to achieve the action's preconditions. For example, if an action's preconditions are a set of relationships all of which must be achieved (i.e., a conjunction), then the action model can indicate the order in which they should be achieved by making a sequence of calls to the planning executive, with each call indicating the next relationship to be achieved. In effect, the action model procedure can contain a "sub-planner" specifically designed to guide the production of plans that achieve the action's preconditions.

Procedural action models suffer from the standard difficulty that their "knowledge" is hidden from the system in the code. That is, the system cannot reason about the preconditions or effects of an action if all that is available is the procedure. This problem can be dealt with by providing declarative information about the action in addition to the procedural action model. For example, the planner needs to know what relationships an action is useful for achieving so that it can determine when to consider including the action in a plan. Hence, a procedural action model needs essentially to have a list of "primary effects" associated with it for that purpose. This declarative information will be an abstraction or an approximation to the effects that the procedure will produce in any given situation, and can be thought of as a model of the procedure that itself is a model of a class of actions.

4. PROCEDURAL SUBPLANNERS

Once a planning system has the facilities for using procedural action models, an obvious and powerful generalization becomes possible. A procedural action model can be considered to be a "subplanner" specifically designed to produce plans for achieving the primary effects of an action. We can generalize this notion by removing the restriction that such subplanners must be models of an action, and consider writing subplanners for any specific class of tasks. For example, in a robot domain a route-finding algorithm could be written that would determine a sequence of rooms for the robot to travel through in order to get from one room into another. The route finder could employ any appropriate search algorithm for determining a suitable route, making use of geometric information, previously computed routes, etc. Such an algorithm could be represented as a subplanner designed to make the relationship (INROOM ROBOT ←X) true.

Often the primary role of a subplanner is to decompose a task by producing a sequence of subgoals to be achieved. The subplanner produces the actual plan by calling the planning executive with each of the subgoals in turn. For example, the route-finder may only determine a sequence of rooms through which the robot is to travel. It would call the planning executive to determine the detailed plan for the movements from room to adjacent room for each step along the route.

Writing subplanners is an easy and natural way of including domain-specific plan generation knowledge in a general-purpose planning system, and it provides the system with the power that is needed to make such a system effective and useful.

5. HIERARCHICAL PLANNING

The robot route-finding example suggests another important theme in automatic planning systems, namely, hierarchical planning. We have been assuming that the planner is given a single set of actions and that all plans must be composed of elements from that set. Hence, if the actions for the robot domain are at the level of detail of "Move forward X meters" and "Turn right Y degrees", then a route consisting of the sequence of rooms that the robot is to go through is not an acceptable plan. It is a metaplan that can be made into a plan by determining the detailed moves and turns that will take the robot from each room to the next. The question arises as to when and if the planner should be involved with details such as these of determining the actual moves and turns for the route. One might argue that we could have just as easily included a "Go to adjacent room X" action in the action set, or for that matter, a "Go to room X" action that would include the route-finding algorithm within it.

How does one decide what level of detail to include in a plan? We can gain insight into that question by considering the purposes for creating a plan. The primary purpose of planning is to determine a suitable method for accomplishing a task and to predict the consequences of applying that method. Finding a suitable method typically means achieving some acceptable degree of certainty that the method can be applied, that it will succeed in accomplishing the task, and that it is less expensive than other feasible methods with respect to some resource such as time or energy. The planner's predictive capability allows the system to answer questions about applying the method without having to expend the resources and deal with the consequences of the actual execution. Planning is necessary at a particular level of detail, then, only to the extent that there is some question as to what method to apply at that level and/or there is information needed about the execution of the method before the execution occurs.

If we can write a "Go to room X" action program that can provide the necessary degree of certainty that a route exists and can provide a sufficently accurate estimate of the cost of moving the robot through the route, then there may be no need to plan the route and the individual moves until it is time actually to execute the plan. On the other hand, if there is uncertainty about the route, such as whether doors are locked or whether clear pathways exist through rooms, then it may be necessary to plan the details of the route to remove the uncertainty.

Even if a "metaaction" such as "Go to room X" cannot answer all the questions that arise before plan execution, there are often advantages to delaying the planning of the metaaction's details until it is certain that it will be included in the final plan. For example, there is no need to plan the details of how to get the robot into some particular room until it is clear that the trip to that room will be part of the plan.

In situations where plans are being constructed for humans to carry out, such as for the SRI Computer-Based Consultant system (CBC) [Hart 75], which assists in the repair of equipment, the use of metaactions becomes even more valuable. In general, the people receiving instructions from the system will have varying levels of expertise and understanding of the steps in the plan. The system can attempt to match its level of instruction to this variability. For example, the CBC might tell a trained mechanic simply "Replace the pump", whereas it might tell a novice "Remove the 4 mounting bolts at the base of the pump using a 3/8 inch open-end wrench". If the person does not understand an instruction, then the system can call the metaaction's subplanner, and respond by providing the more detailed instructions that the subplanner produces.

In order for a planner to include metaactions in plans, it must be provided with "metaaction models" containing the same information and having the same form as the action models. That is, the planner must be able to achieve the preconditions of the metaaction, simulate its execution, and match it to tasks that it is useful for accomplishing. Given such a model, a planner has the option of including a metaaction in a plan without calling its subplanner to determine the detailed plan steps that it represents.

This approach to planning has been explored by Sacerdoti [74, 75] in two systems and has been found to provide significant advantages during both the generation and the execution of plans. In these systems, plans tend to grow in a top-down "breadth-first" manner, in that typically a complete plan will be constructed using high-level metaactions before the detailed steps of any of the metaactions are determined. Since a metaaction's subplanner may itself produce a plan containing metaactions, a multiple-level plan hierarchy is formed, and the planner can make independent decisions for each metaaction as to whether its subplanner should be called.

6. ASSERTIONAL DOMAIN KNOWLEDGE

Another form in which domain specific knowledge can be represented in a planning system is as scenarios or generalized plans. That is, in any given domain, there will typically be many methods for accomplishing tasks for which the order and the identity of the steps involved do not vary for different situations. Such methods provide a planner with the skeleton for an entire subplan, and the task of composing plans using such scenarios is largely one of finding the appropriate scenario and then producing a suitable instantiation of it.

6.1. Scenarios

For example, we have found such explicit scenarios useful in a management support system currently being developed at SRI [Fikes and Pease 75]. In that work, we wish to allow a manager to specify to the system various operational procedures that he uses in his organization. The system can then act as an administrative assistant by planning and monitoring the execution of these procedures at the manager's request. The planning activity in this system is primarily one of instantiation. However, the instantiation process in this case is nontrivial because it involves scheduling the individual steps of the plan and assuring the availability of resources and personnel at specific times.

The example domain being considered for this system is managing the logistics of operations on board a Navy aircraft carrier. One operation of interest in that domain is the flying of training missions. Such a mission involves steps such as preflight and postflight maintenance of the aircraft, fueling the aircraft, briefing and debriefing the pilot, launching and recovering the aircraft, etc. These steps and the order in which they must occur do not vary from mission to mission, hence they can be included in a scenario that is part of the definition of a mission.

A scenario in this system has many "slots" with unassigned values, and the planner's basic task is to find an acceptable set of values for them. Most of these slots specify the start and the end time of some step in the plan or the quantity and identity of some resource that will be used by the plan.

We include at each slot of a scenario a set of constraints on the value to be assigned there. The most common constraints are those that are derived from the temporal partial ordering of the steps (e.g., fueling of the aircraft must occur after the preflight maintenance and before the launch). Default values are included at the slots, usually expressed as functions of other slot values in the scenario. For example, the default value for the start of preflight maintenance is expressed as the time of launch minus some constant. These default values allow the planner to make feasibility estimates and to make scheduling decisions before all of the constraints from the other schedulers have been determined.

Also included at each slot is a specification of what function can be called upon to determine a value for the slot. These are typically calls on planners and schedulers that are responsible for other operational areas in the organization. On board a carrier these would include aircraft maintenance, pilot assignment, aircraft assignment, the flight deck, etc. Hence, the planner that is using such a scenario engages in a negotiation dialogue with the other planners in an attempt to reach agreement on an acceptable schedule.

6.2. Generalized Plans

Another source of assertional domain knowledge is previously produced plans. One would like the plans produced by a planner to be retained as new scenarios so that the system could be considered to be learning new expertise in the task domain.

In some of our earlier work with the STRIPS planning system, we made an attempt at developing such a learning mechanism [Fikes *et al.* 72]. The challenge in such an effort is to have the system derive and store with the new scenario the information required for its use by other parts of the system, including the planner. This information includes all the kinds of information that are provided by action models, namely a set of preconditions for the plan, a description of the effects of the plan's execution, and indications of the class of tasks the plan is relevant to achieving. In addition, for the new scenario to be useful in situations other than just reoccurrences of the one for which it was originally constructed, it must somehow be generalized so that, like the other scenarios, there are slots that can be filled in with values suited to any of a class of situations and goals.

The basic goal of the STRIPS learning work was to generalize and save plans so that they could be used as single steps in future plans. Two aspects of this work are relevant to this discussion, namely, the use of kernels and the manner in which plans were generalized.

In the STRIPS system, a stored plan was called a MACROP (for MACRo OPerator). A MACROP's preconditions were directly available as a side effect of the determination of "kernels" preceding each step of the plan. The kernel preceding step i of a plan is a partial description of the situation that the planner expects to exist after execution of the first $i - 1$ steps of the plan. In particular, it specifies a set of relationships that must be true if the remainder of the plan is to succeed. Hence, in effect, the kernel for each step is the set of preconditions for the remainder of the plan. The kernels for a plan can be computed in a direct manner by considering what relationships were made true by each step in the plan and by knowing what relationships from the state description models were needed to assure the achievement of each action's preconditions and of the final goal.

A plan's kernels provide extremely valuable information for many uses of the plan, and therefore are an important part of the information stored with the plan. First of all, the kernel preceding the first step of the plan specifies the preconditions for the plan. Second, the kernels specify what tests an execution monitor should make after each action to determine whether the plan is proceeding as expected during execution. Third, the kernels are useful for modifying or extending the plan to accommodate a new situation or new task goals.

That is, instead of forming a completely new plan to accomplish some task goal, the planner can be given the option of modifying an existing scenario by adding and/or changing some of its steps. The basic information that is needed to allow such modification to occur is contained in the kernels since each kernel indicates what must remain true between any two adjacent steps in a plan. Hence, the planner can add any number of steps between step $i - 1$ and step i of an existing plan as long as the kernel between those two steps is not violated.

Providing a capability for modifying an existing plan is an important way of improving the power of a planning system. It allows the planner to consider adding steps anywhere in a plan (as opposed to just at the end) to achieve a goal [Waldinger 75]. For example, if a plan has been constructed to move a robot from room A to room B, and then the planner considers a goal of transporting some object from room A into room B, the existing plan can be modified so that the robot transports the object as part of the first trip rather than making a second trip.

This modification capability is also useful when combining two scenarios to achieve a conjunctive goal [Sacerdoti 75]. For example, in the equipment repair domain, the planner might conjoin two scenarios each of which includes removal and replacement of the same subassembly. The planner needs to be able to recognize this redundancy and to combine the scenarios so that the subassembly is removed only once. Finally, a plan modification capability is useful for "debugging" a plan [Sussman 73]. Often, stored scenarios and the methods found in subplanners are heuristic in nature and do not always produce bug-free plans. Such bugs are typically discovered during the planner's simulation of the plan, and when such a discovery is made, the planner can employ its plan modification facilities to remove the bug.

The second comment to be made about the STRIPS learning work relates to the generalization that was done on the plans before they were stored. The goal was to "unbind" the slots in each of the plan's steps so that, whenever possible, they became unvalued slots in the scenario for the entire plan. The logical structure of the plan imposes restrictions on this unbinding process so that some pairs of slots are required to take on the same value (i.e., they become a single slot in the new scenario), and others must retain their binding (i.e., they lose their status as distinct slots in the new scenario). For example, if one step of the plan causes the robot to go to a door, and the next step causes the robot to go through a door, then the door in those two steps must be the same door.

This generalization process essentially parametrizes the plan and thereby provides it with enough generality to make it worthwhile to save. For example, consider a plan that takes a robot from room R1 through door D1 into room R2 and then has the robot bring box B1 from room R2 back into room R1 through door D1. That plan would be generalized so that it would take the robot from any room into any adjacent room through any connecting door and then take any box in the room into any adjacent room through any connecting door. The generalization removes all bindings to the particular rooms, doors, and box, and allows the room into which the box is taken to be different from the one in which the robot was initially located.

We see, then, that another way of expanding the power and effectiveness of a planning system is to provide it with facilities for instantiating and modifying plans that have been previously produced, generalized, and stored.

7. SUMMARY

A planner is needed when a task is presented that the system does not have a prestored method for accomplishing. The planner's role is to combine the methods that are available to the system in order to produce a new "method" that will accomplish the task. The methods being composed may consist of single actions or multiaction scenarios, and the composition process may include instantiating and modifying the existing methods to match the particular situation. In addition to basic means–ends analysis and simulation facilities for composing prestored actions and scenarios, a planner typically has available a collection of subplanners, embodying domain dependent expertise, that are designed to be applied to specialized classes of tasks.

REFERENCES

Derksen, J., Rulifson, J. F., and Waldinger, R. J., The QA4 language applied to robot planning. *Proc. EICC* **41**, 1181–1192 (1972).

Fahlman, S. E., A planning system for robot construction tasks. *Artificial Intelligence* **5** 1, 1–49 (1974).

Fikes, R. E., and Nilsson, N. J., STRIPS: A new approach to the application of theorem proving to problem solving. *Artificial Intelligence* **2** 3, 189–203 (1971).

Fikes, R. E., Hart, P. E., and Nilsson, N. J., Learning and executing generalized robot plans. *Artificial Intelligence* **3** 4, 251–288 (1972).

Fikes, R. E., and Pease, M. C., An interactive management support system for planning, control, and analysis. Computer Science Group Tech. Rep., Stanford Research Inst., Menlo Park, California, 1975.

Hart, P. E., Progress on a computer-based consultant. *Proc. 4th Intern. Joint Conf. Artificial Intelligence, Tbilisi, USSR, September 1975.*

Minsky, M., A framework for representing knowledge. Artificial Intelligence Lab. Memo., Massachusetts Inst. of Technology, Cambridge, Massachusetts, 1974.

Sacerdoti, E. D., Planning in a hierarchy of abstraction spaces. *Artificial Intelligence* **5** 2, 115–135 (1974).

Sacerdoti, E. D., A structure for plans and behavior. Artificial Intelligence Center Tech. Rep. 109, Stanford Research Inst., Menlo Park, California, 1975.

Schank, R. C., Using knowledge to understand. *Proc. Theoretical Issues Natural Language Processing Workshop, MIT, Cambridge, Massachusetts, 1975.*

Sussman, G. J., A computational model of skill acquisition. Artificial Intelligence Lab. Tech. Rep. AI-TR-297, Massachusetts Inst. of Technology, Cambridge, Massachusetts, 1973.

Waldinger, R., Achieving several goals simultaneously. Artificial Intelligence Center Tech. Note 107, Stanford Research Inst., Menlo Park, California, 1975.

On the Concurrency of Parallel Processes

A. N. Habermann

Department of Computer Science
Carnegie-Mellon University
Pittsburgh, Pennsylvania

This chapter contributes to the 10th anniversary symposium of the Computer Science Department at Carnegie-Mellon University by looking at two old problems in concurrent processes in a new light. The first problem is that of restricting the order in which concurrent processes may operate on shared objects. We show how such restrictions can be stated as path expressions. The second problem is that of deadlock states. An $O(mn \log n)$ deadlock detection algorithm is presented, which is based on the heapsort algorithm.

1. INTRODUCTION

Operating system design has been a respectable computer science topic since the invention of multiprogramming and time-sharing. A multiprogramming operating system distributes CPU time and main storage space over several programs. This has the advantage that the execution of one program does not have to wait until a preceding program is finished. In addition, the time that one program must wait for I/O operations is utilized by running part of the next program. Time-sharing is based on a similar idea: several user jobs each receive a fraction of the CPU time and the main store so that these users appear to run simultaneously.

Multiprogramming and time-sharing have in common that several activities (called processes or tasks) are performed concurrently. No harm is done when these processes run concurrently so long as each process operates only on its local objects (i.e., objects that are exclusively accessible to that process). However, concurrent processes must not simultaneously operate on shared objects, or the result is chaos. For instance, two processes must not reserve the same area in the store, or the same I/O device. Restricting the order in which concurrent processes may operate on shared objects is called *synchronization*.

Synchronization used to be viewed as a matter of restricting the execution of concurrent processes. Consequently, it has been customary to code synchronization statements in line in the places where programs may have to wait and where they reactivate other programs. In this chapter we take the view that the necessary synchronization is determined by the nature of the shared objects instead of by the users of these objects. Taking this view, synchronization rules are stated as part of the object definition instead of coded in line. Such a synchronization statement is called a path expression [Campbell and Habermann 74, Habermann 75].

However, the rules specifying the execution order of operations on a shared object do not preclude the possibility of a "deadlock state". This is the situation in which several processes are each waiting for another to release some resource. In its simplest form a process P is holding a resource A and waits for resource B while a process Q is holding resource B and waits for A. A deadlock state occurs if neither process is willing to give up the resource it is holding. Deadlock states are possible only if the resources are nonpreemptible, for a nonpreemptible resource cannot be deallocated until its user is willing to give it up. In contrast, a preemptible resource can be taken away at any time and reallocated at a later time. CPU time and main storage space are examples of preemptible resources; line printers and magnetic tape units are examples of nonpreemptible devices. (Nobody wants his output lines mixed with those of someone else's program!)

Two algorithms for avoiding deadlocks are discussed and compared in the last part of the paper. The first algorithm is straightforward and well known [Habermann 69]. The second algorithm is a variation on the "heapsort" algorithm invented by J. W. J. Williams [Williams 64], and is clearly described by Aho et al. [74]. Floyd's improved version of the algorithm is found in Knuth [73]. The performance of the second algorithm is comparable to Holt's algorithm [Holt 70].

2. COORDINATION OF CONCURRENT PROGRAMS

An example of what can go wrong when two processes simultaneously operate on a shared object follows. Suppose a system has n magnetic tape units: MT1, MT2, . . . , MTn. A MT unit is allocated by calling *allocMT*. This procedure returns the number of a MT unit. A process returns a MT unit by calling *releaseMT(x)*. The parameter x is the number of the MT unit being released. Let the free MT units be recorded in array *MTfree*[1:n]. If there are k MT units free ($0 \leqslant k \leqslant n$), their unit numbers are recorded in the array elements *MTfree*[1:k]. The order of the unit

TABLE I

Possible Statement Sequence

Time	Statement	Action	Result
$t1$	Q1 (by P1)	decrement k	$k' = k - 1$
$t2$	Q1 (by P2)	decrement k	$k'' = k' - 1 = k - 2$
$t3$	Q2 (by P2)	take $MTfree[k'' + 1]$	MTfree$[k']$
$t4$	Q2 (by P1)	take $MTfree[k'' + 1]$	MTfree$[k']$

numbers is immaterial. Programs for *allocMT* and *releaseMT* are

> **procedure**   allocMT =
> **begin**
>   Q1: $k \leftarrow k - 1$;
>   Q2:   **return**(MTfree$[k + 1]$)
> **end**

> **procedure**   release MT(x) =
> **begin**
>   L1: $k \leftarrow k + 1$;
>   L2:   MTfree$[k] \leftarrow x$
> **end**

If two processes simultaneously request a MT unit, it might happen that the statements of procedure *allocMT* are executed in the order shown in Table I.

The problem is that two processes take the same MT unit and the unit recorded in $MTfree[k = k'' + 2]$ is entirely lost. The reader can check that simultaneous execution of *releaseMT* or mixed execution of *allocMT* and *releaseMT* also leads to undesirable situations.

The problem is solved if we impose the restriction that execution of *allocMT* and *releaseMT* must not overlap in time. If two processes try to execute one of these procedures, only one process may go ahead. The other process must wait until the first has finished. This restriction is stated by the "path expression"

> **path**   *allocMT + releaseMT*   **end**

The operator + reads as "or". A path expression allows the execution of only one of its elements at a time. This particular path expression specifies that *allocMT* and *releaseMT* can be executed in arbitrary order, but only one at a time. (It specifies that *allocMT* and *leaseMT* are critical sections [Dijkstra 68].) A path expression defines the execution history of its elements. In this particular case it specifies that the history is an arbitrary string of *allocMT* and *releaseMT* executions in no particular order. All possible histories are described by the regular expression

$$(allocMT \lor releaseMT)*$$

It is obvious that no MT unit can be allocated if there are no free units left. This constraint is expressed by a slightly modified version of the path expression

path *releaseMT* $\geqslant$ *allocMT* **end**

The operator $\geqslant$ resembles the operator + in that both specify that either *releaseMT* or *allocMT* can be executed, but not in overlapping time intervals. It specifies in addition that the number of times that *allocMT* has been executed never exceeds the number of times that *releaseMT* has been executed. This additional constraint allows a history such as

rel. rel. rel. al. al. rel. al. al.,

but it precludes the history

rel. rel. al. al. rel. al. al. rel.,

because, after executing the fourth *allocMT*, the number of executions of *allocMT* exceeds the number of executions of *releaseMT* by one. If the system owns all the MT units in the initial state, this path expression assures that no attempt to allocate a MT unit will succeed when there are none free. (The histories of a path expression in which the operator $\geqslant$ is used correspond to the sentences of a Dyke language [Ginsburg 66].)

The general path expression rule is

A program that attempts to execute a path element is delayed if another path element is being executed or if execution of that element would lead to a nonpermissible history. When execution of a path element is completed, it may happen that now execution of some path elements is permitted while earlier attempts failed. In that case one of the programs waiting for permission to execute such a path element is allowed to proceed.

In other cases it is necessary to enforce a specific order in which the path elements must be executed. For example, a serial device such as a drum or a disk can execute only one command at a time. Therefore, the next device command must not be given until the device has completed the current command; otherwise the current command is overwritten causing disastrous results. The restriction imposed on device commands is stated by the path expression

path send command; execute command; copy device status **end**

The operator ";" is the sequencing operator. It forces sequential execution of its left and right operand. The execution histories defined by this path are described by the regular expression

(send   execute   copy)*

2.1. Path Expressions as Programming Tool

The use of path expressions is not unlike the use of control statements such as **while** B **do** S and **if** B **then** $S1$ **else** $S2$. These tools allow a programmer to abstract from coding details and enable him to concentrate on the logic of his programs. Without control statements, a programmer must define explicit labels in his program and implement control flow by placing **goto** statements in line. Control statements relieve the programmer from this task. Implicit control, defined by the control statements, is now translated into branch instructions by a compiler. Likewise, without path expressions, the programmer must explicitly define semaphores and code the necessary synchronization in line by P and V operations. Using path expressions, it suffices to specify the order in which the operations on a shared object can be performed. A compiler will translate this specification into the necessary semaphores and P, V statements. This section demonstrates the use of path expressions in writing programs for a drum scheduler.

Consider a segment transfer scheduler for a segment request system. The processes of such a system manage their own segments. That is, a process determines all by itself which segments it wants to load into the main store and which segments should be saved in the backup store. If a process needs a segment, it must send a *load* command to the backup store device. If it wants to transfer a segment from the main store to the backup store, it must send a *save* command to that device.

Let us assume that the backup store device is a rotating device with movable read/write heads. Each load or save command concerns a particular track on the device. (If a segment occupies more than one track, a separate command must be given for each track.) The time it takes the movable head to travel from one track to the other is proportional to the distance between those tracks. Therefore, an efficient scheduler does not send the commands to the backup store device in the order in which they arrive, but in the order "nearest track first". That is, the scheduler looks for a command that requests access to a track nearest to the track currently accessed by the read/write head.

C. A. R. Hoare observes [Hoare 74] that the pure nearest-track-first strategy has a potential "starvation" problem. It may happen that requests are serviced at one end of the device, whereas requests for tracks at the other end are never serviced. This problem is solved by the "elevator schedule". In going from one track to the other, the head travels in a certain direction, up or down. The head changes direction if it reaches the last or first track or if there are no requests for tracks in the direction in which it is traveling while there are requests for the other direction. This strategy is close to the nearest-track-first strategy and obviously solves the starvation problem.

The scheduler maintains an array $R[1:n]$ of segment requests and a schedule $S[1:n]$ indicating the order in which the requests will be serviced. The elements of array R are segment requests. There are four operations defined on a segment request element. Their execution is restricted by the path expression

    path   *init*; *read*; *write*; *clear*   **end**

Procedure *init* places a device command in a segment request element, procedure *read* copies this command from the segment request element, and procedure *write* returns the result of executing the command to the request element (indicating whether or not some error occurred). Procedure *clear* removes this result from the segment request element.

These four operations are defined for the individual elements of array R, not for the array as a whole. This implies that an instance of the path expression is attached to each element of array R. It is therefore possible that the state of one element in R currently allows reading, while the state of another element allows writing, etc.

The scheduler provides only one procedure for transferring segments. This procedure is *request*(c, i), where c is the transfer command and i the number of the track involved. Its program is

    procedure   *request*$(c, i) =$
      begin
          init$(R[i]$ with $c)$; *insert*$(i$ into $S)$; $c \leftarrow clear\ (R[i])$
      end

It seems that a user may clear a request element prematurely. This is not so, because the path expression for segment requests makes it impossible that the element be cleared before it has been read and written into. These operations are performed by the scheduler (see below). The use of the procedures *init* and *clear* at the beginning and the end assures that an element $R[i]$ is used serially, because the next request for track i cannot execute procedure *init* until procedure *clear* has been executed.

There are two operations on the schedule: *insert*(i *into* S) and *movehead*. The former is called in procedure *request* when a new transfer request arrives. The latter is used by the scheduler when it moves the read/write head from its current position to the nearest requested track. The selected track is recorded in the variable *head*. The scheduler program is

```
local  c
repeat
    movehead;  c ← read(R[head])
    process(c);  write(c into R[head])
end
```

The scheduler should not be able to move the head if there are no unprocessed requests left. This constraint is enforced by the path expression

path   *insert* $\geqslant$ *movehead*   **end**

It assures that the number of times that the head is moved does not exceed the number of times a request has been inserted into the schedule. (Note that this path expression applies to array S as a whole and not to its separate elements.)

The scheduler is able to read the command in $R[head]$, because this element was initialized in procedure request before it was inserted into the schedule. After processing the command, the result is written into $R[head]$. The user is then able to clear the request element. Once it has been cleared, another request involving this track can be given.

We can think of array S as the stack of floors in a high-rise building: $S[1]$ corresponds to the ground floor and $S[n]$ to the top floor. The value of head corresponds to the current position of the elevator. The direction in which the elevator moves is remembered in variable *dir*, whose value is either up or down. The schedule is organized as two circular linked lists: one for going up and one for going down.

Let *down* be a constant equal to zero and let *up* be a constant equal to $n + 1$. In order to avoid searching for the nearest requested track in the current direction when the head is moved, array S is extended with the elements $S[down]$ and $S[up]$. The number of the requested track nearest to the head going down is recorded in $S[down]$; the one nearest to the head going up is recorded in $S[up]$. In the initial state the lists for both directions are empty. Therefore, $S[down]$ is initialized to *down* ($= 0$) and

$S[up]$ to up $(= n + 1)$. The nearest track in the current direction is found in $S[dir]$. If $S[dir] = dir$, there are no requests left in the current direction. In that case the nearest track requested in the opposite direction is chosen and the direction is reversed (the opposite direction is $n + 1 - dir$). The path expression specifying the constraint on *insert* and *movehead* guarantees that a next request will indeed be found. Once found, the requested track number is copied into *head* and deleted from the up- or down-list. A program for procedure movehead is

> **procedure**   *movehead* =
>   **begin**
>   **if** $S[dir] = dir$ **then** $dir \leftarrow$ opposite(dir) **fi**
> $head \leftarrow S[dir]$; $S[dir] \leftarrow S[head]$
>   **end**

Inserting a request for track i into the schedule amounts to linking this request onto the up- or the down-list. If $i < head$, the request is placed in the down-list; if $i > head$, it is placed in the up-list; if $i = head$, the request is placed in the list for the opposite direction (in order to avoid stalling the head on one track). A program for insert is

> **procedure**   *insert*(x) =
>   **begin local** y
>   **if** $x = head$ **then** $y \leftarrow$ opposite(dir)
>   **else if** $x < head$
>   **then** $y \leftarrow down$;   **while** $S[y] > x$ **do** $y \leftarrow S[y]$ **od**
>   **else** $y \leftarrow up$;   **while** $S[y] < x$ **do** $y \leftarrow S[y]$ **od**
>   **fi fi**
> $S[x] \leftarrow S[y]$; $S[y] \leftarrow x$
>   **end**

The segment transfer scheduler demonstrates the use of path expressions in writing programs. Elaborate coordination problems can be solved if several path expressions are used, each defining the execution history of operations on a different shared object. A path expression attached to a shared object protects this object against erroneous states that otherwise could result from operations applied to the object by concurrent programs. However, it does not preclude that these programs use the shared objects in a wrong way. For example, we could have made a mistake in the scheduler program by programming *write*$(c$ into $R[head])$ before *read*$(R[head])$. The path expression assures that these operations cannot be applied in the wrong order. This provides protection as to the way in which a request element is manipulated, but the scheduler would come to a halt if it attempted to write into a request element.

An important case for which no assistance must be expected from path expressions is that of a deadlock state. A deadlock state arises if one or more programs attempt some operation and we can show that these attempts will fail forever. For example, let the operations on two independent shared objects be controlled by the path expressions

path f; g **end**

path p; q **end**

Suppose all the programs using these objects either call q followed by f or g followed by p. These programs cause a deadlock state, because they are mutually waiting for the other programs to take the necessary initial step.

MT allocation is another example. It may happen that all users are requesting additional units and none are willing to release a unit. This results in a deadlock state that cannot be resolved unless some MT units are released. In the next section we discuss an algorithm for detecting deadlock states.

3. DEADLOCK DETECTION

Consider the general case of allocating resources of m different types to the concurrent processes $P_1, \ldots, P_n$ $(m, n > 1)$. Let $alloc[i, j]$ indicate the number of resources of type j allocated to process P_i. Let vector **rem** = $rem[1:m]$ represent the number of free resources of each type and let $request[i, j]$ indicate the number of resources of type j requested by process P_i. The allocation state is deadlocked if we can show that one or more processes can never get the resources they request. Alternatively, the state is deadlock free if we can show that every process can eventually get all the resources it requests.

It is customary to assume that a process that receives all the resources it requested will return all its resources in due time. A straightforward deadlock detection algorithm proceeds as follows. It first collects all the processes that request no more resources than currently remain. These processes can get all the resources they want, so these can finish. After finishing, the resource pool will have been incremented by the resources these processes are holding at the present time. Add this amount to the current value of **rem** and collect all the processes for which this new amount is sufficient. Repeat this process until either all processes have been moved from the initial trial set or a process remains that cannot be satisfied while **rem** cannot be incremented further. The allocation state is deadlock-free in the former case and a deadlock state in the latter.

The number of times the algorithm starts collecting another subset of processes is proportional to n, so is the number of probes per collection. Since these actions are nested and carried out for each resource type, the simple detection algorithm executed in $O(m*n^2)$ time. However, the algorithm evidently has the characteristics of a sorting algorithm. Since efficient sorting algorithms execute in $O(n*log_2*n)$ time, it should be possible to construct a deadlock detection algorithm that executes in $O(m*n*log_2 n)$ time. We discuss below such an algorithm, which uses Williams' heapsort [Williams 64].

Let $N = \{1, \ldots, n\}$ and let $R_1, \ldots, R_{m+1}$ be a partitioning of N. We design a test procedure which takes a resource type t as parameter. The test succeeds if the union of $R_t, \ldots, R_m$ contains a subset whose requests for *all* the resource types $t, \ldots, m$ can be satisfied; the test fails otherwise. A given allocation state contains a deadlock if $test(1)$ fails because, applied to the whole range for type $t = 1$, the test procedure reveals whether or not the remaining resources suffice to satisfy all the requests of some processes.

The test applied to t first determines the subset S, consisting of all indices $i \in R_t$ that satisfy $request[i, t] \leqslant rem[t]$. Processes in S request no more resources of type t than available. After subtracting S from R_t and adding it to R_{t+1}, the test is applied to $t + 1$. Recursive application of the test results in the construction of a set S whose requests can be satisfied for all the resource types $t, \ldots, m$. The resources allocated to the processes in S are added to **rem**. These resources will be available when the processes in S return their resources after having used the requested resources. If we start with $R_1 = N$ and all others empty, repeated application of the test terminates successfully if all indices have been pushed from R_1 through $R_2, \ldots, R_m$ to R_{m+1}. The test programs are

```
procedure   test(t) =
  begin
    if  t > m   then return(S)  fi
    S ← {i|i ∈ R_t and   request[i, t] ≤ rem[t]}
    R_t ← R_t − S; R_{t+1} ← R_{t+1} + S
    return(test(t + 1))
  end
procedure deadlockfree =
  repeat
    if size(R_{m+1}) = n then return(true)  fi
    if (S ← test(1)) = ∅ then return(false)  fi
    forall  i ∈ S  do   rem ← rem + alloc_i  od
  end
```

The runtime of this program depends on the construction of S, the test for $t + 1$ and the repeated addition to $rem[t]$. Note that successively constructed subsets S in the deadlock test have no elements in common (because S is added to R_{m+1}). This means that the total number of additions to $rem[t]$ is at most equal to the number of elements in N. If R_t is ordered in ascending order of requests for resource type t, the construction of a subset S is proportional to its number of elements. In that case, the construction of all successive subsets is equal to the sum of these numbers, which is equal to $n*m$, because every index is transferred exactly once from R_t to R_{t+1} for $t = 1, \ldots, m$.

However, we pay a price for keeping every R_t sorted for resource type t. The crucial steps are the removal and insertion of a subset S. A sorting version of the test program looks like this:

```
procedure  test(t) =
   begin
      if t > m then return(S)   fi
      S ← ∅
      while  R_t ≠ ∅  and request[first(R_t), t] ≤ rem[t]  do
         k ← remove(first(R_t));   insert(k into R_{t+1});   S ← S + {k}
      od
      return(test(t + 1))
   end
```

The complexity of the test algorithm is determined by the complexity of keeping the subsets R_t sorted. Since the complexity of sorting is more than linear, the complexity of the test algorithm is determined by the sorting procedure. The complexity of the best known sorting algorithm (heapsort) is $O(n* log_2 n)$ [Knuth 73, Aho et al. 74]. Since the sorting is applied for each resource type, the runtime of $test(N, 1)$ is $O(m*n* log_2 n)$ if the heapsort algorithm is used.

3.1. The Deadlock Detection Program

An array $Q[1 : q]$ is a *heap* if

$$Q[j//2] \leqslant Q[j] \quad \text{for} \quad j = 2, \ldots, q$$

(The operator "$//$" stands for integer division.) The heap property is best understood if the array is represented as a binary tree. The root of the tree is element $Q[1]$. The leftmost elements in the tree are $Q[1]$, $Q[2]$, $Q[4]$, $Q[8]$, etc. The offspring of $Q[j//2]$ are $Q[j]$ and $Q[j + 1]$. The heap property means that the value of a parent node is not larger than that of its offspring.

Let $Q[j//2]$ be a node whose left and right subtrees both have the heap property. If $Q[j//2]$ is greater than the values of its offspring, subtree $(j//2)$ is also a heap. Otherwise, the value of $Q[j//2]$ must be "sifted down" to establish the heap property. A recursive version of the sift procedure is

```
procedure sift down(x in Q[1 : q]) =
  begin var  j = 2*x
    if  j < q   then if   Q[j + 1] < Q[j]   then   j←j + 1   fi fi
    if  j ≤ q   then if   Q[j] < Q[x]   then
        exch(Q[j], Q[x]);   siftdown(j in Q[1 : q])   fi
    fi
  end
```

The first statement makes j point to the smaller offspring. If x is not a leaf, the second statement exchanges the values of parent and offspring if the parent has the larger value. In that case the procedure is called recursively.

Since the recursive call is the last statement in the procedure body, the sift procedure can easily be written as an iterative statement. This transcription is left to the reader. If the root element of a heap is removed, the heap falls apart into two separate heaps. The heap property is restored as follows. Take the last element off the heap and put it in the place of the root node. The heap property is probably violated by the new root node. Restoring the heap property amounts to sifting down the value of $Q[1]$. Thus, the restoration is accomplished by

$$Q[1]← Q[k]; \quad k ← k - 1; \quad siftdown(1 \text{ in } Q[1 : k])$$

We can write a similar procedure "siftup" which allows us to add a new element to a heap. The element is first added as $Q[k + 1]$. The *siftup* procedure exchanges it with its parent until the heap property is restored. Writing a program for *siftup* is left to the reader.

The sift algorithms run in $O(\log_2 n)$ time. Since the two sorting steps in *test* are executed in sequence and since both are repeated $n*m$ times, the complexity of the deadlock algorithm is $O(m*n*\log n)$.

The values that are compared in order to sort a subset R_t into a heap are those of the requests for resources of type t. The smaller the request, the closer to the root. The test program uses *siftdown* when it removes an element from R_t and siftup when it inserts an element into R_{t+1}. It suffices to keep the subsets R_t heapsorted instead of totally ordered, because the smallest element is on top of the heap. If its request exceeds $rem[t]$, the requests of all other elements in R_t also exceed $rem[t]$.

The final version of the test program is:

```
procedure  test(t) =
  begin
    if  t > m  then return(S)  fi
    S ← ∅
    while  last_t > 0  and  request[R_t[1], t] ≤ rem[t]  do
      k ← R_t[1];   R_t[1] ← R_t[last_t];   last_t ← last_t − 1
      siftdown(R_t[1] in R_t[1 : last_t])
      S ← S + {k}
      last_{t+1} ← last_{t+1} + 1;   R_{t+1}[last_{t+1}] ← k
      siftup(R_{t+1}[last_{t+1}] in R_{t+1}[1 : last_{t+1}])
    od
    return(test(t + 1))
  end
```

Knuth discusses [Knuth 73] an iterative version of the heapsort algorithm in which the two steps of the algorithm are combined in one loop. This version is due to R. Floyd. The test program is less complicated, because a total ordering is unnecessary. The deadlock detection algorithm is somewhat wasteful in space because of the arrays $R_t[1 : n]$. In fact, only n elements of all these arrays are in use at any moment. However, if all the arrays R_t are packed into one array $P[1 : n]$, it is necessary to move heaps through P. This brings the complexity of the algorithm back to $O(m*n^2)$.

4. CONCLUSION

The order in which concurrent processes may execute operations on shared objects must be restricted so that the values and states of these objects remain meaningful. Path expressions are sufficiently powerful for stating the coordination rules for fairly complicated systems. However, the coordination rules do not preclude the possibility of deadlock states. A straightforward deadlock detection executes in $O(m*n^2)$ time, where n is the number of the concurrent processes. An algorithm based on the heapsort method is able to detect a deadlock (or its absence) in $O(m*n*\log_2 n)$ time. The straightforward algorithm performs better for small n $(n < 8)$; the modified heapsort algorithm performs better for large n $(n > 10)$.

REFERENCES

Aho, A. V., Hopcroft, J. E., and Ullman, J. D., *The Design and Analysis of Computer Algorithms*. Addison–Wesley, Reading, Massachusetts 1974.

Campbell, R. H., and Habermann, A. N., The specification of process synchronization by path expressions. *Lecture Notes in Computer Science* **16**. Springer–Verlag, New York, 1974.

Dijkstra, E. W., Cooperating sequential processes. In *Programming Languages* (F. Genuys, ed.). Academic Press, New York, 1968.

Ginsburg, S., *The Mathematical Theory of Context-Free Languages*. McGraw–Hill, New York, 1966.

Habermann, A. N., Prevention of system deadlocks. *Comm. ACM* **12** 7, 373–377 (July 1969).

Habermann, A. N., Path expressions. Computer Science Dept. Rep., Carnegie-Mellon University, Pittsburgh, Pennsylvania, June 1975.

Hoare, C. A. R., Monitors: an operating system structuring concept. *Comm. ACM* **17** 10, 549–557 (October 1974).

Holt, R. C., On deadlock in computer systems. Ph.D. thesis, Computer Science Dept., Cornell Univ., Ithaca, New York, 1970.

Knuth, D. E., *The Art of Computer Programming* **3**. Addison–Wesley, Reading, Massachusetts, 1973.

Williams, J. W. J., Algorithm 232: Heapsort. *Comm. ACM* **7** 6, 347–348 (June 1964).

A Case Study—Assimilation and Creation of Computer Science Technology in a Developing Country

Renato Iturriaga[†]

Coordinor General del Sistema Nacional de Informacion Palacio Nacional Mexico City, Mexico

Technological development does not have the intrinsic value of scientific research; it has meaning only as an instrument to aid in reaching human goals. It is appropriate in developing countries like Mexico that computer science technology be developed and adapted to aid in the establishment and maintenance of capable, efficient processes of public administration. In the case of INFONAVIT, Mexico's housing agency, a "mechanized bureaucrat" was designed to satisfy the information processing needs of the housing agency; most importantly this was accomplished in a way that also satisfied the administrative constraints dictated by the political and administrative context.

1. THE PROBLEM IN GENERAL

Scientific research is in itself a worthwhile endeavor when it is motivated by the intellectual curiosity of man, with the desire to find the physical or abstract truths that occur in his real or imaginary world. On the other hand, technological development has no value in itself; it has meaning only if it is used to solve actual problems relevant to the society that generates them. Technological results are only instruments to aid in reaching human goals.

Knowledge is universal; technological problems are local. Therefore, scientific research does not have, nor can it have, boundaries; but technological developments correspond to the needs and values of a particular society. Hence, technology is a bridge between a present reality and a reality to be attained. Thus, two societies that enjoy different economic, political, and cultural characteristics, and that are moving toward different

---

[†]On leave of absence, National University of Mexico, Center for Research on Applied Mathematics and Systems (CIMAS).

objectives, frequently have technological needs of a very different nature.

Computer science technology is a powerful agent for change within a community. The profound social impact produced by computers is evident, especially in the highly industrialized countries. At the same time, those countries still in the process of development also require computer science technology in order to accelerate growth. However, due to their limited financial, technical, and human resources, developing countries should exercise great caution in the production and importation of computer science technology.

It would be naive, through some misguided desire for autonomy, to generate locally the technology which has been developed and tested abroad; but it would be equally naive to believe that it suffices simply to bring in external technology to solve local problems. In the computer sciences, this is quite clear. On the one hand, with respect to hardware, it does not seem plausible to undertake locally the development of large digital computers. The industrial, scientific, and technological knowledge necessary seriously to support the design and production of this equipment is not available. Even if, for reasons of national pride, one could reach the capacity to produce this, it would not be economically sound, since it would be impossible in the foreseeable future to match the efficiency that only the United States has in this type of industry.[†]

Mexico may undertake the design and construction of small special purpose computers, peripheral equipment and remote terminals. However, it is still necessary to import many of the electronic components that are necessary for the construction of such equipment.

The situation is quite different with respect to software: (a) Mexico has a growing capacity to design, build, and implement the most complicated software systems. (b) Design premises for control and information systems, developed in the highly industrialized countries, are frequently not applicable to the existing conditions in Mexico. For example, the ratio between labor cost and capital is very different. (c) In the world powers, a great part of the official stimulus for technological development in computer science has been directed toward military and space programs, which are meaningless in developing countries like Mexico.

The use of computers in scientific research is similar throughout the world. Naturally, such use corresponds to the development of each nation. But, as was stated before, the motivation is universal and independent of the characteristics of a particular society.

[†]Charles DeGaulle's ambitious *plan calcule*, which specified how France could be independent in terms of the development and manufacture of software and hardware, was reduced in 1975 when the state-owned French computer manufacturer was sold to Honeywell-Bull-General Electric.

The introduction of new industrial computer applications is regulated by economic factors which appear in a cost–benefit analysis. In this field of application, the development, adaptation, or simply the importation of computer science technology is principally in the hands of private enterprise. However in the developing countries, the government should regulate these processes in two ways: by encouraging computer science knowledge transfer, and by restricting the payments abroad of royalties on software that can be developed locally.

Those countries with an economic and social profile similar to that of Mexico, whose future does not depend on its industrial and military power, but on its capability and wisdom to use its own resources; the countries that look to augment the production of goods and services, but at the same time insist upon a just social distribution; the countries that try to build their development entirely on bases that neither destroy nor give away their patrimony, and because of their limited resources must avoid waste and must unite their efforts; that is, those countries that belong to the so-called third world, require governments capable of planning, coordinating, promoting, and carrying out a range of activities, which, taken as a whole, will lead to their desired goals. This point is of the utmost importance. The government must be capable; hence, in a developing country it is of special importance to improve government efficiency.

For this reason, the developing countries should not, nor have they any reason to, direct their incipient computer science technology toward glamorous international ventures. Instead of constructing a "mechanical astronaut" or, worse, a "mechanical Kamikaze," developing countries should be interested in the construction of a "mechanical bureaucrat", who can serve the society.

In contrast to the goals of the most powerful countries, one of the principal goals for Mexico is to improve the governmental administrative mechanism, and thus make feasible the aforementioned national objectives. Computer science technology is a determining factor.

2. COMPUTER SCIENCE TECHNOLOGY FOR BUREAUCRATIC SYSTEMS

In the strictest sense, computer science is not sufficient to solve the problem of bureaucratic inefficiency. But the related concepts from systems analysis and interdisciplinary methods constitute the best methodological framework for attacking the problem. Bureaucracy may be considered to be a huge political, economic, and administrative system that acts upon society. Such a system is composed of a large number of interrelated subsystems, each one performing a special function. These subsystems have an information flow described in Fig. 1. The same figure shows the principal problem areas and thus some of the possible lines for technological development that may evolve in this field. These are the following:

(1) Methods for gathering and validating data.

(2) The organization of large data bases and information retrieval techniques.

(3) Mathematical models for analyzing and processing data from each bureaucratic function.

(4) Organization of mechanized processes.

(5) Interfacing between subsystem components, as well as between different subsystems.

(6) Mechanisms for interfacing the bureaucratic system with society.

It might appear that the type of computer science technology needed by the government would be similar to that used in private enterprise. However, this is not the case. On a descriptive level, administrative processes might be similar, but the information needs of government are much more complex than those of industry and commerce. Among other reasons, government interacts with all the people, which in a developing country is a heterogeneous group. Thus, the administrative interface of a bureaucracy with the public is much more complex than that between companies and their clients.

The administrative logic of a government imposes a more difficult operation than that of a business enterprise. To begin with, a business is organized around a very clear concept—profits. But a government looks for the optimization of other factors, the optimization, subject, of course, to the constraint of no economic loss. Sometimes such factors are difficult,

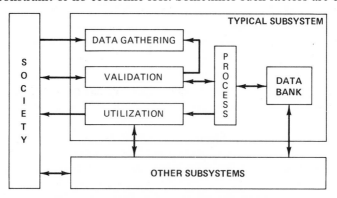

Fig. 1. Information flow in a bureaucratic system.

if not impossible, to measure; this makes the goals of a public administration more difficult to oversee and control than those of a business. The lack of dynamic controls that should be adapted to react to changing situations has given rise to the creation of static controls, which, because of their rigidity, have become the universal characteristic of bureaucracies. Overcoming this is, beyond doubt, one of the main challenges to computer science technology.

For all of these reasons, the software developed for commercial use is not in general useful for government. Thus, technological developments of great magnitude are required.

When scientific or engineering problems are processed by a computer, the solution that the machine produces is very close to the actual solution. Unfortunately this does not happen in administrative problems. In order for the computer output to be converted into a real solution, it is essential to have a complex administrative interface that translates the computer recommendation into a concrete and usable solution to the real problems. For this reason, it is of particular importance to study the relations among the components of the information systems, and their connections with society. Computers, together with their programs, are only pieces of the administrative apparatus. These two in turn are part of society, and thus are subject to the political system. In order for computers in government to be truly useful, it is imperative not only to know how to program them with the most advanced techniques, but also to know how to embed them into administrative processes. These frequently are required to change, but in such a way that the adjustments are feasible within the political, economic, and social framework of the country.

Such feasibility conditions cannot be violated. This frequently causes trivial applications of computers. The real challenge to computer science technology is on the one hand, to develop ingenious programs without infringing on the societal constraints, and yet resolving important problems effectively; and on the other hand, to develop a cybernetic methodology that would permit the structure rationalization and function optimization of both the administrative and political systems, but in such a way that in complying with present restrictions, it could create conditions for modification of these restrictions in the future.

Finally, there is one aspect of major social importance—the human–computer relationship. Computers should be used so as to avoid dehumanization of the bureaucratic system. We will now describe the experience obtained in the design and implementation of various computer supported administrative systems of the INFONAVIT.

3. THE INFONAVIT

The *Instituto del Fondo Nacional de la Vivienda para los Trabajadores* (Institute for the National Fund for Workers Housing) is a public organization whose objective is to solve the housing problem for Mexican workers.

All Mexican employers must pay 5% of the salary of their workers to build and maintain a special fund, from which the financing for construction of workers' housing is obtained, as well as credit loans to purchase them (see Fig. 2). These payments by the employers are collected and deposited by INFONAVIT in an individual savings account for each worker, who has the right to request a loan.

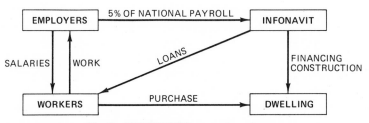

Fig. 2. INFONAVIT's operative scheme.

4. THE POLITICAL FRAMEWORK

INFONAVIT was created by law on May 1, 1972, and it began operations on that same date. Right from the start, it began collecting 5% of the national payroll. As employers paid into the fund, and as workers became aware of it, they immediately pressured for both the construction of housing and for credit with which to purchase the housing. However, at the same time, business groups and unions demanded to participate in the operation and internal control of the institute. This would have impeded immediate results. Low income housing had been ignored for many years. Therefore public opinion was a mixture of hope and skepticism. Also, different political groups suddenly became interested in controlling the powerful economic and social instrument that was being created. As if this were not enough, financial control by statute fixes a maximum of 1.5% for administrative expenses, but it was obvious that during the starting-up period, especially if it was to be escalated very rapidly, more administrative expenses would be needed than for general operation. It soon became clear that it was necessary to create, posthaste, an organization capable of satisfactorily handling information that arrived daily in large volumes. An information system was necessary, not only for administrative reasons, but also for the new public organization to become politically stable. The applicability of computers was evident. For this reason, the author was called upon to coordinate the design, construction, and implementation of the information system which would support the various actions of IN-FONAVIT.

It must be emphasized that the obligation accepted was not only to propose a solution, but actually to implement a solution. We were given complete control of design and implementation of the system. This required a study of the situation from an overall view, including the political, administrative, and technical (computational) issues. It is probably the first time in Mexico that a computer scientist has been given such a global responsibility.

The freedom to decompose the solution of a problem into political, administrative, and technical components is an experience comparable to that of a mathematician who can choose, at will, different notations or spaces of definition to state and solve the various phases of a problem.

To begin our work, we had to consider carefully the following points:

(1)   Most people look upon information as the equivalent of power. Any proposition that implies a large concentration of information would be objectionable.

(2)   In the past, computers had generated many failures; it would be necessary to use them correctly and to show them to be a key part of the solution.

(3)   It was urgent to implement specific projects that would soon show the usefulness of computation, and at the same time to start building the administrative apparatus of the organization. This was necessary because fast results would aid in the political consolidation of the institute.

(4)   In order to make the project as a whole a success, it was necessary to make the number of areas of the institute involved in the project as large as possible. At the same time, it was imperative that our participation not be regarded as a technocratic exercise, having nothing to do with the social objectives of the institute.

5.   ADMINISTRATIVE MEASURES

A strategy was proposed, which, in a broad aspect, included the following points:

(1)   Establish a computing center, whose only function would be the operation of a powerful computer.

(2)   Form interdisciplinary groups at the highest technical level to do the design and implementation of large institutional subsystems.

(3)   Divide the responsibility for collecting, evaluating, and safeguarding of information between the computer center and the designing and programming groups.

These three points permitted a responsibility distribution that averted the concentration of functions, of information, and of power in one single place. This solution is unique in Mexico; the rule has always been that the use of the computer, its programming and the information control are concentrated in one single administrative unit.

In addition to these basic points, a large number of additional points were proposed. To mention a few:

(1)   It was decided to construct a building to house the computer center, which would become a showcase and a symbol of modern technology.

(2)   The National University of Mexico, through its Center of Applied Mathematics and Systems, was invited to participate on technical aspects in the development of programming and file organization.

(3)   We set May 1, 1973, the first anniversary of INFONAVIT, as the deadline to have some of the more important parts of the systems operational.

We established various independent work groups, each one responsible for meeting a proposed goal. We will describe next a project carried out by one of these groups.

6.   THE TECHNICAL ASPECTS

The objective of this system is to gather the data, update the files, and give information related to the individual savings accounts of the workers. The main issues for designing the system were:

(1)   The volume of information. Three and a half million accounts are updated every two months.

(2)   Correct identity. It is very important that all entries made with the same file in the computer correspond to the same corporation or person.

(3)   Error filtering. The source documentation is prepared by over 200,000 employers all over the country. The errors they commit must be detected and corrected.

(4)   Real-time access and communication with other systems. Information on individual accounts must not only be on-line, but must also be available for used by other systems, such as those for granting the loans.

Figure 3 describes the information flow in this system. The data corre-

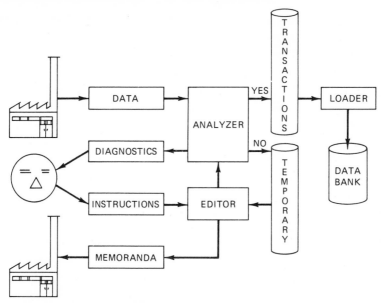

Fig. 3. Information flow for worker's account system.

sponding to employers' quotas are fed into the system by means of an analyzer, which does an exhaustive filtering of errors. Once the data are verified, they are passed into a transactions file; from there a loader puts them into a master data bank. Erroneous or doubtful data are held in a temporary file, where through an editing system, they may be corrected and returned to the analyzer for verification.

The master data bank is organized in a very complex way; it is based on a hierarchical structure, tied to the exterior through "hash" directories, which permit direct access to data by means of the worker's social security number, or by a business ID-code. We are looking for an efficient way to retrieve worker or business data using the name. To support this we are testing various compacting schemes.

The data bank organization is an example of application of technological knowledge to a particular problem. However, it constitutes a nontrivial problem since it involves five and a half million complex individual files.

The original contribution of this project was the design of the analyzer and the editor. The analyzer was constructed from a very pessimistic premise: "The input data will be erroneous most of the time." We made a careful analysis to identify the largest possible number of errors; we found nearly 150 different situations that presented conflicts. These showed up in a striking fact: 95% of the code deals with "exceptions" and only 5% handles the "normal" situations.

The analyzer is the embryo of a mechanical bureaucrat. It corresponds to the clerk who checks the incoming documents necessary to start an administrative process. This program was made as intelligent as possible.

(1)   It uses a lot of common sense; it will not discard a document with a minor error. A lot of analytic and deductive capacity was included in this program so that errors could not only be detected, but in some cases corrected.

(2)   It has the capacity to learn, which eliminates the need of human intervention in situations that have been resolved previously.

The validation process cannot be completely mechanized; it is necessary to have human participation. When the computer detects an error that it cannot correct, the source document has to be checked to rectify possible keypunch errors. However, if the error is in the source document, the originator of the document has to be reached in order to correct the error. In our case that can be in any part of the country. It was this consideration that led us to design a very efficient interface between the computer and the human.

For each set of data the analyzer puts out three types of diagnostics:

(1)   *Errors*. These are situations where the analyzer is certain that a piece of data is wrong and it cannot correct the data. In this case the program holds the data in a temporary file and writes up a very explicit comment on the error. For example, an error occurs when there is discrepancy in the amounts paid.

(2)   *Notes*. In this case, the analyzer is in doubt whether a piece of data is wrong or not; it holds the data in the temporary file and asks for human intervention. For example, if the age of a worker is greater than 73 years, a note is generated. The same is true when the salary of a worker varies more than 50% between two consecutive payments.

(3)   *Comments*. In this case the analyzer found a problem it could resolve; the processing of the data is not stopped, but it records the error found and the action taken. For example, a comment is made when an error occurs in an ID number and it can be corrected by using the name of the worker.

For the human interface two instruments were developed: first, a special language, so simple to use that it was taught to high school graduates without any knowledge of computers. With this language clerks can correct the data in the temporary file and resend the data to the analyzer. The language allows the clerk to instruct the computer to put out a memorandum to the employer that a correction to the source document is requested. The second instrument consists of an operation manual that includes all the possible actions taken by a clerk for all 150 possible diagnostics. This operation manual is actually a program for a human computer. The procedures in this manual, together with the analyzer, constitute the algorithm for validating data.

The relation between the manual and the analyzer is based on the premise that a maximum of routine work should be left to the computer, leaving for the human being the work that requires refined criteria or consultation with the environment. That is why, whenever a manual process that can be programmed is detected, it is included in the analyzer. For example, 500 memoranda or more are sent out daily; each one is created using one of 30 different texts and the particular data of the case.

Some interesting research has resulted from this problem. First, an analysis of the statistical properties of names in Mexico allowed the design of the analyzer facility to recognize names and to correct them in a way similar to a human bureaucrat using his common sense. Also, an algorithm was found to break up any Spanish word into its syllables. This is a syntactic algorithm; it does not rely on the meaning of words.

7. CONCLUSIONS

(1) Computer Science technology has to be adapted to the local conditions of the society using it.

(2) Mexico is not in a condition to, nor does it need to, develop its own technology in hardware. However, it does have the possibility and the necessity of producing and adapting its own technology in the area of software, since software is the link between computers and local problems.

(3) Developing countries require capable governments. Computer science technology can assist the process of public administration to be as efficient as possible.

(4) Computer science technology for a developing country does not need to be underdeveloped technology.

(5) The project of building a "mechanized bureaucrat" can be a nucleus that generates specific research projects as well as solutions to concrete problems.

(6) The operation of a government is more complex than that of private enterprise. Hence, a large part of the computer science technology developed for private administration cannot be applied to public administration. It is important to find the role of the computer in the administration, and to find the role of the administration in the political context. If this is ignored, failure is certain.

(7) One must never forget that the computer is an instrument for man. Therefore, it must be used with imagination and vigor to solve human

problems, without falling into technocratic positions that justify the use of the computer per se.

(8) In INFONAVIT we were able to put into practice some of these ideas. It was necessary to start with political and societal constraints and apply computer technology given these restrictions.

(9) The National University of Mexico was invited to participate. There, the software was developed applying knowledge adapted to local needs. Also, new technology was developed for some specific problems.

(10) As a result of the analysis of the problem, several research projects have started, among which is the study of the structure of the Spanish language.

A New Approach to Recursive Programs

Zohar Manna[†] and Adi Shamir[‡]

Applied Mathematics Department
The Weizmann Institute of Science
Rehovot, Israel

In this chapter we evaluate the classical least-fixedpoint approach toward recursive programs. We suggest a new approach which extracts the maximal amount of valuable information embedded in the programs. The presentation is informal, with emphasis on examples.

1. INTRODUCTION

The classical stack implementation of recursive programs does not always give results that correspond to our naive intuitive expectations. For instance, one might expect the program

$$F(x) \Leftarrow 0 \cdot F(x)$$

over, say, the natural numbers, to be identical to the program

$$F(x) \Leftarrow 0,$$

since for any number y, $0 \cdot y = 0$. Similarly, the program

$$F(x) \Leftarrow \text{ if } F(x) = 0 \text{ then } 0 \text{ else } 0$$

would be expected to yield the zero function. Since the test $F(x) = 0$ is irrelevant, nothing but 0 can be produced as an output. However, stack implementations and the conventional theory of programs dictate that both of these programs be undefined for all inputs. Users of recursion are so accustomed to this implementation that they are no longer surprised at this unintuitive interpretation, and never stop to consider any alternative meanings of recursive programs.

[†]Present address: Artificial Intelligence Laboratory, Stanford University, Stanford, California.

[‡]Present address: Computer Science Department, University of Warwick, Coventry, England.

A recursive program, such as those above, looks like an implicit functional equation relating the values of the function variable F. Such an equation may in general have many possible solution functions (*fixedpoints*). Since there is no unique solution, the semantics of recursive programs is selected rather than implied. The classical stack implementation yields one solution, the *least defined fixedpoint* of the program. As we have seen above, the blind selection of the least defined solution is inadequate, because a recursive program often contains more information than this solution exhibits.

In this chapter we suggest the selection of a different and often more defined solution, which always exists and which contains as much information as possible.

In Section 2 we discuss various possible approaches toward recursive programs, in an attempt to characterize the "best" one. On the basis of this discussion we introduce our new *optimal-fixedpoint* approach in Section 3, which is exemplified in Section 4. Various techniques for proving properties of optimal fixedpoints are presented in Section 5.

This chapter is an informal exposition of the optimal fixedpoint theory. More formal treatment is given by Manna and Shamir [76] and Shamir [77].

2. RECURSIVE PROGRAMS AND THEIR FIXEDPOINTS

Consider, as a typical example, the following recursive program P1 over the natural numbers[†]:

$$\text{P1}: \quad F(x, y) \Leftarrow \text{if } x = 0 \text{ then } y \text{ else } F(F(x, y - 1), F(x - 1, y)).$$

Any solution function to this program must satisfy the relations dictated by the program, i.e.,

$$F(0, y) = y \qquad \text{for all } y,$$

and

$$F(x, y) = F(F(x, y - 1), F(x - 1, y)) \qquad \text{for all } x \neq 0 \text{ and all } y.$$

Let us analyze what functions satisfy these two conditions.

The main part of this program is the functional

$$\tau[F]: \quad \text{if } x = 0 \text{ then } y \text{ else } F(F(x, y - 1), F(x - 1, y)),$$

in which the symbol F is considered as a *function variable*. Given any partial function $f(x, y)$, the result of substituting f for F yields a new

[†]All functions in this program map natural numbers into natural numbers: thus, $x - 1$ is defined to be 0 for $x = 0$.

partial function, denoted by $\tau[f]$. For example, if we substitute the function

$$f(x, y) = y$$

for $F(x, y)$, we obtain the function

$$\tau[f](x, y) = \text{if } x = 0 \text{ then } y \text{ else } f(f(x, y - 1), f(x - 1, y))$$

$$= \text{if } x = 0 \text{ then } y \text{ else } f(y - 1, y) = y.$$

Thus, the function $f(x, y)$ has the interesting property that $f(x, y) = \tau[f](x, y)$; that is, f is a solution function to the functional equation $F(x, y) = \tau[F](x, y)$. Since f does not change under the application of τ, it is said to be a *fixedpoint* of the given recursive program.

An entirely different function that is a fixedpoint of the program is

$$g(x, y) = \max(x, y).$$

Substituting g for F in $\tau[F]$, we obtain

$$\tau[g](x, y) = \text{if } x = 0 \text{ then } y \text{ else } \max(\max(x, y - 1), \max(x - 1, y)).$$

By the definition of max, this can be simplified to

$$\tau[g](x, y) = \text{if } x = 0 \text{ then } y \text{ else } \max(x, y - 1, x - 1, y)$$

$$= \text{if } x = 0 \text{ then } y \text{ else } \max(x, y)$$

$$= \max(x, y).$$

Thus $g(x, y)$ is a fixedpoint of the recursive program P1.

Yet another example of a fixedpoint is the partial function

$$l(x, y) = \text{if } x = 0 \text{ then } y \text{ else } \textbf{undefined.}$$

To show that this function is indeed a fixedpoint of our recursive program, we substitute l in τ, treating **undefined** as any other value. For this purpose we make the general assumption that all functions and predicates appearing in τ are "naturally extended," in the sense that they are **undefined** whenever at least one of their arguments is **undefined**. Thus, we have

$$\tau[l](x, y)$$

$$= \text{if } x = 0 \text{ then } y \text{ else } l(l(x, y - 1), l(x - 1, y))$$

$$= \text{if } x = 0 \text{ then } y \text{ else } l(\text{if } x = 0 \text{ then } y - 1 \text{ else } \textbf{undefined}, l(x - 1, y))$$

$$= \text{if } x = 0 \text{ then } y \text{ else } l(\textbf{undefined}, l(x - 1, y))$$

$$= \text{if } x = 0 \text{ then } y \text{ else}$$

$$\quad\quad \text{if } \textbf{undefined} = 0 \text{ then } l(x - 1, y) \text{ else } \textbf{undefined}$$

$$= \text{if } x = 0 \text{ then } y \text{ else } \textbf{undefined.}$$

These three functions do not exhaust the set of all fixedpoints of the program. An example of an infinite class of fixedpoints (indexed by the function a over the natural numbers) is

$$h_a(x, y) = \textbf{if } x = 0 \textbf{ then } y \textbf{ else } a(x).$$

A function $h_a(x, y)$ can be shown to be a fixedpoint of the program, provided that the function $a(n)$ satisfies

$$a(n) \neq 0 \quad \text{and} \quad a(a(n)) = a(n) \quad \text{for all} \quad n > 0.$$

Examples of functions satisfying this condition are the identity function, any nonzero constant function, or the function that assigns to any natural number n its greatest prime factor.

There are actually infinitely many more distinct fixedpoints, the exact characterization of which is quite complicated. We can thus see that the set of all fixedpoints of the program may contain many functions with extremely diversified behavior. All these functions can be considered as "solutions" to the equation represented by our recursive program.

Some of these fixedpoints are related by the "less defined or equal" relation. We say that a function $r(x, y)$ is *less defined or equal* to $s(x, y)$, or that $s(x, y)$ is *more defined or equal* to $r(x, y)$, if for any pair of natural numbers (a, b), if $r(a, b)$ is defined, then $s(a, b)$ is also defined and has the same value; thus, either $r(a, b)$ is undefined or else $r(a, b) = s(a, b)$. Note that a function $r(x, y)$ may be neither "less defined or equal" nor "more defined or equal" to $s(x, y)$.

This relation introduces some structure into the set of all fixedpoints of a recursive program. A fixedpoint is called *least (defined)* if it is less defined or equal to any other fixedpoint of the program. Dually, a fixedpoint is called *greatest (defined)* if it is more defined or equal to any other fixedpoint.

Among the fixedpoints of the program P1, the fixedpoint

$$l(x, y) = \textbf{if } x = 0 \textbf{ then } y \textbf{ else undefined}$$

stands out. Since any fixedpoint of P1 must be defined as y for $x = 0$, it is clearly the program's least fixedpoint.

Least fixedpoints of recursive programs have long attracted the attention of computer science theoreticians for three main reasons (see, e.g., Manna [74]):

(a) Any recursive program must have a (unique) least fixedpoint. Thus the least fixedpoint can be used to unambiguously define the "meaning" of recursive programs.

(b) The classical stack implementation of recursive programs computes the least fixedpoint of the program.

(c) There are powerful methods for proving properties of the least fixedpoint of recursive programs.

As a result, the least fixedpoint was chosen as the "proper" solution of recursive programs and other fixedpoints were absolutely discarded by researchers from further consideration. However, we have an important objection to this choice: it contradicts the intuitive concept that the more defined the solution, the more valuable it is. Indeed, there are many recursive programs for which the least fixedpoint does not contain all the useful information embedded in the program, information that is contained in more defined fixedpoints.

Consider, for example, the following recursive program P2 for solving the discrete form of the Laplace equation, where $F(x, y)$ maps pairs of integers in $[0,100] \times [0,100]$ into reals:

P2: $F(x, y) \Leftarrow$ **if** $x = 0$ **then** $2y$

   else if $x = 100$ **then** $3y + 300$
   else if $y = 0$ **then** $3x$
   else if $y = 100$ **then** $4x + 200$
   else$\big[F(x - 1, y) + F(x, y - 1) + F(x + 1, y)$
      $+ F(x, y + 1) \big]/4.$

This recursive program has exactly two fixedpoints:

$$f(x, y) = \begin{cases} 2y & \text{if } x = 0, \\ 3y + 300 & \text{if } x = 100, \\ 3x & \text{if } y = 0, \\ 4x + 200 & \text{if } y = 100, \\ \textbf{undefined} & \text{otherwise.} \end{cases}$$

$g(x, y) = 3x + 2y + (x \cdot y)/100$ for $0 \leqslant x, y \leqslant 100$.

There is no doubt that the second (totally defined) fixedpoint $g(x, y)$ contains much more valuable information than the (mostly undefined) function $f(x, y)$. Moreover, it is quite obvious that any programmer writing such a recursive program unconsciously thinks about the function $g(x, y)$ as the "solution" of the functional equation represented by the program. Thus, the arbitrary selection of the least fixedpoint as the "proper solution" seems a poor choice in this case.

This example might suggest a turn to the other extreme—considering greatest fixedpoints rather than least fixedpoints. Unfortunately, there are many programs for which there is no such greatest fixedpoint, as program P1 shows: There is no function that is more defined or equal to all the fixedpoints exhibited.

A more modest approach could be the selection of a *maximal fixedpoint*, i.e., a fixedpoint that is not less defined than any other fixedpoint. However, there are difficulties with this choice too. While any recursive program has such a fixedpoint, it may have more than one. This is demonstrated by program P1, in which the functions $f(x, y)$, $g(x, y)$ and $h_a(x, y)$ are all examples of total, and therefore maximal, fixedpoints of P1. This indicates that P1 is an "underdefined" recursive program—the relations stated between values of F for various arguments (x, y) are not sufficient to determine uniquely one defined value of the fixedpoint. Thus, a randomly chosen maximal fixedpoint is by no means superior to the least fixedpoint $l(x, y)$ in this case.

As an artificial example that illustrates this problem, consider

P3: $F(x) \Leftarrow F(x)$

over, say, the set of the natural numbers. Any partial function over the natural numbers is clearly a fixedpoint of this extremely "underdefined" program. The least fixedpoint of P3 is the totally undefined function, and every total function over the natural numbers is a maximal fixedpoint. In such a case, the least fixedpoint seems the most appropriate solution, since no other fixedpoint can be considered a more "valuable" solution of this program.

3.   THE OPTIMAL FIXEDPOINT

Thus far we have objected to the classical least fixedpoint and the proposed greatest and maximal fixedpoint approaches to recursive programs. We now suggest a new approach—the *optimal fixedpoint approach*. It combines the nice properties of all the above approaches in that the fixedpoint selected always exists and is unique, and it supplies the maximal amount of valuable information embedded in the program. Thus, in the three examples considered so far, the new approach will select the least fixedpoint in the "underdefined" programs P1 and P3, but will select the desired total fixedpoint (which differs from the least fixedpoint) in the Laplace program P2.

In order to develop the new approach we first introduce the notion of "consistency". Two functions are said to be *consistent* if they have identical values for any argument for which both are defined. For example, let

$$f_1(x) = \begin{cases} 0 & \text{if } x = 0, \\ \textbf{undefined} & \text{if } x = 1, \\ 0 & \text{otherwise,} \end{cases} \qquad f_2(x) = \begin{cases} 0 & \text{if } x = 0, \\ 1 & \text{if } x = 1, \\ \textbf{undefined} & \text{otherwise,} \end{cases}$$

$$f_3(x) = \begin{cases} 0 & \text{if } x = 0, \\ 2 & \text{if } x = 1, \\ \textbf{undefined} & \text{otherwise.} \end{cases}$$

Then f_1 and f_2 are consistent, as are f_1 and f_3. However, f_2 and f_3 are not consistent, since for $x = 1$ both are defined and have different values. Note that no two of these functions are related by the "less defined or equal" relation.

Two consistent functions can be regarded as being "approximately the same." One of them may be defined at several arguments at which the other is undefined, and vice versa; but the two functions cannot have contradictory defined values. They can be considered as two incomplete representations of the same knowledge, and one can define a function that is more defined than both of them, thus being superior to both parital representations.

We now define a fixedpoint f of a program P to be *fxp-consistent* if f is consistent with any other fixedpoint g of P. That is, whenever f is defined, say $f(x) = a$, then for any other fixedpoint g, either $g(x)$ is **undefined** or $g(x) = a$. Thus the value a is implicitly defined by the program as the only possible defined solution at x. Every recursive program has at least one fxp-consistent fixedpoint, since the least fixedpoint of the program is less defined than (and thus consistent with) any other fixedpoint of the program. Thus, the classical least fixedpoint is one of these valuable fixedpoints, but only one of many.

The fxp-consistent fixedpoints can be considered as the only genuine solutions of a recursive program, since only they contain uniquely determined values. We can thus concentrate our attention on the subset of fxp-consistent fixedpoints rather than on the set of all fixedpoints of the program. In this restricted set of solutions we are naturally interested in maximally defined solutions of the program. While the greatest fixedpoint approach was not applicable to the set of all fixedpoints of the program, we now fortunately have[†]:

Basic Theorem: The set of all fxp-consistent fixedpoints always contains a (unique) greatest element.

Let us now look at the set of fixedpoints from a different point of view. Previously, we discussed the possibility of selecting a maximal fixedpoint as the "proper" solution of the program. This approach was not applicable, since the program may have infinitely many such solutions with no information common to all of them, and no one of which seems superior to the others. A natural way to resolve this problem is to find a fixedpoint which extracts the unanimity among these maximal fixedpoints, thus being a satisfactory representative of all of them. Such a fixedpoint can be obtained by considering the fixedpoints which are less defined or equal to all the maximal fixedpoints. For these fixedpoints we again have:

[†]The informal nature of our exposition does not enable us to prove the results presented in this section. Formal proofs may be found in Manna and Shamir [76].

Basic Theorem: The set of fixedpoints that are less defined or equal to all maximal fixedpoints of the program has a (unique) least element.

We have thus arrived at two possible definitions of the "most desired solution" of a recursive program, the first by ascending as much as possible from the least fixedpoint in the set of fxp-consistent fixedpoints, and the second by descending from the maximal fixedpoints.

It is quite natural to relate these two "desired solutions" of a recursive program. Surprisingly enough, these two fixedpoints always coincide, and we call the fixedpoint thus defined the *optimal fixedpoint* of the program.

By the definition of the optimal fixedpoint, it follows that any recursive program has a unique optimal fixedpoint. If the program has only one fixedpoint that is fxp-consistent, the optimal fixedpoint coincides with the classical least fixedpoint. On the other hand, if the program has a unique maximal fixedpoint, the optimal fixedpoint coincides with it. In all other cases, the optimal fixedpoint "floats" somewhere in the set of all fixedpoints. We illustrate this with the diagram in Fig. 1, which summarizes some of the structural properties of the set of fixedpoints of recursive programs. In this diagram an upper section (Fig. 2a) represents the set of all fixedpoints that are more defined than or equal to f; similarly, a lower section (Fig. 2b) represents the set of all fixedpoints that are less defined than or equal to f. The "strategic position" of the optimal fixedpoint is clearly visible.

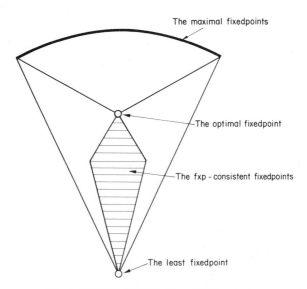

Fig. 1.   The fixedpoints of a recursive program.

(a)   (b)

Fig. 2.

4. A DETAILED EXAMPLE

Consider the following family of recursive programs over the natural numbers:

$$P_{i,j}: \quad F(x) \Leftarrow \textbf{if } x = 0 \textbf{ then } i \textbf{ else } j \cdot F(F(x-1)).$$

We shall investigate the structure of the set of fixedpoints for a few recursive programs in this family, thus illustrating the behavior of the optimal fixedpoint approach in various situations. In order to systematically analyze the possible values of fixedpoints for some $x = a$, we evaluate the term $F(a)$ by repeatedly substituting $\tau[F]$ for various occurrences of F. Note that we make use of the fact that F represents a fixedpoint of the program, but not necessarily the least fixedpoint or the optimal fixedpoint.

4.1. Program $P_{0,j}$

$$P_{0,j}: \quad F(x) \Leftarrow \textbf{if } x = 0 \textbf{ then } 0 \textbf{ else } j \cdot F(F(x-1)).$$

Let us analyze the possible values of F for successive arguments x:

$$F(0) = \textbf{if } 0 = 0 \textbf{ then } 0 \textbf{ else } j \cdot F(F(0-1)) = 0,$$

$$F(1) = \textbf{if } 1 = 0 \textbf{ then } 0 \textbf{ else } j \cdot F(F(1-1))$$
$$= j \cdot F(F(0)) = j \cdot F(0) = j \cdot 0 = 0,$$

$$F(2) = \textbf{if } 2 = 0 \textbf{ then } 0 \textbf{ else } j \cdot F(F(2-1))$$
$$= j \cdot F(F(1)) = j \cdot F(0) = j \cdot 0 = 0.$$

It can be shown easily (by induction) that $F(x) = 0$ for any natural number x. Thus for any j, the program $P_{0,j}$ has exactly one fixedpoint:

$$f(x) = 0 \qquad \text{for any natural number } x.$$

It is clearly the program's least fixedpoint as well as the program's optimal fixedpoint.

The behavior of the programs changes drastically when we take i to be 1 rather than 0.

4.2. Program $P_{1,0}$

$P_{1,0}:$ $F(x) \Leftarrow$ **if** $x = 0$ **then** 1 **else** $0 \cdot F(F(x-1))$.

The value of $F(0)$ is clearly 1, by a direct application of the recursive definition. For $x = 1$, however, we get

$F(1) = $ **if** $1 = 0$ **then** 1 **else** $0 \cdot F(F(1-1))$

$= 0 \cdot F(F(0)) = 0 \cdot F(1)$.

We now have exactly two possible values for $F(1)$:

$F(1) = $ **undefined**   or $F(1) = 0$.

Selecting the first possibility, $F(1) = $ **undefined**, we obtain

$F(2) = $ **if** $2 = 0$ **then** 1 **else** $0 \cdot F(F(2-1))$

$= 0 \cdot F(F(1)) = 0 \cdot F(\textbf{undefined})$

$= 0 \cdot \big(\textbf{if undefined} = 0 \textbf{ then } 1 \textbf{ else } 0 \cdot F(F(\textbf{undefined} - 1))\big)$

$= 0 \cdot \textbf{undefined} = \textbf{undefined}$.

Continuing in this way, we get the fixedpoint

$$f(x) = \begin{cases} 1 & \text{if } x = 0, \\ \textbf{undefined} & \text{otherwise.} \end{cases}$$

However, if we select the second possibility, $F(1) = 0$, we have to continue in the following way:

$F(2) = $ **if** $2 = 0$ **then** 1 **else** $0 \cdot F(F(2-1))$

$= 0 \cdot F(F(1)) = 0 \cdot F(0) = 0 \cdot 1 = 0$,

and so on. We thus get the fixedpoint

$$g(x) = \begin{cases} 1 & \text{if } x = 0, \\ 0 & \text{otherwise.} \end{cases}$$

The functions $f(x)$ and $g(x)$ are clearly the only possible fixedpoints of the program. Since $f(x)$ is less defined than $g(x)$, $f(x)$ is the program's least fixedpoint, while $g(x)$ is the program's optimal fixedpoint.

4.3. Program $P_{1,1}$

$P_{1,1}:$ $F(x) \Leftarrow$ **if** $x = 0$ **then** 1 **else** $1 \cdot F(F(x-1))$.

The value of $F(0)$ is necessarily 1. Evaluating $F(1)$, we get

$F(1) = $ **if** $1 = 0$ **then** 1 **else** $F(F(1-1))$

$= F(F(0)) = F(1)$,

and thus any natural number (as well as the value **undefined**) is a solution of this equation. If we choose $F(1) = $ **undefined**, we get (exactly as in program $P_{1,0}$) the fixedpoint

$$f(x) = \begin{cases} 1 & \text{if } x = 0, \\ \textbf{undefined} & \text{otherwise.} \end{cases}$$

Since any other fixedpoint of $P_{1,1}$ must also be 1 for $x = 0$, $f(x)$ is clearly the program's least fixedpoint.

Suppose we choose $F(1) = 0$. We then continue with

$$F(2) = \textbf{if } 2 = 0 \textbf{ then } 1 \textbf{ else } 1 \cdot F(F(2-1))$$

$$= F(F(1)) = F(0) = 1,$$

$$F(3) = \textbf{if } 3 = 0 \textbf{ then } 1 \textbf{ else } 1 \cdot F(F(3-1))$$

$$= F(F(2)) = F(1) = 0,$$

and so on. We thus get the fixedpoint

$$g(x) = \begin{cases} 1 & \text{if } x \text{ is even,} \\ 0 & \text{if } x \text{ is odd.} \end{cases}$$

If we take $F(1) = 1$, we obtain

$$F(2) = \textbf{if } 2 = 0 \textbf{ then } 1 \textbf{ else } 1 \cdot F(F(2-1))$$

$$= F(F(1)) = F(1) = 1,$$

and so on. We thus obtain the fixedpoint

$$h(x) = 1 \quad \text{for any natural number } x.$$

If we take $F(1) = 2$, we get

$$F(2) = \textbf{if } 2 = 0 \textbf{ then } 1 \textbf{ else } 1 \cdot F(F(2-1))$$

$$= F(F(1)) = F(2)$$

and again we may choose any desired value for $F(2)$ (including the value **undefined**).

It is possible to continue this detailed analysis and find infinitely many more fixedpoints of $P_{1,1}$. But in order to characterize the optimal fixedpoint of this program it suffices to consider just one more fixedpoint:

$$k(x) = x + 1 \quad \text{for any natural number } x.$$

Since the optimal fixedpoint should be less defined than both maximal fixedpoints $h(x)$ and $k(x)$, it cannot be defined for any $x > 0$ (for any such x both $h(x)$ and $k(x)$ are defined and $h(x) \neq k(\dot{x})$). Therefore the program's optimal fixedpoint coincides in this case with the program's least fixedpoint $f(x)$.

4.4. Program $P_{1,2}$

$P_{1,2}:$ $F(x) \Leftarrow$ **if** $x = 0$ **then** 1 **else** $2 \cdot F(F(x - 1))$.

As before, all fixedpoints of $P_{1,2}$ are defined as 1 for $x = 0$. For $x = 1$ we have

$F(1) =$ **if** $1 = 0$ **then** 1 **else** $2 \cdot F(F(0)) = 2 \cdot F(1)$.

We have arrived at an equation (for the value of $F(1)$) which has exactly two solutions:

$F(1) =$ **undefined**   or $F(1) = 0$.

If we decide to take the value $F(1) =$ **undefined**, we again get the fixedpoint

$$f(x) = \begin{cases} 1 & \text{if } x = 0, \\ \text{\textbf{undefined}} & \text{otherwise,} \end{cases}$$

which is the program's least fixedpoint.

Choosing the other possibility, i.e., $F(1) = 0$, we get

$F(2) = 2 \cdot F(F(1)) = 2 \cdot F(0) = 2,$

$F(3) = 2 \cdot F(F(2)) = 2 \cdot F(2) = 4,$

and finally

$F(4) = 2 \cdot F(F(3)) = 2 \cdot F(4).$

The values for $F(2)$ and $F(3)$ were implied, once we chose $F(1) = 0$. But for $F(4)$, we again have to choose between the two possible solutions of the equation, namely,

$F(4) =$ **undefined**   or $F(4) = 0$.

If we choose $F(4) =$ **undefined**, then an argument similar to the one used previously shows that for any $x > 4$, $F(x) =$ **undefined**. Thus we have the fixedpoint

$$g(x) = \begin{cases} 1 & \text{if } x = 0, \\ 0 & \text{if } x = 1, \\ 2 & \text{if } x = 2, \\ 4 & \text{if } x = 3, \\ \text{\textbf{undefined}} & \text{otherwise.} \end{cases}$$

However, if we choose $F(4) = 0$, we must continue as follows:

$F(5) = 2 \cdot F(F(4)) = 2 \cdot F(0) = 2,$

$F(6) = 2 \cdot F(F(5)) = 2 \cdot F(2) = 4,$

$F(7) = 2 \cdot F(F(6)) = 2 \cdot F(4) = 0,$

and so on. The periodic function thus obtained is defined for any natural number x as

$$h(x) = \begin{cases} 1 & \text{if} \quad x = 0, \\ 0 & \text{if} \quad x = 1 + 3i, \\ 2 & \text{if} \quad x = 2 + 3i, \quad i = 0, 1, 2, \ldots, \\ 4 & \text{if} \quad x = 3 + 3i. \end{cases}$$

To summarize, the recursive program $P_{1,2}$ has exactly three fixedpoints, each generated by a different selection of a solution to the above equations:

$$f(x) = \begin{cases} 1 & \text{if} \quad x = 0, \\ \textbf{undefined} & \text{otherwise,} \end{cases}$$

$$g(x) = \begin{cases} 1 & \text{if} \quad x = 0, \\ 0 & \text{if} \quad x = 1, \\ 2 & \text{if} \quad x = 2, \\ 4 & \text{if} \quad x = 3, \\ \textbf{undefined} & \text{otherwise,} \end{cases}$$

$$h(x) = \begin{cases} 1 & \text{if} \quad x = 0, \\ 0 & \text{if} \quad x = 1 + 3i, \\ 2 & \text{if} \quad x = 2 + 3i, \quad i = 0, 1, 2, \ldots, \\ 4 & \text{if} \quad x = 3 + 3i. \end{cases}$$

Note that f is less defined than g and g is less defined than h. The only maximal fixedpoint of this program is h, and thus it is also the program's optimal fixedpoint.

4.5. Program $P_{1,3}$

$$P_{1,3}: \quad F(x) \Leftarrow \text{if } x = 0 \text{ then } 1 \text{ else } 3 \cdot F(F(x - 1)).$$

As before, $F(0) = 1$, and there are exactly two possible values for $F(1)$:

$$F(1) = \textbf{undefined} \quad \text{or} \quad F(1) = 0.$$

The first possibility leads to the same least fixedpoint as before:

$$f(x) = \begin{cases} 1 & \text{if} \quad x = 0, \\ \textbf{undefined} & \text{otherwise.} \end{cases}$$

The second possibility leads to

$$F(2) = 3 \cdot F(F(1)) = 3 \cdot F(0) = 3,$$
$$F(3) = 3 \cdot F(3).$$

Here we have the same choice once more,

$$F(3) = \textbf{undefined} \quad \text{or} \quad F(3) = 0.$$

If we choose $F(3) = \textbf{undefined}$ we get the fixedpoint

$$g(x) = \begin{cases} 1 & \text{if } x = 0, \\ 0 & \text{if } x = 1, \\ 3 & \text{if } x = 2, \\ \textbf{undefined} & \text{otherwise.} \end{cases}$$

However, if we choose $F(3) = 0$ we continue with

$$F(4) = 3 \cdot F(F(3)) = 3 \cdot F(0) = 3,$$

$$F(5) = 3 \cdot F(F(4)) = 3 \cdot F(3) = 0,$$

and so on, and we obtain the third possible fixedpoint:

$$h(x) = \begin{cases} 1 & \text{if } x = 0, \\ 0 & \text{if } x = 1 + 2i, \quad i = 0, 1, 2, \ldots, \\ 3 & \text{if } x = 2 + 2i. \end{cases}$$

The optimal fixedpoint of $P_{1,3}$ is clearly $h(x)$.

4.6. Program $P_{1,4}$

$$P_{1,4} : \quad F(x) \Leftarrow \textbf{if } x = 0 \textbf{ then } 1 \textbf{ else } 4 \cdot F(F(x - 1)).$$

This program behaves entirely differently from the cases considered previously. For $x = 0$, we still get $F(0) = 1$. For $x = 1$, we get

$$F(1) = 4 \cdot F(F(0)) = 4 \cdot F(1),$$

and we have the same choice as before,

$$F(1) = \textbf{undefined} \qquad \text{or} \qquad F(1) = 0.$$

If we take $F(1) = 0$, we continue with

$$F(2) = 4 \cdot F(F(1)) = 4 \cdot F(0) = 4,$$

and therefore

$$F(3) = 4 \cdot F(F(2)) = 4 \cdot F(4) = 4 \cdot 4 \cdot F(F(4 - 1)) = 16 \cdot F(F(3)).$$

Here we encounter a new problem: We do get an equation for the value of $F(3)$, but $F(3)$ is contained in another occurrence of F on the right-hand side of the equation. Since we do not know the global behavior of this function, we cannot simply solve this equation. However, based upon results in number theory, it can be shown that any fixedpoint of this program must be **undefined** for $x \geqslant 3$. Therefore, the program $P_{1,4}$ has exactly two fixedpoints:

$$f(x) = \begin{cases} 1 & \text{if } x = 0, \\ \textbf{undefined} & \text{otherwise,} \end{cases}$$

and

$$g(x) = \begin{cases} 1 & \text{if } x = 0, \\ 0 & \text{if } x = 1, \\ 4 & \text{if } x = 2, \\ \textbf{undefined} & \text{otherwise.} \end{cases}$$

Since f is less defined than g, f is the program's least fixedpoint and g is the program's optimal (and maximal) fixedpoint. In contrast to programs $P_{1,0}$, $P_{1,2}$, and $P_{1,3}$, the optimal fixedpoint is not a total function, even though it is still more defined than the least fixedpoint.

4.7. Program $P_{1,5}$

Finally, we consider

$$P_{1,5}: \quad F(x) \Leftarrow \textbf{if } x = 0 \textbf{ then } 1 \textbf{ else } 5 \cdot F(F(x-1)).$$

For $x = 0$ we clearly have $F(0) = 1$. For $x = 1$, we have, as usual, the choice between $F(1) = \textbf{undefined}$ and $F(1) = 0$. If we take the second possibility, we get $F(2) = 5$. The difficulty arises when considering the possible values of $F(3)$:

$$F(3) = 5 \cdot F(F(2)) = 5 \cdot F(5) = 25 \cdot F(F(4)) = 25 \cdot F(5 \cdot F(F(3))).$$

This equation is too difficult to be solved immediately.

Based upon considerations which are beyond the scope of this chapter, we can find the following two fixedpoints of $P_{1,5}$:

$$g_1(x) = \begin{cases} 1 & \text{if } x = 0, \\ 0 & \text{if } x = 1 + 2i, \quad i = 0, 1, 2, \ldots, \\ 5 & \text{if } x = 2 + 2i, \end{cases}$$

and

$$g_2(x) = \begin{cases} 1 & \text{if } x = 0, \\ 0 & \text{if } x = 1 + 3i, \\ 5 & \text{if } x = 2 + 3i, \quad i = 0, 1, 2, \ldots, \\ 25 & \text{if } x = 3 + 3i. \end{cases}$$

The optimal fixedpoint must be less defined than both of these two total (and therefore maximal) fixedpoints, so it can be defined only at arguments of the form $x = 1 + 6i$ and $x = 2 + 6i$, for $i = 0, 1, 2, \ldots$. However, the function thus obtained is not a fixedpoint of the program (e.g., try $x = 7$). It can be shown that the only two fixedpoints of $P_{1,5}$ that are less defined than this function are

$$f(x) = \begin{cases} 1 & \text{if } x = 0, \\ \textbf{undefined} & \text{otherwise,} \end{cases}$$

and

$$h(x) = \begin{cases} 1 & \text{if } x = 0, \\ 0 & \text{if } x = 1, \\ 5 & \text{if } x = 2, \\ \textbf{undefined} & \text{otherwise.} \end{cases}$$

The function $f(x)$ is clearly the program's least fixedpoint. The fixedpoint $h(x)$ is fxp-consistent, since all its values are uniquely determined by the equations.

Since the optimal fixedpoint must be either $f(x)$ or $h(x)$, and the more defined function $h(x)$ is fxp-consistent, $h(x)$ is the program's optimal fixedpoint. Note the similarity between the optimal fixedpoints of $P_{1,4}$ and $P_{1,5}$—both are defined only for $x = 0$, $x = 1$, and $x = 2$; in $P_{1,4}$ this is due to the lack of possible fixedpoints, while in $P_{1,5}$ it is due to their multiplicity.

One could continue to check all programs $P_{1,j}$ with j greater than 5. However, we believe that the preceding examples sufficiently illustrate the variety of possible cases in the new optimal-fixedpoint approach. It is especially interesting to note that although the least fixedpoint of all programs $P_{1,j}$ is the same, the sets of all fixedpoints, as well as the optimal fixedpoints, of these programs differ widely. We summarize this situation in Fig. 3, where we exhibit the sets of fixedpoints of programs $P_{1,0}$ to $P_{1,5}$. The least fixedpoint of any such program is represented by the lowest dot, while the optimal fixedpoint is represented by the dot surrounded by a circle.

In the examples considered so far, various techniques were used to find the correct value of the optimal fixedpoint. Some of these techniques are easily mechanizable, while others require deep mathematical knowledge. Unlike the least fixedpoint of a recursive program, the optimal fixedpoint need not be a computable function. Thus there cannot be a "complete" computation rule that always computes the optimal fixedpoint, but we can still hope to find good computation techniques that are applicable to large subsets of commonly used programs. The examples discussed in this section give the flavor of a few such techniques.

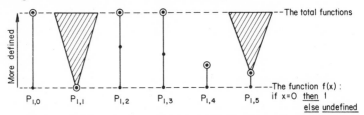

Fig. 3. The structure of the set of fixedpoints of programs $P_{1,0}$ to $P_{1,5}$.

5. PROOF TECHNIQUES

In this section we illustrate several techniques for proving properties of optimal fixedpoints. We wish to show that optimal fixedpoint f of a given recursive program P has some property $Q[f]$ without actually computing the fixedpoint. The property Q is a functional predicate, which may characterize the overall behavior of f. For example, $Q[f]$ can state that f is a total function, or that f equals some given function g, or that f is monotonically increasing over some ordered domain, etc.

Generally speaking, there are three elements involved in the process of proving properties of fixedpoints: A function f, a domain D, and a desired property Q. Any one of these three elements can be used as the basis for induction.

The two classical methods for proving properties of least fixedpoints use induction on the function and on the domain. In the *computational induction* method [deBakker and Scott 69], one first proves the property Q over D for a very simple function f_0, and then successively treats better approximations f_i of f. In the *structural induction* method [Burstall 69] one uses induction over the elements of the domain D, leaving f and Q unchanged.

While these two general methods, appropriately modified, can also be used to prove properties of the optimal fixedpoint in some cases, we suggest a new induction method (called *assertion induction*), which uses the property Q as the basis for induction. Even though this third type of induction has been totally ignored in the least-fixedpoint approach, it turns out to be a very useful technique in the optimal-fixedpoint approach.

What we actually prove in the assertion induction method is that any fixedpoint f of the program belonging to some given subset S of partial functions has the property $Q[f]$. The fact that the optimal fixedpoint g possesses the desired property is derived either as a special case (if $g \in S$), or as a result of some further argumentation (based on the definition of g as the greatest fixedpoint that is fxp-consistent).

Note that S may contain functions that are not fixedpoints of the program, and these functions need not have the property Q. The assertion induction method only shows that all functions in S that are fixedpoints of the program have property Q. The role of the subset S is to rule out certain unwanted fixedpoints that do not have the desired property Q.

5.1. The Assertion Induction Method

Given: A recursive program P: $F(x) \Leftarrow \tau[F](x)$, a property $Q[F]$, and a subset S of partial functions.

Goal: To prove that $Q[f]$ holds for any fixedpoint f of P such that $f \in S$.

Method: Find a sequence of predicates $Q_i[F]$, $i = 0, 1, 2, \ldots$, such that

(a) $Q_0[f]$ holds for any $f \in S$.
(b) If $Q_i[f]$ holds for some $f \in S$ and $\tau[f] \in S$, then $Q_{i+1}[\tau[f]]$ holds.
(c) For any $f \in S$, if $Q_i[f]$ holds for all i, then $Q[f]$ also holds.

This method can be justified by the following argument: By part (a), any fixedpoint $f \in S$ has property $Q_0[f]$. By part (b), if a function $f \in S$ has property $Q_i[f]$, and $\tau[f] \in S$, then $\tau[f]$ has property $Q_{i+1}[\tau[f]]$. But if f is a fixedpoint, then $f = \tau[f]$ so $\tau[f] \in S$, and f has property $Q_{i+1}[f]$. By induction, any fixedpoint $f \in S$ has the properties $Q_i[f]$ for $i = 0, 1, 2, \ldots$. Thus, part (c) implies that f has property $Q[f]$. Note that since f is replaced by $\tau[f]$ in the induction step, an f which is not a fixedpoint of τ is not guaranteed to have all the properties Q_i.

We illustrate this method with the following recursive program over the natural numbers:

P4: $F(x) \Leftarrow \textbf{if } F(x + 1) > 0 \textbf{ then } F(x + 1) + 1 \textbf{ else } 0$.

The least fixedpoint of this program is everywhere **undefined**. We would like to prove that the optimal fixedpoint of this program is the constant function

$f(x) = 0$ for any natural number x.

We first prove two properties of the fixedpoints of P4 which enable us to choose the subset S of partial functions properly:

(i) For any fixedpoint f of P4 and for any natural number x,
     $f(x + 1)$ is **undefined** if and only if $f(x)$ is **undefined**.

To show this, assume that $f(x + 1)$ is **undefined**; then clearly

$\tau[f](x) = \textbf{if } f(x + 1) > 0 \textbf{ then } f(x + 1) + 1 \textbf{ else } 0$

cannot be defined. Since $f(x) = \tau[f](x)$, $f(x)$ is also **undefined**. On the other hand, if $f(x + 1)$ is defined, then $\tau[f](x)$ is also defined, and since $f(x) = \tau[f](x)$, $f(x)$ is defined.

(ii) For any fixedpoint f of P4 and for any natural number x,
      $f(x + 1) = 0$ if and only if $f(x) = 0$.

This can be shown in exactly the same way as in part (i) above.

These two properties characterize two possible fixedpoints of the program P4: f which is everywhere **undefined** and g which is everywhere zero. Our aim now is to show that the recursive program has no other fixedpoints, and therefore while f is the program's least fixedpoint, g is the program's optimal fixedpoint.

The above two properties imply that any fixedpoint of P4 is either totally defined or totally **undefined**, and that for any total fixedpoint h, either $h(x) = 0$ for all x or $h(x) \neq 0$ for all x. Therefore we define S as the set of all total functions which are everywhere greater than zero, and try to prove that P4 has no fixedpoint in S.

In order to achieve this, we formally define the predicate $Q[f]$ to be always "false". The sequence of intermediate predicates we use is

$Q_i[f]$ is true if and only if $f(x) > i$ for all natural numbers x.

(a)   By the definition of S, any $f \in S$ is everywhere greater than zero, and therefore $Q_0[f]$ holds.

(b)   Suppose $Q_i[f]$ holds for some i and $f \in S$. Then by definition, $f(x) > i$ for all natural numbers x. Using this property, we can simplify the expression $\tau[f](x)$:

$$\tau[f](x) = \textbf{if } f(x + 1) > 0 \textbf{ then } f(x + 1) + 1 \textbf{ else } 0$$
$$= f(x + 1) + 1.$$

Since $f(x + 1) > i$, we have $\tau[f](x) > i + 1$. Therefore $Q_{i+1}[\tau[f]]$ also holds.

(c)   Suppose that some total function $f \in S$ satisfies $Q_i[f]$ for all i. Then for any natural number x, $f(x) > i$ for all i, and this is clearly a contradiction. Therefore any such f also satisfies $Q[f]$ which is always "false".

This completes the induction step, and the method thus guarantees that S does not contain any fixedpoint of P4.

Thus far we have introduced the new assertion induction method. As mentioned above, the two classical proof methods can also be used to prove properties of the optimal fixedpoint. We show here an appropriately modified version of the structural induction method.

5.2.   The Structural Induction Method

The structural induction method is intended to prove that a fixedpoint f of a recursive program P has some "pointwise" property $Q[f](x)$ for all x in the domain D. The main idea is to partition D into subsets $S_0, S_1, \ldots$ such that

$$D = \bigcup_{j=0}^{\infty} S_j$$

and to prove that $Q[f](x)$ holds for all $x \in S_i$ using induction over the index i. Thus, one has to show that for any i, if $Q[f](x)$ holds for all x in

$$\bigcup_{j=0}^{i-1} S_j,$$

then $Q[f](x)$ holds for all $x \in S_i$.

This implication is usually proved by freely replacing any occurrence of f by $\tau[f]$ (since f is a fixedpoint) and applying the induction hypothesis to the resultant expression. This method can also be used to prove properties of optimal fixedpoints, but one usually has to apply some additional specific reasoning techniques, such as equation solving or case analysis of possible values.

We illustrate this method with the following program P5 over the natural numbers:

P5: $F(x) \Leftarrow \textbf{if } x = 0 \textbf{ then } 0 \textbf{ else } F(x - F(x))$.

We would like to prove that the optimal fixedpoint f of P5 satisfies

$$Q[f](x): \quad f(x) = 0$$

for any natural number x.

We partition the domain of natural numbers in the following way:

$$S_0 = \{0\}, \quad S_1 = \{1\}, \quad S_2 = \{2\}, \ldots .$$

The fact that $Q[f](0)$ holds (i.e., $f(0) = 0$) is a direct consequence of the definition of P5.

Assume that we have already shown that $Q[f](x)$ holds for all x in

$$\bigcup_{j=0}^{i-1} S_j$$

(i.e., for all $0 \leqslant x \leqslant i - 1$). We now prove that $Q[f](x)$ holds for all $x \in S_i$ (i.e., for $x = i$). Since f is a fixedpoint of P5 and $i > 0$, we have

$$f(i) = f(i - f(i)).$$

We use case analysis in order to find all the possible values of $f(i)$.

One possible value of $f(i)$ is clearly **undefined**. In order to check whether $f(i)$ has any possible defined value, assume that $f(i) = k$ for some natural number k. Substituting this value into the definition of $f(i)$, we get

$$k = f(i) = f(i - f(i)) = f(i - k).$$

We consider two possible cases:

(a)   If $k = 0$, we obtain the requirement

$$0 = f(i)$$

and this value is clearly consistent with our assumption that $f(i) = k = 0$. Thus zero is a possible value of $f(i)$.

(b)   If $k > 0$, we obtain the requirement that

$$f(i - k) > 0,$$

but since $i > 0$ and $k > 0$, $i - k < i$, and this contradicts what we know (in the induction hypothesis) about the optimal fixedpoint:

$$f(x) = 0 \qquad \text{for all} \quad x, \quad 0 \leqslant x \leqslant i.$$

Therefore $f(i)$ cannot have the value k for any $k > 0$.

We have thus shown that the only two possible values of $f(i)$ are **undefined** and 0. By the definition of the optimal fixedpoint, we can now deduce that $f(i) = 0$. Since this holds for any natural number i, the optimal fixedpoint is everywhere defined as zero.

6.   CONCLUSION

In this chapter we have presented the optimal-fixedpoint approach toward recursive programs. While it is clearly appealing from a theoretical point of view, it has a drawback in practice: it may be either impossible or extremely hard to find the optimal fixedpoint of some recursive programs. While we cannot develop perfect implementations, we can try (perhaps using heuristic techniques) to extract as much information from the program as possible. Such an implementation will yield the optimal fixedpoint for certain classes of recursive programs; it will compute some intermediate fxp-consistent fixedpoint for other classes; and in the worst case will yield the least fixedpoint of the program (as computed by the classical stack implementation). By insisting on finding a more informative solution of a recursive program than the least fixedpoint, it is natural that the efficiency of computation rules is reduced and the complexity of proof techniques is increased.

The development of this new approach is still under way, both in its theoretical and practical aspects.

ACKNOWLEDGMENTS

We are indebted to Nachum Dershowitz, Steve Ness, and Richard Waldinger for their critical reading of the manuscript.

REFERENCES

Burstall, R. M., Proving properties of programs by structural induction. *Computer J.* **12** 1, 41–48 (February 1969).

deBakker, J. W., and Scott, D., A theory of programs. Unpublished memo, August 1969.

Manna, Z., *Mathematical Theory of Computation.* McGraw-Hill, New York, 1974.

Manna, Z., and Shamir, A., The theoretical aspects of the optimal fixedpoint. *SIAM J. Comput.* **5** 3, 414–426 (September 1976).

Shamir, A., The fixedpoints of recursive programs. Ph.D. thesis, Applied Mathematics Dept., Weizmann Institute of Science, Rehovot, Israel, 1976.

Time and Space[†]

Albert R. Meyer

Laboratory for Computer Science
Massachusetts Institute of Technology
Cambridge, Massachusetts

Michael Ian Shamos

Department of Computer Science
Carnegie-Mellon University
Pittsburgh, Pennsylvania

Time and space are fundamental parameters for measuring the efficiency of algorithms, and the notion of trading off one for the other is a familiar one in the programmer's informal repertoire. Nonetheless, providing satisfactory mathematical definitions of computational time and space and establishing formal relationships between them remains a central problem in computing theory. In this chapter we examine the interplay between time and space determined by a variety of machine models and explore the connection between time and space complexity classes. We consider a number of possible inclusion relationships among these classes and discuss their consequences, along with recent results indicating that mechanical procedures may be available for reducing the space used by programs. This rosy picture is darkened somewhat by a counterexample due to Cobham, which states that minimum time and space cannot always be achieved by a single program.

1. INTRODUCTION

If I had had more time, I could have written you a shorter letter.

Blaise Pascal[‡]

Every programmer has observed that he can often reduce the storage required by a program at the expense of its running time. This can sometimes be done by compressing the data in clever ways; the added cost

†This research was supported in part under NSF grant GJ 43634X, contract number DCR 7412997 A01.
‡This quotation was kindly supplied by Theodore J. Ronca, Jr.

is the time taken to perform the encoding and decoding. Other times, it may be necessary to redesign the entire algorithm or use a different data structure for representing the problem in order to decrease storage. With extraordinary luck, the new representation may permit a reduction in both storage and execution time—a recent example is Hopcroft and Tarjan's linear-time planarity algorithm [Hopcroft and Tarjan 74], which masterfully exploits the list representation of graphs. In this chapter we will survey some of the theoretical results that bear on the question of whether the ability to exchange time for space is a general phenomenon in computation or merely a fortuitous property of some unrepresentative programs. We will indicate how to define computational space and time for several models of automata and try to present a convincing case that the notion of a time–space tradeoff transcends any specific machine or programming language.

To clarify the concepts of time and space, we look first at the problem of recognizing palindromes. A palindrome is a character string that is identical to its reverse, such as the owl's complaint "TOOHOTTOHOOT". Given a string, how much time and space are needed to determine whether or not it is a palindrome?

To gain an intuitive grasp of the question, let us use a familiar theoretical model and imagine that the input string is provided on a two-way, read-only input tape. That is, we can scan the tape one square at a time and move it in either direction one square at a time, but not change anything on it. One method is to begin at the left end of the string, "remember" the character there, and move to the right end to see if the character matches. Now, at the right end, we can pick up the second symbol from the right, travel back down the tape, and compare it with the second symbol from the left. This procedure is repeated until either every character is checked or a mismatch is found.

How much time does this method require to determine whether a given string is a palindrome? If the string to be checked is a palindrome N characters long, we will need $N/2$ trips across it, having average length approximately $N/2$. A reasonable definition of computation time is the number of primitive operations performed, in this case the number of moves made during the trips, or about $N^2/4$.

The amount of space used is not so apparent. Indeed, it may seem at first glance that no space at all is required other than the tape itself. However, during the scan we must remember in some way which square of the tape to stop at in order to check the current character. This requires being able to store numbers up to size N, which means that we have auxiliary space somewhere for about $\log N$ symbols, or we will get lost while trying to examine the string. What about the space occupied by the program that is controlling this procedure? We will ignore such space for the purposes of this discussion because the size of the program is a constant, independent of the length of the input string. The justification is that no matter how long the program is there exist inputs so large that the program will be small by comparison.

A faster way to accomplish palindrome recognition is to copy the input tape into auxiliary memory and then compare the copy, character by character, with the input tape read backwards. This method requires a number of steps only proportional to N, but now the number of symbols that must be stored in memory rises to N as well.

Is there a single method that recognizes palindromes simultaneously in time proportional to N and space less than proportional to N? We shall return to this question in the last section.

2. TIME AND SPACE IN VARIOUS MACHINE MODELS

Let us make these intuitive concepts of time and space more precise, choosing initially the Turing machine model because it is simple and well-known. Let Turing machine M have a finite-state control, a two-way read-only input tape, and k semi-infinite work tapes, as in Fig. 1. This is the definition given by [Hopcroft and Ullman 69]. Assume that an input string x is given, symbol by symbol, on sequence of consecutive nonblank squares on the read-only tape. Let $T_M(x)$ be the number of moves made by M before halting, when presented with input x. We define the time complexity $T_M(N)$ of M as

$$T_M(N) = \max\{ T_M(x) \mid \text{length}(x) = N \},$$

that is, the largest number of steps taken by M on any input of length N. Similarly, we define the space complexity $S_M(N)$ as the maximum number

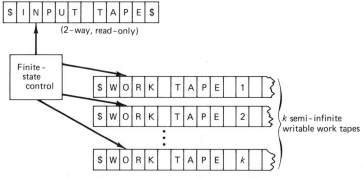

Fig. 1. A multitape Turing machine.

of *work tape squares* scanned by M on any input of length N. From now on we will dispense with the subscript M if no ambiguity results.

The first hint of a formal connection between time and space is that $T(N)$ and $S(N)$ are not independent.

Let M be a Turing machine with k work tapes. For convenience, assume that M halts on every input and that $S(N) \geqslant \log N$. (The latter assumption holds in most cases, since, speaking informally, M needs this much space to detect which part of its input is being read.)

Theorem 1:   There is a constant $\epsilon > 0$ such that for all N,

$$\epsilon \log T_M(N) \leqslant S_M(N) \leqslant k T_M(N).$$

Sketch of proof: Since M has only k work tapes, each with a single read–write head, it can visit at most k new work tape squares at each step, so obviously $S(N) \leqslant kT(N)$. To prove the other inequality, consider the number C of distinct configurations in which M can find itself. If M has k work tapes, m internal states, and a tape alphabet of a symbols, then a configuration is determined uniquely by the state, the position of the read head on the input tape, the positions of the work tape heads, and the contents of the storage tapes. Thus $C \leqslant m(N+2)(S(N))^k a^{S(N)k}$. Now, if M ever enters the same configuration twice it will not halt, so $T(N) \leqslant C$, and the result follows by taking logarithms.

Either of the bounds of Theorem 1 can essentially be achieved. For example, there is a machine M that runs for precisely 2^N steps while using precisely N tape squares for any input of length N, so that $S_M(N) = \log_2 T_M(N)$. There also exists a machine L, which visits new work tape squares with all but one of its work tape heads at every time step, so that $S_L(N) \geqslant (k-1)T_L(N)$ for such a machine.

While either of the bounds may be tight for specific machines, we are interested in solving problems (computing recursive functions), for which there are many Turing machines that will work, each with possibly different complexities S and T. One of the machines may use very little time, and another may use little space, but Theorem 1 says nothing about this possibility, since it applies to a single specific machine.

Let us now see how invariant the quantities time and space remain as we modify the machine model.

2.1. Turing Machine Variants

A natural way of generalizing the Turing machine is to drop the restriction that the work tapes be one dimensional. Such variant Turing machines (VTMs) might be supplied with a finite-number of finite dimensional work "tapes" each of which could be scanned by a finite number of read–write heads. For example, a VTM with a single two-dimensional tape scanned by three heads is illustrated in Fig. 2. In a single step, each of the heads may independently change the symbol in the square it is scanning and move up, down, left, or right. It may be helpful to think of a two-dimensional VTM as having pieces of paper on which to compute as a human might.

In order to be able to compare VTMs and ordinary multitape TMs, we supply the VTMs with a one-dimensional input tape as well as their work tapes. Time and space for VTMs are defined exactly as before, namely, as the number of steps performed and the number of work tape squares scanned.

Theorem 2: [Hartmanis and Stearns 65]. For any VTM V with time complexity $T_V(N)$, there is a Turing machine M, which computes the same function as V, using time that is at most proportional to $(T_V(N))^2$.

In particular, this means that whatever can be done by VTMs in time bounded by a polynomial in N can also be done by ordinary Turing machines in polynomial time. It is known, incidentally, that $n + 1$-dimensional VTMs are a bit faster than n-dimensional VTMs; adding a reasonable technical condition that simulations be "on-line", it has even been shown that the quadratic slowdown of Theorem 2, when ordinary Turing machines simulate VTMs, cannot be improved [Hennie 66].

The result for space is even more attractive:

Theorem 3: For any VTM V there is a Turing machine M, with possibly more states and a larger tape alphabet, which computes the same function as V, using no more space than V.

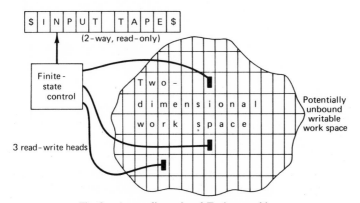

Fig. 2. A two-dimensional Turing machine.

Thus, as we increase the dimensionality of the working storage, space remains invariant and time is preserved to within a polynomial.

2.2. Counter Machines

We turn now to a model that does not outwardly resemble a Turing machine, but is equivalent in that it can compute any function that a TM can compute. A *counter machine* is composed of the following:

(1) A finite-state control.

(2) A two-way read-only input tape.

(3) A finite collection of counters, each of which can contain an arbitrary integer.

(4) Three instructions to control the counters:

    (a) Increment a counter by one.

    (b) Decrement a counter by one.

    (c) Test to determine whether a counter is zero.

All the counters can be tested or modified in different ways at each time step.

The time used by a counter machine is the number of steps that pass before the machine halts, a direct extension of the Turing machine definition of time. One straightforward definition of the space used in processing an input is the largest absolute value attained by any of the counters. Let CMspace($f(N)$) denote the family of formal languages that can be recognized by a counter machine using at most space $f(N)$ on inputs of length N. Define TMspace($f(N)$), CMtime($f(N)$), and TMtime($f(N)$) similarly. Then

Theorem 4: [Fischer *et al.* 68]. For $f(N) \geqslant N$,

$$\text{CMspace}(f(N)) = \text{TMspace}(\log f(N)).$$

Thus this somewhat arbitrary space measure for counter machines turns out to be the same as Turing machine space except for a logarithmic distortion of scale. In fact, Theorem 4 makes it clear that a better definition of space for counter machines should have been the *size of the radix representation* of the largest value in a counter, in which case CM space and TM space would turn out to be the same.

Curiously, CM time also relates directly to CM space. Abusing notation in a hopefully perspicuous way, let CMtime(poly($f(N)$)) denote the family of languages recognizable by a counter machine using a number of steps bounded by any polynomial in $f(N)$ on inputs of length N.

Theorem 5: [Fischer *et al.* 68]. For $f(N) \geqslant N$,

$$\text{CMtime}(\text{poly}(f(N))) = \text{CMspace}(f(N)).$$

If Theorem 5 muddies which is time and which is space for counter machines, it serves with Theorem 4 to make the point that these quantities still reflect the underlying quantity of Turing machine space.

2.3. Space and Time in Formal Language Theory

The Chomsky hierarchy of formal languages is defined by structural considerations alone. Regular, context-free, context-sensitive, and type-0 grammars are distinguished by the form of their production rules. These grammars and their relation to automata are one of the standard topics for courses in the theory of computation. Hopcroft and Ullman [69] provide an introductory textbook treatment.

Time and space enter in an elegant and unexpected way. Kuroda [64] and Landweber [63] showed that the context-sensitive languages are precisely those that can be recognized by a nondeterministic Turing machine operating in linear space, a so-called *linear bounded automaton* (LBA).

The concept of a nondeterministic computation enters here in an essential way. A Turing machine or similar automaton is *nondeterministic* when the state of the machine and symbols read by its heads determine, not necessarily a *unique* next step of computation, but possibly more than one permissible next step. Thus, a nondeterministic machine has many permissible complete computations which it may perform in response to a single input word. It is said to *accept* an input word if *at least one* of its possible computations leads to acceptance of the input; the time (or space) required to accept an input word is taken to be the minimum number of steps (or tape squares) among all accepting computations.

Note that there is nothing probabilistic in these notions of nondeterministic computation. Nondeterministic automata simply specify a family of possible computational behaviors any one of which may lead to successful acceptance. (The adjective "multipath" has been suggested as more appropriate than "nondeterministic" to describe these automata, but, unfortunately, it has not been accepted by the research community.) The possible computations can be thought of as possible proofs in a formal proof system. Following each line or step of a proof, several next steps may be possible, and a theorem is proved just when there is some possible sequence of steps of proof which lead to it. The definition of time required by a nondeterministic automaton to accept an input is thus analogous to the number of steps in the shortest proof of a theorem.

The way in which a nondeterministic machine "performs" a computation is quite different from that of ordinary deterministic computers, and there is no direct or efficient means known by which nondeterministic computations can be carried out by ordinary computers. For this reason nondeterministic computation may seem an artificial concept, but it has proved to be a fruitful one. Indeed some of the most difficult and important questions in the theory of computation involve the relation between deterministic and nondeterministic time and space. The two most celebrated problems of this kind are the following:

1. *The LBA problem*—whether deterministic and nondeterministic LBAs accept the same family of languages.

2. *The P = NP problem*—whether P, the family of languages recognizable by Turing machines in time bounded by a polynomial, is equal to NP, the family of languages recognizable by *nondeterministic* Turing machines in time bounded by a polynomial.

For a discussion of the profound consequences of a solution (affirmative or negative) of the $P = NP$ problem see Cook [71a] and Karp [72], and for the LBA problem see Hartmanis and Hunt [74] . For example, if $P = NP$, then there exist far more efficient algorithms than any now known for such classical operations-research optimization problems as the knapsack or traveling salesman problems and a host of other apparently intractable computations.

The languages determined by regular grammars and recursive grammars can also be characterized by bounds on time or space although the bounds degerate—the regular languages are precisely the family TMspace(1) and the recursive languages are precisely those recognizable without any bounds on time or space. The context-free languages cannot be characterized precisely in terms of time or space. (For example, it is known that there are context-free languages that require space proportional to log N, but there are languages recognizable in space log N that are not context-free [Lewis *et al.* 65, Alt and Mehlhorn 76].) There *is* an elegant characterization of context-free languages in terms of pushdown automata, however, and we shall indicate in Section 2.9 how a simple extension of the pushdown automaton model ties together the notions of time and space.

2.4. Stack Automata

Explaining the relation between the syntactic structure of grammars and the complexity of recognizing the languages they generate can be counted among the fundamental insights of formal language theory. There is another such relation between a peculiarly structured computer model called a stack automaton and Turing machine space.

Stack automata were initially proposed as a variant of pushdown automata that had additional abilities to cope with certain constructs in computer languages like ALGOL. Basically they are pushdown automata that can "peek" at the pushdown store without modifying it. Specifically, a stack automaton is composed of the following:

(1) A finite state control.
(2) A two-way read-only input tape.
(3) A pushdown stack with a two-way head. The head is free to move up and down the stack reading symbols, but it may write a symbol only when it is at the top of the stack. Symbols are never removed from the stack.

Actually this describes only one species, called a two-way deterministic nonerasing stack automaton (Fig. 3), among a bestiary of stack automata that have been collected. Let 2DNESA denote the class of languages accepted by two-way deterministic nonerasing stack automata. Notice that there is no *a priori* bound imposed on how much the stack may grow during a computation. In fact, the stack may grow to be more than exponentially longer than the input, even in halting computations. However, the structural limitation on this large storage space imposed by the stack discipline diminishes its value to that of considerably less Turing machine space.

Theorem 6: [Hopcroft and Ullman 67].

2DNESA = TMspace($N \log N$).

That 2DNESA should contain languages of only bounded computational complexity might have been anticipated by students of automata theory, but that 2DNESA should have an *exact* characterization in terms

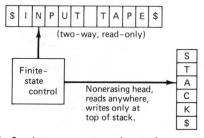

Fig. 3. A two-way, nonerasing stack automaton.

of Turing machine space complexity, and that the space on the Turing machine should be so much smaller than that on the stack, is remarkable. The proof of Theorem 6 is one of the little gems of automaton theory; it has the unusual aspect that the equivalence is nontrivial in both directions. The theorem itself reveals an instance in which the concept of space appears unexpectedly in a fundamental role.

2.5. Vector Random-Access Machines

We saw earlier that, roughly speaking, time on counter machines corresponds to logarithmic space on Turing machines (Theorems 4 and 5). There is another model of computation, however, in which time bears an even closer relationship to TM space—the vector random-access machine (VRAM):

(1) A finite-state control.

(2) A two-way read-only input tape.

(3) A finite number of registers, each holding a bit vector of potentially unbounded length.

(4) An instruction set comprising the operations of assignment, binary addition and multiplication, bitwise OR and NOT, with indirect addressing (that is, the contents of a register may be used as the address of an operand).

(5) A test-for-zero operation.

This model differs from more primitive ones in that multiplication is regarded as an elementary operation and data can be accessed directly instead of through the laborious mechanism of tape storage. VRAMs were intended as a model that better reflects "real" computers in many circumstances. The indirect addressing feature is familiar in actual machine languages, although it turns out to play an unimportant role in the following theorem, that is, the theorem is true even if indirect addressing is disallowed.

Theorem 7: [Pratt and Stockmeyer 76, Hartmanis and Simon 74]. For $f(N) \geqslant N$,

$$\text{VRAMtime}\big(\text{poly}\big(f(N)\big)\big) = \text{TMspace}\big(\text{poly}\big(f(N)\big)\big).$$

The set of languages recognizable by VRAMs operating in polynomial time is thus the same as the set of languages recognizable by Turing machines in polynomial space. This is another result in which the proofs of containment in both directions are nontrivial. The method employed is to show that each machine can simulate the other, but these simulations are difficult. The trouble stems from the fact that on a VRAM, multiplication takes one unit of time, no matter how long the bit vectors are. So in polynomial time one can create bit vectors that are exponentially long, and the TM performing the simulation cannot simply maintain a copy of the VRAM memory, or it would not operate in polynomial space. Again we have an instance in which time and space may appear in each other's guise.

2.6. Recursive Functions

Another way to specify computable functions, which at first sight seems quite different from Turing machines or grammars, is by means of recursive definitions. For example, if $A(x, y) = x + y$, then we can define another function $M(u, v)$ on the nonnegative integers by the equations

$$M(0, v) = 0,$$

$$M(u + 1, v) = A(v, M(u, v)).$$

It is not too hard to see that, despite the apparent circularity of recursively defining M in terms of itself, the function M is uniquely determined by these equations and in fact $M(u, v) = u \times v$.

These equations for defining M from A conform to a scheme of recursive definition known as *primitive recursion*. Computable functions can be classified by the form of recursive schemes sufficient to define them, just as formal languages can be classified by forms of grammars or automata sufficient to generate them.

One such classification was proposed by Grzegorczyk [53]. Grzegorczyk's class $\mathcal{E}^2$ is defined by starting with the functions of addition and multiplication, and then constructing new functions by composing, substituting constants and new variables, and applying primitive recursion to functions already obtained. The application of primitive recursion is constrained so that only functions bounded above by functions already obtained may be constructed. A completely different description of $\mathcal{E}^2$ is provided by the following result.

Theorem 8: [Ritchie 63]. $\mathcal{E}^2$ equals the class of functions on the nonnegative integers that are computable by Turing machines using space proportional to the length in radix notation (e.g., arabic numerals) of integers presented as inputs.

Results similar to Theorem 8 can be proved about Grzegorczyk's classes $\mathcal{E}^3$, $\mathcal{E}^4$, ..., and other classes which have been studied such as the primitive recursive functions or the double recursive functions [Cobham

64, Meyer and Ritchie 72]. Such computational characterizations of recursive definitions help to clarify their expressive power and have contributed to the solution of some technical problems relating different classifications [Meyer and Ritchie 67]. Thus we see another example of an independent line of research about recursive functions converging on underlying concepts of time and space.

2.7. Boolean Networks and Table Look-Up Time

Boolean networks (also called logical or combinational networks) are one of the standard models used by digital hardware designers. Such a network with n input lines and one output line provides a recipe for computing a boolean function from the n zeros or ones that are presented at the inputs to a single zero or one at the output.

The number of "gates" at which atomic operations combining zeros and ones are performed in the network provides an obvious measure of the cost or size of a network (Fig. 4). The *combinational complexity* of a boolean *function* is defined to be the minimum size of any network that computes the function.

This measure of complexity of boolean functions has an intuitive appeal beyond its familiarity in hardware design. Digital computation as currently understood means the manipulation of discrete symbols that ultimately can be coded as strings of zeros and ones. The basic operations by which

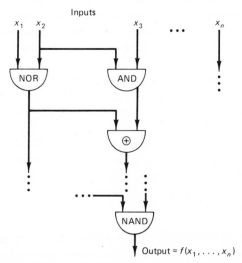

Fig. 4. An n-input boolean network with two-input gates.

such symbols are combined or compared must also ultimately reduce to the atomic operations performed on pairs of zeros and ones at gates. In this sense one would expect the combinational complexity of a boolean function to reflect the irreducible minimum effort necessary to compute the function.

A particular boolean function always has a fixed finite number of zero–one valued arguments and so only represents a finite computational problem. But it is a simple matter to extend the measure of combinational complexity to any infinite problem of interest—recognizing the infinite set of prime numbers, for example. Define the combinational complexity of the set of primes to be a function of N equal to the combinational complexity of the boolean function of N arguments, which has value one if and only if the values of the arguments comprise the N-bit representation in binary notation of a prime number.

Notice that at first sight this formulation of the complexity of recognizing languages is very different from the Turing machine approach. To recognize some formal language L we require a single Turing machine which correctly handles the possibly infinite whole of L. Moreover, the Turing machine time or space complexity of a language L may grow as rapidly as any recursive function of the input length N. On the other hand, the combinational complexity of L only reflects the complexity of larger and larger finite segments of L, since entirely different networks may be used for different values of N. The combinational complexity of any L can never be much greater than $2^N/N$ because any boolean function of N arguments may be computed by a circuit of this size. (Remember that simply expanding a boolean function into disjunctive normal form would already yield an upper bound on combinational complexity of $N2^N$.) Furthermore, Turing machine complexity only makes sense for computable or at best recursively enumerable languages L, whereas combinational complexity has a perfectly definite meaning for any language L whatsoever.

The connection between these complexities can be made by providing Turing machines with oracles. An oracle Turing machine has, in addition to the usual paraphernalia of input and work tapes, an *oracle tape* on which an infinite sequence of zeros and ones may be presented. The oracle tape has a single read-only two-way head, which may move between adjacent squares on the oracle tape. The same pattern on the oracle tape is preserved for each input given on the input tape. In this way the oracle Turing machine can be thought of as having a fixed infinite table of answers or subresults available on its oracle tape. Of course, if the head on the oracle tape is far away from a desired entry in the table, the lookup may take a long time.

Let Combinational($T(N)$) denote the family of languages whose combinational complexity is at most proportional to $T(N)$. Let Oracle TM-time($T(N)$) denote the family of languages that can be recognized within time $T(N)$ by some oracle Turing machine provided with some appropriate oracle tape.

Theorem 9: [Pippenger and Fischer 77, Schnorr 75]. For $T(N) \geqslant N$,

$$\text{OracleTMtime}(T(N)) \subset \text{Combinational}(T(N) \log T(N)),$$

and

$$\text{Combinational}(T(N)) \subset \text{OracleTMtime}(\text{poly}(T(N))).$$

Thus the time measure for oracle Turing machines, which models the time required to perform computations by table look-up, matches well with another intuitively appealing concept of complexity based on boolean networks.

If we regard the size of a network as being analogous to storage space, then Theorem 9 provides still another example in which a space measure for one model corresponds to a time measure on another. Curiously, a reverse correspondence also holds in this case. The time required by a network is usually defined to be the maximum depth of the network, that is, the length of the longest path from any input wire to the output wire. Using this definition, Borodin [75] has observed that the network–time complexity of any language corresponds (to within a quadratic polynomial) to the oracle Turing machine space required to recognize the language.

As an aside it seems worth mentioning that the first containment given in Theorem 9 provides an interesting technique for hardware design. In some cases it is easier to see how to program a Turing machine to perform certain computations efficiently than it is to design a small circuit. The proof of Theorem 9 provides a simple means of translating an efficient Turing machine into a comparably economical circuit.

2.8. Tapes and Heads

Thus far, time has proved to be invariant from machine to machine to within a polynomial of low degree. But for accurate guidance in concrete cases, we need to have a much more exact idea of the effect of machine structure on speed of computation. Unfortunately such results are few and difficult to obtain; we shall mention two.

Turing machines as we have defined them with several one dimensional tapes but only one head per tape can obviously be simulated without time loss by Turing machines with only a single tape but with several independent heads on the tape. (Simply divide the single tape into "tracks" and let each head attend to only one track.) The converse, that multitape machines can simulate multihead machines without time loss, is also true but seems to require an intricate simulation requiring nine times as many tapes as heads to be simulated [Fischer *et al.* 72]. It is not known whether the number of tapes can be kept down to the number of heads. Neither is it known if the result can be extended to two-dimensional tapes.†

Recently Aanderaa [74] settled the question posed by Hartmanis and Stearns [65] of whether $k + 1$ one-dimensional tapes are faster than k one-dimensional tapes. By means of a sophisticated analysis, Aanderaa was able to show that there are languages recognizable in time exactly N, so called "real-time" recognizable languages, on $k + 1$ tape Turing machines that cannot be recognized in time $N +$ constant on machines with only k tapes. It remains open whether three tapes are more than a *constant multiple* faster than two tapes. It is also not known whether Aanderaa's results extend to two-dimensional tapes. In the one-dimensional case, we at least know that many tapes cannot be too musch faster than two tapes: Hennie and Stearns [66] have shown that TMtime($T(N)$) $\subset$ Two-tape TMtime($T(N) \log T(N)$).

2.9. Auxiliary Pushdown Machines

Rounding out the menagerie of machine variants is the auxiliary pushdown automaton (APDA) of Cook [71b], which is made up of the following:

(1) A Turing machine, possibly nondeterministic, with a two-way read-only input tape and a finite number of work tapes.

(2) A pushdown stack subject to the same restrictions as those on a conventional PDA.

Since an APDA (Fig. 5) has an embedded Turing machine, it is clear that the pushdown store is unnecessary in that it does not expand the class of languages recognizable by an APDA. In fact, the pushdown store is less powerful than a single additional work tape, but its inclusion will be justified by Cook's measure of APDA space. He counts only the number of *work tape* squares scanned during the computation—space on the stack, potentially unbounded, is free!

---

†(Added in proof.) A solution to this problem has recently been announced by Seiferas and Leong at Penn State.

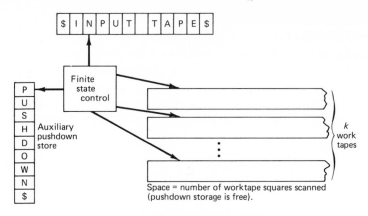

Fig. 5. An auxiliary pushdown automaton.

Theorem 10:   [Cook 71b]. If $T(N) \geqslant N$, then

$$\text{APDAspace}(\log T(N)) = \text{TMtime}(\text{poly}(T(N))).$$

Cook's theorem thus asserts that any language recognizable in time T on a Turing machine can be recognized in space $\log T$ on an APDA, and conversely space S on an APDA can be simulated in time exponential in S on a Turing machine. These results apply, it turns out, equally well to nondeterministic APDAs.

Again the proof involves clever simulations of APDAs by Turing machines and vice versa, and again the simulations cannot be carried out by "step-by-step" simulations since, for example, an APDA operating within space $\log N$ may actually run for 2^N steps, whereas Theorem 10 asserts that such an APDA can be simulated by a Turing machine running in time $\text{poly}(N)$. Giuliano [72] and Ibarra [71] extend Cook's methods to define auxiliary stack automata and obtain similar results; a combination stack-PDA is the basis for further generalizations by van Leeuwen [76].

While the addition of free pushdown storage may seem contrived, it motivates an important unanswered question in automaton theory. Theorem 1 says that, for Turing machines, space is bracketed between T and $\log T$. For an APDA, space is equal to $\log T$. The open question is whether or not the containment holds when the pushdown store is removed and only an ordinary Turing machine remains. This is tantamount to asking whether any Turing machine that uses time $T(N)$ can be "reprogrammed", or transformed, into another Turing machine that uses only space $\log(T(N))$ but possibly more time. (Theorem 1 implies that as much as $\text{poly}(T(N))$ time might be used after such reprogramming.) In the next section we discuss some of the implications of such a time–space tradeoff.

3. INCLUSION RELATIONS AMONG COMPLEXITY CLASSES

Although we do not know whether TMtime(T) is contained in TMspace(log T), or vice versa, or even whether the classes are comparable, there is nothing to prevent our examining the several alternatives.

POSSIBLE RESULT 1: TMtime(T) $\subset$ TMspace(log T).

If PR1 is true, then by Theorem 1 it is actually the case that TMspace(log T) and TMtime(poly(T)) are the same. Hence the two fundamental complexity measures of time and space would be measures on different scales of the same underlying quantity. Further, if PR1 is true, an immediate consequence is a positive solution of the LBA problem mentioned in Section 2.3.

On another front, PR1 might provide some help in certain mechanical theorem-proving tasks. For example, a new mechanical procedure significantly improving Tarski's decision method for the theory of the real field has recently been developed [Collins 75]. This procedure requires time and space that both grow doubly exponentially (like 2^{2^N}). PR1 would imply that space for this procedure could at least be reduced to ordinary exponential growth, and since space, not time, is often the limiting factor in practical mechanical theorem proving, such a reduction might make a few more short theorems accessible to the method.

We cannot pass by this example of mechanical theorem proving without also mentioning one of the triumphant results of complexity theory: within the past four years ways have been found to *prove* that most of the classical theorem-proving problems of mathematical logic, even if they are solvable in principle by Turing machines, are of exponential time complexity or worse. (See Meyer [75] for a summary of these results.) This includes the above problem of proving theorems about the real field, so that the general task of proving such theorems mechanically is inherently intractable [Fischer and Rabin 74] .

To speculate on a speculation, let us remark that if PR1 is true, it might be possible to refine the correspondence between Turing machine measures and boolean network measures mentioned in Section 2.7, to show that network depth is the logarithm of network size. This would imply the existence of fast boolean circuits of depth proportional to log N for finding shortest paths in graphs, parsing context-free languages, inverting matrices, and dividing binary numbers [Csanky 76, Valiant 75]. For each of these problems the best currently known networks require depth proportional to $(\log N)^2$.

Since PR1 is a very powerful conjecture, let us consider instead some weaker possibilities:

POSSIBLE RESULT 2:   TMtime(poly(N)) $\subset$ TMspace(N).

Here we assume not a logarithmic reduction but only that polynomial time algorithms can be run in *linear* space (on a possibly different Turing Machine). If PR2 is true, then, in a very general and far-reaching sense, any computer program using time N^k (which might simultaneously be using space N^k as well) can be rewritten to use only space linear in N. The cost of this improvement is that the resulting program may use exponential time. Such an effective transformation would be a programming technique of vast importance, leading potentially to optimizing compilers of great power. We confidently expect that it would be an idea fully as useful as such fundamental computer science concepts as recursion and iteration.

POSSIBLE RESULT 3:   TMspace(N) $-$ TMtime(poly(N)) is nonempty.

That is, there may exist some problem that can be solved in linear space but not in polynomial time. PR3 would imply that many problems for which no fast algorithms are known are, in fact, computationally infeasible because they cannot be done in polynomial time. Among these are (1) minimizing the number of states in a nondeterministic finite automaton and deciding the equivalence of regular expressions [Meyer and Stockmeyer 72], (2) deciding first-order predicate calculus in which equality is the only predicate [Stockmeyer 76], and (3) determining which player has a winning strategy in some simple games on graphs such as generalized versions of HEX and the Shannon switching game [Even and Tarjan 76].

All of the above possibilities are implied by PR1. Let us see what would happen if the inclusion in PR2 were reversed.

POSSIBLE RESULT 4:   TMspace(N) $\subset$ TMtime(poly(N)).

This is an electrifying possibility, since it would mean that $P = NP$, that deterministic and nondeterministic Turing machines operating in polynomial time accept the same set of languages. PR4 would also imply that all the apparently infeasible problems mentioned after PR3 could in fact be solved in polynomial time.

If any of the possibilities PR1–PR4 are true, then interesting conclusions follow. Pessimistically, however, there is a fifth choice. It may be that there is a problem in TMtime(poly(N)) that cannot be solved in linear space. Some work of Cook [74], Cook and Sethi [74], and Jones and Laaser [76] suggests that this "uninteresting" possibility may be the correct one, and our intuition (albeit a faulty barometer) about difficult problems tends to support this view.

It is disappointing that we know so little about time and space as to be unable to distinguish between the blatantly contradictory hypotheses PR3 and PR4. It is positively irksome, though, that we know definitely that the classes of polynomial time and linear space are not the same [Book 72]. We can prove this by showing that there exist transformations that preserve polynomial-time recognizability but not linear-space recognizability, but no example is known of a problem that belongs to one class and not the other. Yet such a problem must exist![†]

3.1. Space Is More Valuable Than Time

We come now to the recent result of Hopcroft *et al.* [75], which is the strongest theorem known regarding time and space. Informally, it says that having space T is strictly more valuable than having time T:

Thorem 11:   TMtime($T \log T$) $\subset$ TMspace(T) .

This theorem is the first solid example we know that guarantees the existence of a mechanical procedure for reducing space. It asserts, for example, that programs that run in time $N \log N$, even if they use space $N \log N$, can be reprogrammed to use only linear space. The price we pay is that the time required for the new algorithm may be exponential. A weakness of the result is that it appears to apply only to ordinary multitape Turing machines with one-dimensional tapes, and not to VTMs, but the theorem is a very good beginning. It was proved by means of a particularly clever simulation on one-dimensional tapes and will undoubtedly be a focal point of future work on space and time.

For completeness we mention an earlier result of this kind, which applies to the highly restricted model of classical Turing machines with only a single one-dimensional tape: for these machines time T^2 can be simulated in space T [Paterson 72].

3.2. Space–Time Tradeoff

The central question at this point is whether there are any *inherent* time–space tradeoffs. Theorem 11 shows how to reduce space in certain cases, but it does not claim that the time *must* increase. It may be that

[†](Added in proof.) Some further surprising connections between time and space have recently been observed by Kozen [76] and Chandra and Stockmeyer [76].

minimal time and space are achievable by the same program. At present, there is only one known counterexample to this enticing possibility, due to Cobham [66]:

Theorem 12: If a Turing machine that performs palindrome checking uses time $T(N)$ and space $S(N)$, then $T(N) \times S(N)$ is at least proportional to N^2, and this bound is achievable in each of these cases:

(a) $T(N) = 2N$,
(b) $T(N) = N^2/\log N$,
(c) $T(N) = N^{(1+r)}$, where r is a rational between zero and one.

This quadratic lower bound for the product of time and space actually applies more generally to all manner of machine models besides Turing machines. The proof rests on analyzing the number of different internal configurations which a palindrome-checking automaton must assume as it crosses boundaries between tape squares on its input tape. The proof does not apply, however, if the input head can jump between non-adjacent input tape squares in a single step. The ideas of the proof do not seem to extend to yield larger than quadratic lower bounds.

Nonetheless, Cobham's theorem is the only instance in which we can prove the existence of a tradeoff that most programmers (and theorists) believe occurs in some form or other. Thus the palindrome problem, which we first explored in order to develop an intuitive feeling for computational time and space, provides the first piece of evidence that we must give up one in order to reduce the other.

REFERENCES

Aanderaa, S. O., On k-tape versus $(k - 1)$-tape real time computation. *SIAM-AMS Prog.* 7, 75–96 (1974).
Alt, H. and Mehlhorn, K., Lower bounds for the space complexity of context-free recognition. In *Automata Languages and Programming, Third International Colloquium*, (S. Michaelson and R. Milner, eds.) 338–354, Edinburgh Univ. Press, 1976.
Book, R. V., On languages accepted in polynomial time. *SIAM J. Computing* **1**, 281–287 (1972).
Borodin, A., Some remarks on time-space and size-depth. Computer Science Dept. Rep., Univ. of Toronto, Toronto, Ontario, 1975.
Chandra, A., and Stockmeyer, L., Alternation. *Proc. 17th IEEE Symp. Foundations of Computer Science 1976*, 98–108.
Cobham, A., The intrinsic computational difficulty of functions. *Proc. Intern. Cong. Logic, Methodology, Philos. Sci., 1964*, 24–30.
Cobham, A., The recognition problem for the set of perfect squares. *Rec. 7th IEEE Symp. Switching and Automata Theory, 1966*, 78–87.
Collins, G. E., Quantifier eliminations for real closed fields by cylindrical algebraic decomposition. In (*Automata Theory and Formal Languages 2nd G.I. Conference*), *Lecture Notes in Computer Science*, Vol. 33, 134–183. Springer Verlag, New York, 1975.

Cook, S. A., The complexity of theorem proving procedures. *Proc. 3rd ACM Symp. Theory of Computing. Shaker Heights, Ohio, May 1971*a, 151–158.

Cook, S. A., Characterizations of pushdown machines in terms of time-bounded computers. *J. ACM* **18** 1, 4–18 (1971b).

Cook, S. A., An observation on time-storage trade off. *J. Computer and System Sciences* **9** 3, 308–316 (1974).

Cook, S. A., and Sethi, R., Storage requirements for deterministic polynomial time recognizable languages. *Proc. 6th ACM Symp. Theory of Computing, Seattle, Washington, April 1974*, 33–39.

Csanky, L., Fast parallel matrix inversion algorithms. *SIAM J. Computing* **5** 4, 618–623 (1976).

Even, S., and Tarjan, R. E., A combinatorial problem which is complete in polynomial space. *J. ACM* **23** 4, 710–719 (1976).

Fischer, M. J., and Rabin, M. O., Super-exponential complexity of Presburger arithmetic. *SIAM-AMS Proc.* **7**, 27–41 (1974).

Fischer, P. C., Meyer, A. R., and Rosenberg, A. L., Counter machines and counter languages, *Mathematical Systems Theory* **2**, 265–283 (1968).

Fischer, P. C., Meyer, A. R., and Rosenberg, A. L., Real-time simulation of multihead tape units, *J. ACM* **19** 4, 590–607 (1972).

Giuliano, J. A., Writing stack acceptors. *J. Computer and System Sciences* **6**, 168–204 (1972).

Grzegorczyk, A., Some classes of recursive functions. *Rozprawy Mat.* **4**, 1–45 (1953).

Hartmanis, J., and Hunt, H. B., III, The LBA problem and its importance in the theory of computing. *SIAM-AMS Proc.* **7**, 1–26 (1974).

Hartminis, J., and Simon, J., On the power of multiplication in random access machines. *15th IEEE Computer Soc. Symp. Switching and Automata Theory*, 13–23 (1974).

Hartmanis, J., and Stearns, R. E., On the computation complexity of algorithms. *Trans. Amer. Math. Soc.* **117**, 285–306 (1965).

Hennie, F. C., On-line Turing machine computations. *IEEE Trans. Computers* **EC-15**, 35–44 (1966).

Hennie, F. C., and Stearns, R. E., Two-tape simulation of multitape Turing machines. *J. ACM* **13** 4, 533–546 (1966).

Hopcroft, J., and Tarjan, R., Efficient planarity testing. *J. ACM* **21** 4, 549–568 (1974).

Hopcroft, J. E., and Ullman, J. D., Nonerasing stack automata. *J. Computer and System Sciences* **1** 2, 166–186 (1967).

Hopcroft, J. E., and Ullman, J. D., *Formal Languages and Their Relation to Automata.* Addison–Wesley, Reading, Massachusetts, 1969.

Hopcroft, J., Paul, W., and Valiant, L., On time versus space and related problems. *Proc. 16th IEEE Symp. Foundations of Computer Science, 1975*, 57–64.

Ibarra, O. H., Characterizations of some tape and time complexity classes of Turing machines in terms of multihead and auxiliary stack automata. *J. Computer and Systems Sciences* **5**, 88–117 (1971).

Jones, N. D., and Laaser, W. T., Complete problems for deterministic polynomial time. *Theoretical Computer Science* **3** 1, 105–117 (1976).

Karp, R. M., Reducibility among combinatorial problems. In *Complexity of Computer Computations* (R. E. Miller and J. W. Thatcher, eds.), 85–104. Plenum, New York, 1972.

Kozen, D., On parallelism in Turing machines. *Proc. 17th IEEE Symp. Foundations of Computer Science 1976*, 89–97.

Kuroda, S. Y., Classes of languages and linear-bounded automata. *Information and Control* **7**, 207–223 (1964).

Landweber, P., Three theorems on phrase structure grammars of type 1. *Information and Control* **6** 2, 131–136 (1963).

Lewis, P. M., II, Stearns, R. E., and Hartmanis, J., Memory bounds for recognition of context-free and context-sensitive languages. *Rec. 6th IEEE Symp. Switching Circuit Theory and Logical Design, 1965*, 191–202.

Meyer, A. R., The inherent computational complexity of theories of ordered sets. *Proc. Intern. Cong. Mathematicians* **2**, 477–482 (1975).

Meyer, A. R., and Ritchie, D. M., The complexity of loop programs. *Proc. 22nd Nat. Conf., ACM, 1967*, 465–469.

Meyer, A. R., and Ritchie, D. M., A classification of the recursive functions. *Z. Math. Logik Grundlagen Math.* **16**, 71–82 (1972).

Meyer, A. R., and Stockmeyer, L., The equivalence problem for regular expressions with squaring requires exponential space. *13th IEEE Computer Society Symp. Switching and Automata Theory, 1972*, 125–129.

Paterson, M. S., Tape bounds for time-bounded Turing machines. *J. Computer and System Sciences* **6** 2, 116–124 (1972).

Pippenger, N., and Fischer, M. J., Relationships among complexity measures. Manuscript, IBM Watson Research Center, Yorktown Heights, New York, 1977 (to appear).

Pratt, V., and Stockmeyer, L., A characterization of the power of vector machines. *J. Computer and System Sciences* **12** 2, 198–221 (1976).

Ritchie, R. W., Classes of predictably computable functions. *Trans. Amer. Math. Soc.* **106**, 139–173 (1963).

Schnorr, C. P., The network complexity and the Turing machine complexity of finite functions. Manuscript, Fachbereich Mathematik, Univ. of Frankfurt, 1975.

Stockmeyer, L., The polynomial-time hierarchy. *Theoretical Computer Science* **3** 1, 1–23 (1976).

Valiant, L. G., General context-free recognition in less than cubic time. *J. Computer and System Sciences* **10** 2, 308–315 (1975).

van Leeuwen, J., Variants of a new machine model. *Proc. 17th IEEE Symp. Foundations of Computer Science 1976*, 228–235.

C.mmp: A Progress Report on Synergistic Research

Allen Newell and George Robertson

Computer Science Department
Carnegie-Mellon University
Pittsburgh, Pennsylvania

C.mmp has become a synergistic research effort in which almost ten distinct research efforts have become intertwined, so that they both support each other and depend on each other in ways that are both gratifying and scary. These efforts include: the hardware effort of C.mmp; the operating system, HYDRA; the implementation language, BLISS–11; the hardware performance monitor; the driving application, HEARSAY–II (a speech-understanding system); a second implementation system, L*; the development of a dynamically microprogrammed PDP–11/40; the development of specialized processors; and the problem of decomposition of algorithms into parallel form. The end is not in sight, in fact. We attempt here an integrated picture of this total research endeavor, making clear what the important scientific issues are and relating these to the current state of progress. Our interest in such an endeavor includes its role as a model for how experimental computer science can be accomplished. We reflect on this as well.

1. INTRODUCTION

The C.mmp project has violated Forgie's Principle and the question is whether we shall thereby win or lose.

Forgie's Principle is no doubt known by other names. It surfaced during a study of the feasibility of speech understanding systems [Newell *et al.* 73]. One of the members of that study group, Jim Forgie of Lincoln Laboratories, enunciated the following:

Never demand more than one breakthrough in a proposed R & D effort.

The soundness of the principle is self-evident, as is the fact that its violation has occurred more than once in the annals of research on systems. To propose research goals that demand more than one scientific or technical breakthrough is to ask for the nth power of a rare event—that is, for almost certain failure. It was a principle of wondrous utility to the study group, being wielded to crush many otherwise glorious proposals that the group entertained during its deliberations.

C.mmp is a multiminiprocessor consisting of many minicomputers accessing a common primary memory through a cross-point switch [Wulf and Bell 72] . Around this experimental computer system cluster a substantial number of research efforts—at least ten by the counting scheme of this chapter. These efforts are almost all independent in that they have independent research goals to contribute to a variety of aspects of computer science. They also form a synergistic mass in the way they use each other. Synergy implies dependence; the success of each depends in some measure on the success of all, though not uniformly. Thus, within this cluster of research efforts there surely occurs a violation of Forgie's Principle. Yet, the risks so run are offset to some degree by the potential gains.

This chapter has several purposes. The total research effort is in midstream and a progress report is worthwhile. Reports on the individual efforts, many of which have already appeared, do not present a view of the whole and its interconnections. Thus, an attempt to describe the entire cluster and to argue its synergy seems worthwhile. Also at stake in the C.mmp effort are some important general scientific propositions that adhere to the total effort more than to any of the particular component efforts. At least, so we will argue. It is worthwhile to formulate these propositions. Finally, some important issues of research strategy and management are also at stake in C.mmp; indeed, our opening remark on Forgie's Principle reflects this concern. We wish to formulate and argue several of these propositions about how computer science research can be profitably pursued.

Before turning to the subject matter of the chapter, we need to be sure the term "synergy" is in the reader's good graces. The term refers to the simultaneous action of separate agents, which together have greater total effect than the sum of their individual effects. Its common scientific usage occurs, for example, in pharmacology, where drug X is said to have a synergistic effect with drug Y if the normal effect of Y is increased when X is also present. Thus alcohol is synergistic with some tranquilizers. For some reason the term has become a favorite of wordmongers in attempting to describe some situation in glowing terms, and seems thereby to have fallen into a certain disrespect. But for us it describes exactly our concern: whether a set of independent but associated research efforts can operate to produce some greater result—can be synergistic. It is not our intention to convey special virtue simply by the use of a term. If synergy is there, let it operate. And if risks are there as well, let them be understood by those whose aim is to make the research a success.

Our plan is straightforward. We first give a very brief descriptive overview of the entire research effort, which provides a modicum of history and introduces all of the separate subefforts. Then we state the basic scientific propositions that adhere to the entire system and relate them to the individual efforts. After this we shift to the level of research strategy, and discuss the style of research represented by the whole project, along with its risks and benefits as we see them at this point in time.

2. OVERVIEW

Figure 1 shows the projects that currently exist around C.mmp. Others will come into existence, but this is enough for present purposes. Most of these projects have an independent research life. Their research goals are independent of C.mmp and of one another. They could, then, be discussed in any order. But it will add the coherence of familiarity to take them from the bottom up, starting from the hardware system and moving toward the systems that are being programmed on it.

2.1. C.mmp: The Computer Structure

The intellectual history of C.mmp starts with two events. The more specific was an ARPA-initiated study to look at computers for the use of the artificial intelligence community in its experimental work. The CMU contribution was a paper design for a machine, called C.ai, which was a large classical multiprocessing system with 10^8 words of memory and a substantial number of PDP–10-like processors [Bell and Freeman 72]. The more general event was the emergence of minicomputers into a cost–performance region in which it was economical to put many of them together to obtain computing power. We already had half a dozen minicomputers scheduled into the environment for a variety of purposes. The cross-point switch design from C.ai crystallized a design effort on a classical multiprocessing structure with minicomputers, which would not only be within the ambit of technology but be cost-effective as well.

The structure of the system is shown in Fig. 2. There are up to 16 processors working through a cross-point switch to 16 memory ports giving access to one million 16-bit words of memory. The processors are PDP–11s. Initially they were 11/20s; from now on they will be 11/40s (which are about twice the processing power of 11/20s). Every memory access requires a trip across the switch, the round trip requiring 250 nsec.

Project   1971   1972   1973   1974   1975

C.mmp hardware

HYDRA

BLISS–11

Hardware monitor

HEARSAY–C.mmp

L∗C.

System software

PDP–11/40E

Specialized Pc's

Decomposition

Fig. 1. The projects that comprise the C.mmp effort. Key: ==, intensive effort; − −, continuing effort; ∗, special event.

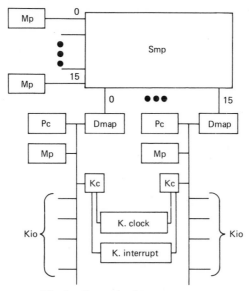

Fig. 2. C.mmp hardware structure.

Relocation registers augment each processor; they map the 18-bit address into a 25-bit address. The relocation device costs a significant but not overwhelming fraction of the cost of a processor (an 11/40 costs about $13,000 and modifications cost about $5000). It is the major additional cost per processor, since the processor remains basically an unmodified PDP–11. Unfortunately, the processors are not completely unmodified, so that they do become dedicated to C.mmp. Table I provides a list of facts about the hardware and its specification.

C.mmp is not locked into using a particular processor; in fact it has two versions of the PDP–11 on it, the 11/20, which was the main PDP–11 available at design time, and the 11/40. The relocation and processor modifications are unique to each processor type. Thus, due to the higher speed of the 11/40, its relocation scheme will include a cache to avoid memory interference problems; whereas the 11/20 does not need one. The system can be configured into subsystems since each of the $16 \times 16 = 256$ switches may be permanently set, either by software or manually (in the latter case producing complete isolation).

Secondary memory for the pages of active jobs is provided by a set of disks each of which holds 128 pages (of 4096 words). The page occupies exactly one track around the disk, and the transfer from disk to primary memory begins instantly, without the delay for the initial starting address

TABLE I

C.mmp Hardware Fact Sheet

Processors: DEC PDP–11 family with slight CMU alterations

‡ Different models can be used concurrently (e.g., 11/20, 11/40, 11/45)

Status: 5 PDP–11/20 processors operational; 1 PDP–11/40 operational; interfaces for additional PDP–11/40s in preparation

Relocation Unit: CMU designed and built
‡ Interfaces UNIBUS to cross-bar switch's processor ports
‡ Relocates processor and I/O addresses
‡ Provides address and data parity generation and validation

Cross-Bar Switch: CMU designed and built
‡ Switches 16 processor ports to 16 memory ports on a single-word request basis
‡ Allows up to 16 simultaneous memory accesses and arbitrates request conflicts
‡ Provides software control (with hardware override) of 256 cross points, permitting arbitrary system partitioning

Memory: Ports—CMU designed and built, Modules—AMPEX 1865 core
‡ 16 ports, each housing up to 8 memory modules
‡ Each module provides 8K words of 18 bit core memory (16 data bits, 2 parity bits per word)
‡ Access time—250 nsec, cycle time—650 nsec
‡ Rewrite implemented in each module, and overlapped with accesses to other modules

Status: 656K words distributed in 16 ports

Interprocessor Control: CMU designed and built
‡ Provides interprocessor interruption at 3 priority levels
‡ Allows each processor to start and stop an arbitrary subset of the 16 processors

Time Base: CMU designed and built
‡ Provides global time source with resolution to 1 μsec

Peripherals: Standard PDP–11 devices are plug-to-plug compatible
Status
‡ 2M words swapping storage
‡ 60M words disk storage (moving head)
‡ 6 DECtape drives
‡ High-speed links to PDP–10 and front-end terminal handler
‡ Interface to ARPA network
‡ Line printer
‡ Miscellaneous small peripherals

characteristic of most rotating memories. Thus a page is transferred to primary memory in exactly one revolution of 16 msec.

2.2. HYDRA: The Operating System

HYDRA is a capability-based operating system, which provides a basic set of facilities [Wulf *et al.* 74] . Figure 3 gives a picture of its structure. It contains a kernel, which holds the minimum facilities necessary to protect and dispense the resources. The facilities for all other functions—schedulers, command languages, file systems, etc.—occur in modules called *policy modules* and *subsystems*. There can be many of each of these, so that each user community can perceive a distinctly different operating system.

Protection is an essential ingredient of an operating system and especially for HYDRA, where quite distinct protection policies may need to be enforced for different subordinate operating systems (sub-OSs). Some central source of protection rights must thus be able to assign appropriate access rights to these sub-OSs, in such a way that these subsystems can themselves assign rights. This requirement for a flexible protection system leads to a capability-based operating system, which allows the access rights of a process to vary so that the process has only those rights required for the function or program that the process is currently executing [Jones and Wulf 75] .

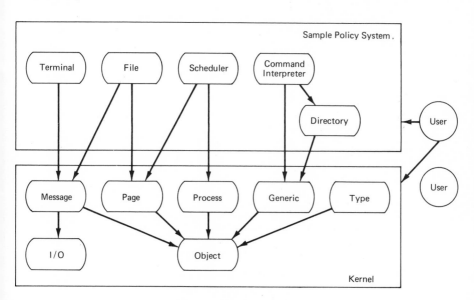

Fig. 3. HYDRA structure.

Another important dimension of an operating system is the type of control it affords over the resources it distributes. While it is easy enough to provide crude partitioning, it is difficult to provide guarantees on the exact amount of resources and service available to particular users (or user communities). This is an important concern of HYDRA, and ties closely to making sub-OSs effective.

Work on the HYDRA kernel started even before the hardware was available, using a simulator on the PDP-10. Thus, the kernel has been operational for some time. Since January 1975, a single policy module and subsystem has been operational, along with the kernel, providing regular services to a slowly growing user community. This is providing the basic shake-out of the system. But exercising the flexibilities of HYDRA is still on the future agenda.

2.3. BLISS-11: The Implementation Systems

BLISS-11 is a PDP-11 version of the BLISS language [Wulf *et al.* 75]. Some characteristics appear in Table II. BLISS, created originally some years ago for the PDP-10 [Wulf *et al.* 71], is a language for implementing

TABLE II

BLISS-11 Characteristics

Systems implementation language—machine-oriented

Algebraic expression language—ALGOL-like

Control structures for structured programming
    Minor extensibility with macros

Typeless

Macro and data structure access definition facilities

Compiler-based
    Deposits target system
    Noninteractive
    Minimal run-time support

Highly optimized code

Provides for linkage to other languages

Provides escape to machine code

Provides almost total accessibility

Uses cross-compiler and linker on PDP-10

---

software systems. Its incarnation on the PDP–11 was motivated in part by the need for an implementation language for HYDRA. But it was more fundamentally motivated by an independent interest in the efficiency of the code produced by compilers. These are related, of course, since the requirement for efficiency shows up sharply in an operating system. To use a higher level language for an operating system is to court disaster if the compiler does not produce extremely good code.

Bliss–11 is a cross-compiler, running on the PDP–10 and producing PDP–11 code. This code is fully instantiated on the PDP–10 and shipped as absolute bit strings to C.mmp. This arrangement permitted programs to be run on an evolving hardware configuration very early in its development.

As Table II shows, Bliss is an algebraic language. Its main language features that adapt it to the task of implementing systems are good facilties for manipulating addresses and for defining new data structures. It also is a language without **goto**'s (i.e., without the ability to jump from one arbitrary point in a program to another arbitrary point); this is closely related to optimization, since it makes the formal structure of the program more clearly indicate the underlying computational structure.

2.4. Performance Analysis and the Performance Monitor

As the complexity of computers has increased, so has the necessity of measuring and analyzing their performance under operational conditions. The essential instrument in such an enterprise is a hardware device for time-stamped samples of register contents at the level of the basic cycle of the memory and the processors. Many such devices have been built. The requirement on such hardware performance monitors is to correlate the behavior of the hardware with that of the hierarchy of software that is concurrently defining the performance state of the system. Many hardware monitors only permit low-level statistics to be gathered.

The complexity of a multiprocessor increases the need for a hardware monitor, for the performance of the system is even less understandable at the level of the running program than with a complex uniprocessor. We have designed and built our own hardware performance monitor [Fuller *et al.* 73] . Some of its characteristics are given in Table III. It resides on the UNIBUS, like any other device, and normally monitors a single processor and its interactions with memory. It can be used to monitor a single memory and its interactions with all processors. With a wide range of data accessible and a rich way of specifying events to be monitored, it allows monitoring of very complex software events.

TABLE III

Hardware Monitor Characteristics

Two modes of operation
Monitor UNIBUS of single processor
Monitor memory port at switch—all processors
Data accessible
16 bits of data path, 18 bits for UNIBUS address
Probes in Pc
Processor status word
Instruction/operand fetch bit
16 miscellaneous inputs (hi-impedance probes)
Event driven
Primitive events sensitive to program state—boolean exp. of:
Brackets on address range
Data field and pattern specification
PSW and misc. inputs
Accumulated events
Primitive event has counter with limit register
When counter reaches limit, accumulated event is fired
Events buffered in two MOS shift registers
Nine words wide, 64 deep
Uses DR11B for DMA transfers
Can interrupt Pc on special events if desired
Software can dynamically change hardware-monitor state

2.5. HEARSAY–II: A Speech-Understanding System

For the last several years the artificial intelligence group at CMU has been working to develop a system capable of understanding connected speech. This work has been one of our main efforts and is a part of a concerted effort by ARPA to attain this important technical goal [Newell *et al.* 73]. Table IV reproduces the performance goals for a speech-understanding system (SUS) adopted by this effort, to be achieved in November 1976. Analogous efforts are going on at Bolt, Beranek, and Newman and at System Development Corporation jointly with Stanford Research Institute.

The first SUS, called HEARSAY–I [Reddy *et al.* 73] was brought up in 1972. Its successor, HEARSAY–II [Lesser *et al.* 74], is now operational, although with a way to go to gain the required performance. Besides HEARSAY–II, there are other alternative SUSs being developed here, one called DRAGON [Baker 75] and another called HARPY. This multiplicity of systems is a deliberate tactic for system development, and we will talk about it a bit later. The SUSs are being developed primarily on the

TABLE IV

Speech-Understanding System Goals

The system should

(1)	accept continuous speech
(2)	from many
(3)	cooperative speakers of the general American dialect,
(4)	in a quiet room
(5)	over a good quality microphone
(6)	allowing slight tuning of the system per speaker,
(7)	but requiring only natural adaptation by the user,
(8)	permitting a slightly selected vocabulary of 1000 words,
(9)	with a highly artificial syntax,
(10)	and a task like the data management or computer status tasks (but not the computer consultant task),
(11)	with a simple psychological model of the user,
(12)	providing graceful interaction,
(13)	tolerating less than 10% semantic error,
(14)	in a few times real time on a dedicated system.

PDP–10. But we are also carrying along a parallel development on C.mmp. The development of HEARSAY–II, called HEARSAY–C.mmp, is the main effort, but a version of DRAGON is also being developed on C.mmp.

HEARSAY plays the role on C.mmp of a *driving* application, that is, of a large application that promises to utilize the capabilities of C.mmp in a strong way and whose attainment will be an important scientific or technical event in its own right.

Figure 4 shows the conceptual organization of HEARSAY–II, which is independent of implementation on the PDP–10 or C.mmp. Called the blackboard control scheme, it consists of a central data structure (the blackboard) surrounded by a large number of functionally independent processes, each corresponding to a source of knowledge about how to decode the speech signal.

The HEARSAY structure of Fig. 4 is already a proposal for a multiprocess structure, derived from substantive considerations rather than considerations of computer structure implementation. It is not thereby given how to map this into a process structure or how to map that process structure into the underlying processor structure. Its realization on the PDP–10 preserves the multiprocessor structure, and simulation studies have been

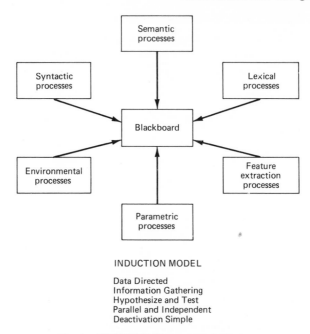

Fig. 4. HEARSAY–II conceptual structure.

done to analyze the basic costs [Fennell 75]. Table V indicates how HEARSAY–C.mmp maps into C.mmp. The precondition for the activation of each knowledge source is a separate process; and there is a pool of processes, each of which can take on the identity of any knowledge source. The mapping of processes to processors is a function of HYDRA, the operating system kernel.

TABLE V

HEARSAY–C.mmp Fact Sheet

Written in L∗C. (C)

Includes SL∗ (Sail environment in L∗) for knowledge sources

Each precondition is a separate HYDRA process

Pool of processes for knowledge sources

Knowledge source process assumes correct identity by overlaying

Basic HS–C. (with no KSs) is 45K (16 bit words)
 Nine pages (4K words each) are shared among all processes
 Three pages are local to each process

2.6. L*: A Second Implementation System

HEARSAY is implemented on the PDP–10 in SAIL, a language for implementing systems, developed at the Stanford AI Laboratory [van Lehn 73]. However, HEARSAY is being implemented on C.mmp within an implementation system called L*, which has been developed at CMU for implementing AI systems [Newell *et al.* 71].

In many ways L* is at the opposite pole from implementation systems such as BLISS–11 and SAIL, as a comparison of Table VI (for L*) with Table II (for BLISS–11) shows. (SAIL is at the BLISS end of the scale, although with more of a runtime environment.) L* is an interactive symbol manipulation system and grows the target system from within the implementation system. BLISS–11 has no symbol manipulation facilities, runs in a compiled mode, and produces an object system that is an independent module of code from the implementation system itself. BLISS–11 produces highly efficient code; L* obtains efficiency only by successive analysis and selective compilation. Although neither system dictates a programming

TABLE VI

L* Characteristics

Systems implementation system—machine-oriented

Symbol manipulation language
    List, stack, string, and association processing capabilities
    Extensible syntax (dynamically modifiable user interface)
    Essentially context-free syntax
    Longest recognizable name recognition

Control structures natural to list structured programs
    Extensible control structures

Universal type system (dynamic)—many type-driven features

Extensible data structures

Interactive
    Grow target system rather than deposit
    Complete programming environment
        Editing, debugging, performance monitoring, compiling, assembling, etc.

Interpretive with selective optimization/compilation

Provides for linkage to other languages

Machine language is supported in L* as a language environment

Provides total accessibility

Exists on C.mmp
    Uses PDP–10 file system until HYDRA file system available

approach, BLISS–11 encourages modular decomposition and, to some extent, structured programming; while L* encourages iterative design (i.e., design and implementation in a sequence of successive operating approximations). The HYDRA effort has proceeded as an example of modular decomposition using BLISS–11, while the HEARSAY–C.mmp effort has proceeded as an example of iterative design using L*.

L* was developed on the PDP–10 and has been used there for implementing several AI systems. It also exists for a stand-alone PDP–11, as well as for C.mmp under HYDRA.

2.7. General System Software

All computer systems require a set of software facilities. Prominent among these are the operating system and implementation languages, which already exist in HYDRA and BLISS/L* for C.mmp. But much is required beyond this in the way of editors, other language processors, and

TABLE VII

Software under Development

Item	Source group	Status
System status	HYDRA	Planned
Hardware monitor use by users	HYDRA	Planned
HELP facility	HYDRA	Planned
Failsafe of disks	HYDRA	Under design
File system	HYDRA	Designed, mostly implemented
Editors		
TECO	HYDRA	Implemented
SOS	L*	Implemented
ARPA-net	HYDRA	Designed, partly implemented
Languages		
BLISS–11	BLISS	Implemented
L*C. (C)	L*	Implemented
FORTRAN	HYDRA	Designed, mostly implemented
ALGOL–68	ALGOL–68	Designed, partly implemented
ALPHARD	ALPHARD	Under design
MACRO–11	HYDRA	Planned
Microcode		
HYDRA pieces	HYDRA/Micro	Designed, mostly implemented
BLISS–11	BLISS/Micro	Designed, mostly implemented
L*	L*/Micro	Designed, mostly implemented

utilities of various sorts. They are what transform a hardware system into a useful computing engine.

There is a small effort associated with C.mmp for obtaining this software. This does not count as a major independent research effort, as do the other projects we have mentioned so far. However, the problem that it addresses is sufficiently important to the overall issues we will raise, that it must be included.

Table VII lists the software systems now under development and consideration for C.mmp [Reid 75] . It also shows their source and their status, whether implemented, under active development, or simply in the planning stage.

2.8.   The PDP–11/40E: Dynamically Microprogrammed Processor

Like many processors, the PDP–11/40 is microprogrammed. Additional microcode to accomplish supplementary functions such as floating point arithmetic can be affixed. Independently of C.mmp, the question arose of whether the 11/40 could be extended so its microcode would be dynamically loadable and used for user-defined extensions. A study of this was initiated, resulting in a successful modification [Fuller *et al.* 76]. This required adding to the PDP–11 several additional facilities, notably a subroutine-call mechanism and a shift/mask unit. The characteristics of

TABLE VIII

PDP–11/40E. Characteristics

PDP11/40
Microcoded—256 (56 bit) words implement 11/40
Max memory size = 124K words (16 bit)
Cycle time = 0.99 μsec (reg-to-reg add time)
Basic PDP11 instruction set + five new instructions
Memory management option + dual address space option
PDP11/40E—the extensions
1024 word writable control store (80 bit words)
Shift mask unit
ALU can use
Branching can use
16 word (16 bit) stack for temps and microsubroutine calls
16 bit emit field for arbitrary constants
Characteristics
Horizontally encoded
140 to 300 nsec basic cycle time
Memory reference time = 780–1180 nsec
16 bit data paths
Basic NOVA emulator can be written in 189 microwords

this machine are given in Table VIII (along with a few basic characteristics of the PDP–11 for those unfamiliar with it).

The possibility that the 11/40E should be used on C.mmp was, of course, entertained from the start, although the project had its own interest and momentum. In fact, this has transpired and all of the 11/40 processors for C.mmp will be equipped with a dynamic microstore. This microstore will be used not only to speed up the basic system routines in HYDRA, but also for user-defined language systems, such as L* and BLISS, and even specific applications, such as speech.

2.9. Specialized Processor Design

Although designed for the PDP–11, the switch and memory present a well-defined interface to the processor that permits one to consider adding specialized processors. The main constraint is expressed in the use of 18-bit data paths and relatively slow access time (750 nsec).

The evolution of C.mmp is still at a state where specialized processors are mostly a gleam. Also, the availability of the PDP–11/40E implies that early attempts will take the form of microcoding the 11/40. The main existing project, designing an L* processor, takes this route. Note that it is one thing to add a small section of microcode to help an existing software system (here L*) to be efficient, and quite another to consider the design of an L* processor, even if one wanted to embed it in the 11/40 microcode.

2.10. Parallel Decomposition of Algorithms

Whatever the reasons for getting a multiprocessor system, one inherits the problem of decomposing algorithms to run with concurrent control paths. Although each multiprocessor system presents a distinct face to the problem of decomposition, the general issue is ubiquitous to all parallel systems. Thus one hopes, within each architectural instance, to contribute to the general scientific understanding.

There is an active group around C.mmp working on the question of parallel decomposition [Fuller 76] . The major means of doing this is to consider a collection of benchmark tasks that pose different problems of decomposition. Table IX lists the problems that are under active consideration with some of their characteristics.

There is also substantial concern at CMU for basic mathematical investigation into the general questions of decomposition. Until recently, this work has only been potentially related to the specific issues of decompositions relative to the C.mmp architecture. The situation is something like that in the area of specialized processors: the early state of

TABLE IX

Benchmark Characteristics

Pattern classification
    Algorithm used on ILLIAC–IV
    Large data base (5M words)—ERTS data
    Stresses swapping characteristics of C.mmp

Solution of partial differential equations
    Obvious set of decompositions with interesting trade-offs
        For example, chaotic versus lock-step
    Stresses scheduler (compute bound)

Tech chess program
    Searching in parallel
    Can the advantages of alpha–beta be retained with
    concurrent processes?

Integer programming
    How do you decompose optimization algorithms?
    Stresses scheduler (compute bound)

Searching for $f(x) = 0$
    New algorithm designed explicitly for multiprocessor
    architecture (as opposed to array processor)

C.mmp discourages users who have no reason to make a large investment in the underlying system. However, with the recent work of Kung [75] on a search algorithm specifically designed for multiprocessors with characteristics like those of C.mmp (as opposed to those of ILLIAC IV, for example), contact has begun between the theoretical work and the experimental test bed.

3. SCIENTIFIC ISSUES

The foregoing listing of projects has provided some picture of the total activity around C.mmp at the present time. Many of these, indeed most, have an independent scientific motivation for existing and some even speak to scientific audiences that are unconcerned with multiprocessing. BLISS–11, with its emphasis on optimized compilation; L*, with its focus on implementation philosophies; and HEARSAY, which is primarily an attempt to recognize connected speech; all fit this category. From one point of view this state of affairs is hardly surprising. Computing systems, except in special circumstances, are facilities on which many independent investigators pursue their separate destinies. But on the other hand, the mutual relations between these efforts on C.mmp is far closer than that of the usual collection of independent research efforts that jostle each other to share a common computing facility. In this section we wish to examine these relations.

We believe there are a set of scientific questions that are addressed by the total C.mmp effort. Of necessity, these questions are rather general. The results from C.mmp cannot be definitive for them. Rather, they will provide a single data point, which, along with data points from other computer systems of differing characteristics, can add up to important scientific lessons. In discussing each of these questions, it will become evident how they depend on substantial subsets of the projects of Fig. 1.

3.1. Effective Power and Power per Dollar

In the trade-off view of life, technological systems provide opportunities and benefits on the one hand and raise problems and costs on the other. It is imperative to have a clear view of both sides of the equation.

There are, as far as we can see, four possible reasons for desiring a multiprocessing system: power, power per dollar, modularity, and reliability. By power we mean operations per second. This is usually measured in millions of instructions per second (mips), but is also measured in millions of bits per second (megabaud) when referring to channel bandwidths, where the operations are transmissions of bits from one place to another.

As to power, given a technology capable of producing uniprocessors of power p, then it will always appear possible to produce a system of power $n \times p$ by constructing a multiprocessor, thus obtaining a system with peak power greater than can be achieved by other means.

As to power per dollar, given that there is larger market demand for systems of low power than of high, the cost efficiencies of mass production may differentially affect the production of small computers over big ones. Thus, it will come to pass at various times that the cost of n processors of power p will be less than the cost of a single processor of power $n \times p$, even though the latter may be constructable. Multiprocessors will then seem economically attractive.

This is a denial of Grosch's law, which states that the power of a computer is proportional to the square of its cost. Thus, to build a multiprocessor with power $n \times p$ out of n units of size p and cost c would cost $n \times c$. According to Grosch's law, to build a uniprocessor of power $n \times p$ would cost $n^{1/2} \times c$, which is less than the multiprocessor cost. Grosch's law was discovered and verified during eras when mass production techniques were not being differentially applied to systems by size, and so the conflict may be explainable. (There is good verification up to 1963 [Knight 63].) This points up, however, the ephemeral nature of this gain—that its existence is transient and dependent on many factors.

As to modularity, to the extent that varying amounts of physical resources (processors, memories, and switches) can be assembled to match the exact demands of a task environment, a multiprocessor can provide economies. Excess capacity need not be provided since the system can be expanded (or contracted) with experience.

As to reliability, redundancy has always been its mainstay at a hardware level. Multiprocessors suitably organized (and organization may itself be a problem) afford redundancy of processors and presumably of memory. Whether that redundancy is of use in the total reliability of a computing system (where, e.g., the error rate of disks may dominate) is an important issue.

So much for the opportunities. On the debit side, it seems clear that a multiprocessor is always more complex and has more constraints on its programming than an equivalent uniprocessor. Tasks must be decomposed, data communicated, synchronization attained, and protection assured—all within the particular constraints provided by the multiprocessor hardware. To be sure, to be put on a computer at all, every problem must be decomposed (e.g., communication is required between the parts). But the multiprocessor adds a layer of structure that is not problem dependent, and thus is unwanted complexity.

All these problems can presumably be overcome. That is why one creates software systems. But to overcome the problems requires development resources as well as some of the resources of the system on a continuing basis, eroding the gain that was the reason for constructing the multiprocessor. Hence, we can define the fundamental issue with respect to multiprocessor systems as:

> Does the effective power or effective power per dollar exceed what one can get with an equivalent uniprocessor system?

There is nothing new here, for the general arguments about multiprocessors pro and con have often been rehearsed. But it seems to us important to emphasize the fundamentals. The development of multiprocessors is a three-step affair. The first step is the perceived gain computed in terms of basic hardware performances and costs. This may seem quite large. The second is the construction of the actual hardware device. This creates a serious handicap with respect to obtaining, for actual problems, the promised power, power per dollar, or perhaps even reliability. All the complexity in the computer structure must be overcome. In the third step, then, one throws away parts of this putative gain in order to obtain an effective system. The end result remains in doubt for some time until the total system finally shapes up. This seems to us a more honest view of multiprocessor research than one sometimes put forth, which makes it appear to provide new opportunities at the user level.

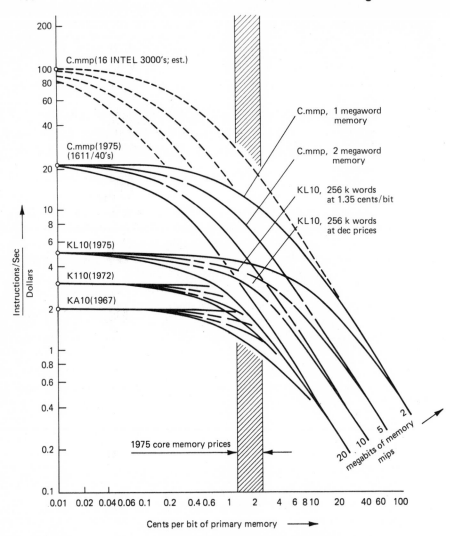

Fig. 5. C.mmp cost/performance characteristics.

Turning to C.mmp, what can be said about the fundamental definition of the research problem? First, of the major foci, the main one is the power per dollar. Minicomputers, and now microcomputers, have entered into the realm where, on the most elementary calculation, multiprocessors should be cost-effective. Figure 5 attempts to give some reality to this. It shows the mips deliverable from various versions of the C.mmp, taking the sequence of PDP–10 machines as comparison. (The KA10 is the current PDP–10 processor at CMU, the KI10, the one currently available from DEC, is about twice the speed, and the KL10, which will be available soon, is about twice the speed of a KI10.) Some of the numbers in this figure are quite firm, being based on measured mips both for the KA10 and C.mmp with PDP–11/20s. Likewise, that one PDP–10 instruction can be equated with one PDP–11 instruction is a measured result, both statically and dynamically. The extrapolations to the other machines, the KI10 and KL10 on the large machine side, and the 11/40 on C.mmp on the multiprocessor side, are softer (the 11/40 assumed does not have the dynamic microstore).

Figure 5 shows the perceived gain—it is the first step. Given our three-step view of multiprocessor research, it should be clear that this first step cannot stand alone. Figure 5 does not show what the effective power (respectively, power/dollar) is of C.mmp. Some of that power (maybe even a substantial fraction) will have to be sacrificed to get a workable system.

As of January 1975, C.mmp was made available to users. It had a functioning HYDRA kernel and a primitive policy module and subsystem. We had taken the second step; we now actually have the ability to run problems. We are now almost a year on our way to obtaining effective power. The system operates for users 19 hours a day and is moderately stable (one hour mean time between crashes); there is a modest user community; they are developing general software support, and running HEARSAY–C.mmp, Dragon, and other benchmark programs.

But only when user experience has been gained with a range of user programs will the effective power be calculable. Such a dependency means precisely that all of the research projects mentioned above are involved in the success of the basic system.

The other goals of multiprocessors—peak power, reliability and modularity—seem to us to play a more subdued role on C.mmp. In all cases, we will be revealing indications about whether the type of structure represented by C.mmp could offer significant advantages if an appropriate one were built with these other goals in mind. C.mmp, even at a full 6 mips, is not a large machine in absolute terms; what is to be learned is whether the structure is a good candidate for a large machine. Our C.mmp environment does not force us to devote extreme attention to attaining high reliability; however, we will find out a great deal about how to make software and hardware cooperate in attaining a highly reliable system. We will probably find out least about modularity, since we are not considering a class of specialized tasks of graded size. (An example of multiprocessor research that is strongly focused on reliability and modularity is the BBN Pluribus IMP [Heart *et al.* 73] .)

3.2.   The Usefulness of Flexible Operating Systems

There is a fundamental relationship between a designer of an instrument and its user. The designer works first, out of some domain of materials. He has, as we say, *designer's prerogative*. He reduces some of the potentiality of the material to actuality and passes the result on to the user. The user, then, has lost some options, but presumably has gained a more effective device. However what the designer produces cannot be completely specific, for it is an instrument. That is to say, the user himself further specifies its use in each concrete situation in which he finds himself. Thus, instruments tend to have controls and adjustments, by means of which the designer passes along to the user some freedom to be bound later when the situation is more specific. The designer gives up his prerogative to bind certain specific aspects in advance (which he had by virtue of being first).

This relation between designer and user, which seems to have no direct name in English, is cascaded in modern computing systems. The device physicist plays designer to the computer engineer, who in turn plays designer to the operating system programmer, who in turn plays designer to the application system builder, who in turn plays designer to the user. How many such levels there are is not determined by nature, but by our own inventive ways of organizing tasks. But at each step some capabilities are bound and others are passed on to the next stage for further specification.

What has allowed this deep hierarchy to grow up in computer systems is that, unlike any other instrument known, a designer can pass on to his user a set of capabilities in no way diminished from the set he received, but only shaped so that a different set of activities is easy to perform. The reasons for this are deeply embedded in the nature of universal computational systems and are familiar to us all. Our interest here rests on a particular division that currently characterizes the field.

Operating systems are now an established station in the sequence of successive designers/users. The operating system transforms the computer system, as designed by the engineers, into a different more useful machine for a community of users. It has come to include a collection of functions that contribute to the commonweal: allocation of resources, protection and security, handling of common devices (such as peripherals), command languages, language processors, debugging facilities, etc. Since the late fifties, almost all computers have run under some sort of operating system and the success of computing is testimony to the fruitfulness of establishing this station.

The question is whether this current decomposition of designs/users can be improved upon—in what environments and under what conditions.

HYDRA, in one of its aspects, embodies the hypothesis that what is now the single station of operating systems can be decomposed with advantage. Specifically, HYDRA makes a structural split between the kernel (of which there is only one) and a collection of programs that it calls subsystems and policy modules. The kernel contains the essential aspects of those functions which cannot be performed by any subset of the community singly because they involve interactions and interests of the entire community. These are the allocation of resources (space, cycles, devices) and protection. All other functions, and the elaboration of the basic kernel functions in forms useful to subcommunities, are left to the policy modules and the subsystems. There can be many of these corresponding to many distinct subcommunities with different demands. To put the matter succinctly: from a user's point of view, C.mmp should come to consist of a number of operating systems with distinct user-oriented properties.

There are a number of reasons for kernelization of operating systems, and it has become a rather popular design philosophy. One of the main reasons is protection; another is assurance of correctness; a third is to keep as little function bound as possible to permit experimentation and evolution. It will be possible to evolve a sequence of functional capabilities on a kernel such as HYDRA; while some versions are being tried and debugged, others are safely serving users. All of these reasons are important and are mirrored in HYDRA. Another advantage of kernelization, however, concerns us: that user communities, and even specific applications, will wish to specialize their operating systems—almost to personalize them. Furthermore, those who create these specialized operating systems are *not* to be the same as those who design and modify the kernel. There is to be an additional station in the designer/user chain.

Demonstration of this hypothesis clearly depends not only on the operating system and its designers, but also on groups of users who form the secondary station—who build their own operating systems under HYDRA, operating systems that have distinct properties.

Given our research environment at CMU, some groups will arise whose direct aim will be to explore variations in operating systems on C.mmp under HYDRA. These groups will not constitute evidence in favor of the hypothesis. For they will only be experimenting with operating systems, not trying to be a community that is using an operating system and finds it advantageous to specialize it.

A genuine tension exists that may in fact defeat the hypothesis. There is great benefit in uniformity in computing facilities. If we all use the same language, or the same editor, or the same file system, or whatever, then the learning and the acquisition of skill is done once and for all. The benefits of standardization are real. Opposed to these, of course, are the benefits of adaptation of the facilities to the task. The complaints of users about the limited facilities of a system when they bump up against the boundary are also real enough.

In its initial phase, the SUS provides the most likely opportunity for the adoption of a specialized operating system. SUS is a large system. It seeks to exploit the resources extensively, and in ways that are special compared to the anonymous user. At this early stage, when both HYDRA and HEARSAY–C.mmp are just coming up in their first incarnations, one would not expect such specialization. However, it is worthwhile to examine the situation briefly.

A sub-OS is composed of a policy module, which provides scheduling and paging policies, and a collection of subsystems that provide user facilities, such as directory structures, file systems, and terminal systems. Each of these could need specialization or redesign. In HEARSAY, the scheduling will eventually need to support dynamic priority changes to allow for focusing the attention of a collection of cooperating processes. Another example is the paging policy, which is initially tailored to a diverse collection of small processes. The HEARSAY processes are large and share most of their memory. Thus, for HEARSAY, the paging policy should be tailored to a collection of large processes with much sharing. HYDRA will allow all the above specializations to be constructed and to coexist with other sub-OSs [Levin *et al.* 75]. It remains to be seen whether such flexibility is actually exploited and what the factors are that de-termine whether such exploitation succeeds or fails.

3.3. The Decomposition of Algorithms for Parallel Execution

The decomposition of problems so they can be solved by algorithms with parallel control streams would seem to be an essential component of making multiprocessors effective. This is surely right, but the matter requires some additional investigation. In this we need to keep clear on the three separate reasons for wanting multiprocessors: power, power/dollar, and reliability. In all cases, of course, parallelism in tasks is only useful to a multiprocessor if there are processors that are idle.

If the concern is with the total power deliverable, then the right unit of analysis is the single task. Given the availability of many processors, the right question is the trade-off between total time to completion and total processing effort: how much extra processing must be done (or will be lost by forced idleness) to speed up the task by running it as a set of parallel computations?

If the concern is with cost effectiveness, i.e., with power/dollar, the right unit is not the individual task but the population of tasks. The role of decomposition in this case is not so clear. If we look at the set of all problems of interest to the world (or some suitably large universe) in a given epoch, a major characteristic is one of independence—independent problems thought up by independent people doing independent things. Tight coupling is a rarity. This is why the basic model for general computing is a series of independent jobs. If there is a natural pool of independent jobs available for a multiprocessor, then we must ask when it is necessary to pay attention to decomposition. If the pool is sufficiently big so that jobs are always available, waiting to be run, of what use is decomposition, which can only provide still more jobs in the pool?

A multiprocessor system is more than just a collection of processors. It also consists of a hierarchy of memories to feed those processors. In the typical situation, there is an inward migration of unprocessed jobs to the processors and an outward migration of finished (or interrupted) jobs to make way for new ones. These migrations are subject to the limited capacities and flow rates of the memory hierarchy as well as to the variability of job duration and transfer time. This results in each specific architecture and job population having some pattern of idle processors.

Given a population of problems, the decomposition of problems can have one of several effects. If it cannot change the population characteristics significantly, then it is unclear of what use it is. It can skew the size/time relations, and then it may help or hinder, depending on the existing population. By generating the problems internally (rather than externally at the user) it can change the pattern of loading on the memories and channels, again with effects running either way. Finally, if the decomposed processes share memory, because they are intrinsically related, this can upset the usual assumptions of independent jobs and change radically the effective balance between memory and power requirements.

All of the relations do not make decomposition unimportant. They do indicate that it needs to be analyzed against a background population of given characteristics, and not as an isolated job.

3.4. How to Get Software Facilities on Unique Systems

Creating software for computer systems is well established as a major problem in computer science, with many facets and distinct subproblems. The C.mmp research effort hardly touches all of these—but it does touch some, and in a fundamental way.

C.mmp, like any other computer being used for experimental purposes, can be an arena in which experimentation on software implementation can occur. Indeed, in our list of projects there are two implementation systems, BLISS–11 and L*, with contrasting philosophies, already in operation. There may well be others, in particular, ALPHARD [Wulf 74], which is a language for structured programming. To a first approximation these represent independent research efforts that could be going along on any machine. It is useful to have them in a common environment mainly for purposes of comparison and cross fertilization.

There is at least one aspect of the software problem, however, in which all of the projects are involved together, either in a direct or indirect way. This difficulty arises, not because the machine is experimental, but because it is unique enough that no software system can simply be inherited.

The question is of very general significance. A good case can be made that a major source of the software problem is the rapid evolution of hardware systems, so that each new system (or generation of systems) poses the problem of bringing up anew the range of software that is necessary for satisfactory operation. When said this way, i.e., when referred to as the "reprogramming problem", there is conveyed a flavor of useless repetition. But that is not the case. If it were, the software problem would not be so vexing. For the evolution of machines is toward vastly increased power and vastly increased qualitative capability at the level of the computer structure. With each new generation we ask the software to do substantially more than we have asked of software before. With all the sniping that OS/360 has engendered, it attempted to provide many more capabilities than its predecessors, and to exploit substantially increased hardware capabilities. Thus at each stage we have faced the issue of doing new things with our software and doing the old things in richer environments.

There is a collection of approaches being tried on C.mmp: using a high-level implementation system (BLISS–11); using an interactive symbolic implementation system (L*); coupling to a system that already has good software (the PDP–10); structuring the operating system so that the construction of utility software is relatively easy; and relying on a sophisticated computer user community to generate appropriate software spontaneously in a decentralized fashion. All these are being tried simultaneously and we may ultimately know something about which approach provided the bulk of the useful software on the system. We have discussed these issues somewhat more thoroughly elsewhere [Newell and Robertson 75].

3.5. How to Get Power by Multiple-Level Optimization

It has been proposed [Reddy and Newell 76] that it may be possible to get very large speed-up factors over initial versions of a system if the system is implemented as a deep hierarchy of independent levels, all of which may be optimized. We leave the main argument to that chapter. However, the applications being implemented on C.mmp have the right character for this kind of speed-up.

Consider the speech-understanding system as a target. The hierarchical levels employed to achieve this target include the technology (e.g., PDP–11s, switch design), the architecture (e.g., central switch), the micro-store for the 11/40E, the operating system implementation system (BLISS–11), the operating system kernel (HYDRA), the sub-OS, the implementation system for the application (L*), the organization of the application system, and the heuristics and algorithms used within that organization. The bottom levels (the technology and the architecture) are already fixed; and at least one software level (BLISS–11) is already highly optimized. But the remaining levels are still open and are somewhat, although certainly not completely, independent. The hypothesis is that if the application is important enough, and enough time and effort is available, each of the levels can be optimized with the final goal in view, with the resulting gains for each level being multiplicative (to the extent of independence).

We hope there will be several application systems of enough complexity and importance to warrant becoming test examples of multiple level optimization.

4. RESEARCH STRATEGY ISSUES

Given a description of the research projects and some of the scientific issues that the collection of projects addresses, we can now formulate some propositions about the research strategy and management techniques being used. As with the scientific issues, we will attempt to discuss only those propositions that relate to the entire collection, since it is clear that each project has its own strategy and its own management philosophy.

4.1. Experimental Computer Science

Determining the proper role of basic research in computer science has been a major issue since the very beginning of a computer industry. In the very early days there were only experimental machines and there was no computer industry. The universities and research institutes engaged in the full range of research. ENIAC, the IAS machine, and ILLIAC I typify that era. With the development of a computer industry came a very large shift. Industry has become the developer of technology and of all really expensive systems, while the universities have become the locus of the theoretical and mathematical aspects of the science. This split is taken as proper by many—as indicating the appropriate division of labor.

One only has to look at the other sciences to realize what an anomalous situation this is. They have control over the phenomena they study, even when the equipment required to generate the phenomena is expensive. Particle physics, for example, has large accelerators that are designed and built by the scientists who study them. Astronomers have large telescopes. When, as with NASA and the exploration of space, other considerations play a dominant role and science loses control of the phenomena it will study, the strains are all too apparent. We argue that computer scientists must also have control over the phenomena they study; that is, that they should design and build the computer systems that give rise to the phenomena. For it is the ability to design and construct highly novel systems at whatever limits of technology seem appropriate that will determine whether computer science becomes a proper experimental science.

There is some evidence to support the apparent necessity, if not desirability, of this division of labor between industry and computer science. Universities seem to bog down in constructing large systems. The production of large systems requires much manpower and organization, neither of which seem congenial to the typical university environment. A university utilizes graduate students for producing its systems. Although relatively inexpensive labor for the talent involved, it remains manpower dedicated to goals of education and self-development, and one with high training requirements. Thus, so goes the argument, small systems might be produced in universities, but not large systems. (It should be noted in passing that industry also bogs down in constructing large systems; but this is a separate issue, which is beyond the scope of this chapter.)

Another argument for the division of effort is that much of the work involved in producing a large system is not research. The researcher may be interested only in one aspect of the system, say in initial design and construction of the system. He may be uninterested in completing the system and satisfying end-user demands. Alternatively, a researcher might be interested in end-user feedback to evaluate his product (e.g., an operating system), but not be interested in (or capable of) designing and constructing the system in the first place. And most generally of all, there is simply a lot of work that is well inside the art that must be done to build a big system.

Finally, the split is deemed proper since after all the basic purpose of building hardware and software is for the delivery of computing facility to users. This is certainly not the function of universities.

How does C.mmp address this basic issue? C.mmp is an entry to show that computer science can successfully gain access to the primary phenomena it studies. Starting with a technological base provided by industry, the projects associated with C.mmp provide experiments with all levels of a large system that has many novel aspects. It is an example of the sort of experimentation computer science needs to be able to do—not occasionally, but routinely.

C.mmp is not the only such example, of course. It joins examples such as those of ILLIAC I, II, III and IV in providing evidence. However, these latter machines (though not ILLIAC I) have often been cited by some as prime examples of the difficulties of such experimentation in universities. The question is whether C.mmp can provide a positive instance.

C.mmp is an experiment to produce a given point in technology space, i.e., a given type of multiprocessor organization. It opens up a certain range of phenomena to exploration and understanding. Scientifically, it is worth doing only if it is new, if these phenomena have not already been explored. Now C.mmp is not the first multiprocessor. Even putting aside all the dual processors that form the bulk of Enslow's [74] book, there have been at least two genuine multiprocessors, the Burroughs D825 [Anderson et al. 62] and the Bell Laboratories SAFEGUARD computer [Crowley 75], which existed or were under development before C.mmp was created. These machines were created by industry. The D825 had four processors (48-bit words) accessing shared memory and peripherals through a cross-point switch. The SAFEGUARD system consisted of up to ten processors (32-bit words) of approximately 1.5 mips each, an immensely powerful system.

Why do not these two multiprocessor systems demonstrate that, indeed, it is more appropriate for industry to build such systems rather than the universities? In fact, they provide a clear answer: neither of the systems has been used to make major contributions to our understanding of the science. No contribution to the scientific literature exists from the D825 beyond the initial sketchy paper. In the SAFEGUARD system a major effort has been made to get at least the outlines of the project into the mainstream (the reference is an entire special issue of the *Bell System Technical Journal*), but it appears that no further work will be done with the system. With all due respect to these earlier systems, one can confidently expect a more permanent contribution to our scientific understanding from C.mmp than from either of these, precisely because it remains an experimental system that is motivated toward scientific goals and not driven exclusively by an application.

No claim is made for C.mmp's uniqueness. Other machines, such as the ILLIACs, share this property of scientific openness. An interesting example in this regard is the BBN Pluribus Imp [Heart et al. 73], a multiprocessor of up to 14 processors which is highly modular and highly reliable. Created within a research and development environment (the ARPA research program on information-processing techniques), this project has yielded a continuing stream of scientific papers and some important ideas. The project is, however, directed to an application (message processing in the ARPA network) and it remains to be seen whether this ultimately serves to constrain the scientific lessons to be learned from the Pluribus Imp.

Before leaving the topic of experimental machines, it is worth noting that the cost of experimental systems has decreased substantially. Thus the total costs of all hardware, engineering, and software (BLISS–11, HYDRA) of C.mmp from the start of the project in 1972 until June 1975 were approximately $1.25 million, or about $400,000 per year. Although this is still a substantial sum, it is much less than would have been required a decade ago. Furthermore, it is much less than the sort of industry-produced application systems on which such experimental projects can be expected to shed light (e.g., the SAFEGUARD multiprocessor system ran into the hundreds of millions).

We have devoted substantial space to the issue of experimental computer science, and C.mmp's possible contribution to it, because we believe it critical that computer scientists be able to generate their own phenomena in order to explore them.

4.2. What about Forgie's Principle?

In the C.mmp effort, we have violated Forgie's Principle in many ways. The most obvious examples include the HEARSAY dependence on the success of L* and HYDRA, and the HYDRA dependence on the success of BLISS–11. Slightly less obvious are dependencies in the opposite direction, such as HYDRA depending on L* to carry some of the load imposed by HEARSAY before HYDRA fully matures. There are other examples as well.

This violation of the principle has already cost something. It has led to one of the few sources of tension in the environment, between the speech group and the HYDRA group where the deadline for the speech effort is quite inflexible. But there have clearly been many benefits as well. For example, the early feedback from users to the HYDRA designers has led to improvements in HYDRA and verification of its basic philosophy. Also, the applications have had the advantage of a general user facility that the HYDRA group has provided. These advantages work in both directions at all the levels of the system development.

The final verdict on whether the advantages outweigh the costs is necessarily still not in. It too must wait until the complete user facility is finished and the applications have proven themselves. The trade-off lies ultimately between the additional capabilities created by pushing the art at many places, and the increased probability of critical failure in a series system of many components each subject to risk.

4.3. Research by Multiple Alternative Systems

It is frequently suggested that a good research strategy is to build several systems with each trying to solve the same problem in different ways. The major concern in using this strategy is duplication. A researcher shies away from duplication because he always wants to be doing something unique. The funding agencies dislike this strategy because any duplication appears wasteful. But we will argue that this strategy should be used in certain circumstances.

Duplication is beneficial when the research effort must succeed. This is the same argument used by reliability theorists when observing that multiprocessors are potentially more reliable because of duplication at the hardware level. A good example of this was the Manhattan project during World War II, where three distinct methods for the production of enriched uranium were developed in parallel to ensure success. The relevance of this to Forgie's Principle should be clear. If you have created multiple dependencies that jeopardize success, then infuse the effort with some redundancy —do not permit the total effort to be entirely in series.

Duplication, in the sense of simultaneous alternative methods to achieve the same goals, also helps to avoid becoming blind to better avenues of research. When a researcher chooses only one hypothesis or one system to build, he runs the risk of becoming intellectually attached to it. When several working hypotheses are explored simultaneously, his allegiance is attached to discovering which of the hypotheses is true, and he is much less likely to be a victim of his own selective attention to evidence. This is an old idea, of course, but it is nonetheless true. A famous defense of it can be found in an early paper by the geologist T. C. Chamberlain [65].

One of the problems of working in isolation is that a researcher is never sure of what can and cannot be done. With multiple alternative systems, each system provides inputs to the other in the form of insights into what is possible and what problems are difficult. Often, just knowing that a result is possible is sufficient to be able to obtain it oneself. The knowledge of successful nuclear chain reactions is an oft-quoted example.

Finally, multiple alternative systems provide an easy way to assess one's scientific competition. Friendly competition within a single environment provides a much richer set of research results because of the resulting communication of the underlying reasons for the success of competitive approaches. Depending upon scientific competition from other environments often leads to little or no communication between the competitors, indeed to a barrier to communication.

The best example of local use of this research strategy is the Speech Understanding Systems project. This project has evolved into at least four distinct systems being developed in parallel: HEARSAY–II, DRAGON/HARPY, HEARSAY–C.mmp, DRAGON-C.mmp. The competition among these systems has led to much more understanding about the performance characteristics of such systems. It has also led to a much broader view of the world than would be possible if just one such system were being developed. In fact, the total ARPA Speech Understanding Systems effort is also built around a concept of multiple alternative systems (BBN, CMU, and SDC/SRI) working toward a common goal.

On C.mmp, the best example of the multiple systems approach involves the two implementation languages (BLISS and L*). As described earlier, these two languages represent radically different approaches to system implementation. Much can and has been learned by contrasting them, and this is much easier since they exist in the same environment and are being used for similar problems.

HYDRA was developed without multiple alternative systems, and we have paid some price for doing so. We contend that if two operating systems had been developed in parallel, say HYDRA and one considerably more conservative, the end product would have been better. The major impact would have come through having a fully operational operating system several months earlier, so that user experience with a multi-processor could have occurred significantly earlier and so that the development of other components of the total effort could have proceeded concurrently with HYDRA. This would have increased the feedback to HYDRA.

It is only fair to state the main arguments against this opinion. The first one, and the main general argument against using multiple approaches, is the total effort required. The manpower would have been cut in half for each of the operating systems being developed; the final end product (HYDRA) would have taken twice as long to produce. The second argument is more closely tied to operating systems per se. If users had begun to use and adapt to an early, more conservative and less capable system, abandoning it would have been like pulling teeth. A costly, and possibly acrimonious, competition might have developed in which the early system would be upgraded by hack after hack to show that the eventual system was not yet demonstrably better in operation, so that the shift to the new system should be delayed even longer. Conceivably, the advanced system would have been derailed, and with it the research goals of the operating system.

Not withstanding these counterarguments, our conclusion is that the multiple alternative systems approach can be an effective antidote to a violation of Forgie's Principle. When faced with a demand for several major breakthroughs, the potential impact of the breakthroughs on each other can be decreased by providing more insurance that each breakthrough can be made. This is possible if each breakthrough is being attacked using several approaches simultaneously. The impact is also lessened by the greater general understanding of the issues that arises from multiple approaches. We believe that the effort drain for multiple efforts occurring in the same environment is over-rated, since much of the effort involved in any large project is in cranking up, building up a head of steam, and constructing various tools and foundations. The final systems can often be launched from such a base with remarkably little effort. As to the other, more specific, difficulty of changing operating systems in midstream, we unfortunately have little more to offer than exhortations of goodwill.

4.4. Single-Purpose versus General-Purpose Systems

The general notion of a well-managed reseach effort suggests that any instrument built to carry out a particular research effort should be used only for that research. Also, any support that must be developed to help build the instrument should be tailored only to that purpose. For most research projects, this is the cost-effective way of doing business. To violate it implies that one is paying for more generality than is warranted. The tools for other research may sometimes be bootlegged this way, and this may often be a good thing from a higher point of view. But for the specific project in question, our instinctive belief is that means should be shaped strictly to ends.

In the case of research on computer systems, this single-purpose system approach can lead to serious failings. A new computer system is an unexploited resource; it can only be totally exploited if enough energy is devoted to it. The necessary energy can only be mustered if many people devote their efforts to the task. With a single purpose computer system, only those researchers interested in that purpose will use that system. With a general-purpose computer system, many people will take an interest in providing tools for accomplishing their separate aims. This will lead to a rich collection of support tools and a more complete exploitation of that computer system. With the single system approach, necessary tools and techniques—even fundamental solutions—remain undiscovered for lack of manpower.

We are treating C.mmp as a general-purpose system, even though we have accepted the role of speech understanding as a driving application. Since a primary goal of the total effort is to verify that this computer structure is superior in effective power per dollar, we must reach a state where effective power can be measured. The shortest path to producing an effective computing engine, even for the major applications, requires much manpower working on many diverse things. It should be possible, after the fact, to identify what efforts finally made the major contributions to the total understanding of the multiprocessor issues.

5. CONCLUSIONS

We have described a wide range of projects associated with C.mmp. Our hope is that this is only the beginning and that additional projects will participate in the effort. This hope arises from the belief that a synergistic community of projects is important for a major experimental computer science research effort.

We have also discussed a collection of scientific issues to which we believe the entire set of projects contribute. To date, none of these issues has been resolved. They remain open until the C.mmp system has been completely assimilated into the user environment and the applications have proved themselves. At that point, the effectiveness of the total system will be measurable and the contributions of the various projects will be more easily identifiable.

Although the scientific issues remain in the balance while the evolution of C.mmp continues, some of the important research management issues can be asserted with conviction. Experimental systems are both appropriate and necessary for research in computer systems, so that computer scientists can generate and control the phenomena they study. Multiple independent efforts are worth the risk. And finally, one should hedge against the potential disaster implied in Forgie's Principle by the use of alternative competing subsystems.

ACKNOWLEDGMENTS

Whatever scientific substance this chapter contains has been made possible by the people who have done the work on C.mmp and the multiple projects surrounding it. We are only commentators and reporters. All these others deserve the scientific credit. There are too many of them to name here. In each part of Section 2 the references give the principal authors of the specific efforts; but many others have been involved as well.

We would like to thank Anita Jones, Dave Jefferson, Bill Wulf, Sam Fuller, Roy Levin, and Joe Newcomer for their comments on this chapter.

NOTE ADDED IN PROOF

Considerable progress has been made toward the goal of making C.mmp a user facility. As of August 1977, the system runs in a stable configuration with five PDP-11/20s and eleven PDP-11/40s with approximately 2.4M bytes of primary memory. All of the 11/40s are equipped with writable control stores. The mean time between failures is about ten hours for a modest user community; the system is available to users about 20 hours each day. Also, several of the user utilities mentioned in Table VII are now implemented and in use. These include a system status procedure, a HELP facility, a file system, an ARPA-net interface, and an implementation of ALGOL-68. In fact, multiple alternative subsystems are in routine use. There are two directory subsystems and several file subsystems.

REFERENCES

Anderson, J. P., Hoffman, S. A., Shifman, J., and Williams, R. J., D825—A multiple computer system for command and control. *Proc. FJCC* **22**, 86–96 (1962).
Baker, J. K., Stochastic modeling as a means of automatic speech recognition. Ph.D. thesis, Computer Science Dept., Carnegie-Mellon Univ., Pittsburgh, Pennsylvania, 1975.
Bell, C. G., and Freeman, P., C.ai: a computer architecture for AI research. *Proc. FJCC* **41**, 779–790 (1972).

Chamberlain, T. C., The method of multiple working hypotheses. *Science* **15** 92 (1890); reprinted in *Science* **148** 3671, 754–759 (1965).

Crowley, T. H., (ed.), SAFEGUARD. *Bell Syst. Tech. J., Special Suppl.* (1975).

Enslow, P. H. (ed.), *Multiprocessors and Parallel Processing*. Wiley, New York, 1974.

Fennell, R. D., Multiprocess software architecture for AI problem solving. Ph.D. thesis, Computer Science Dept., Carnegie-Mellon Univ., Pittsburgh, Pennsylvania, 1975.

Fuller, S. H., Price/performance comparison of C.mmp and the PDP-10. *Proc. 3rd Symp. Computer Architecture, January 1976.*

Fuller, S. H., Almes, G., Broadley, W., Teter, J., Forgy, C., Karlton, P., and Lesser, V., The PDP-11/40E microprogramming reference manual. Computer Science Dept. Rep., Carnegie-Mellon Univ., Pittsburgh, Pennsylvania, January 1976.

Fuller, S. H., Swan, R. J., and Wulf, W. A., The instrumentation of C.mmp: a multi-mini-processor. *Proc. COMPCON, New York, March 1973*, 173–176.

Heart, F. E., Ornstein, S. M., Crowther, W. R., and Barker, W. B., A new minicomputer/ multiprocessor for the ARPA network. *Proc. NCC* **42**, 529–537 (1973).

Jones, A. K., and Wulf, W. A. Towards the design of secure systems. *Software—Practice and Experience* **5** 4, 321–336 (October 1975).

Knight, K. E., A fast sort of country: a study of technological innovation—the evolution of digital computers. Ph.D. thesis, Computer Science Dept., Carnegie-Mellon Univ., Pittsburgh, Pennsylvania, 1963.

Kung, H. T., Searching on C.mmp. Talk at the 10th Anniversary Symp., Computer Science Dept., Carnegie-Mellon Univ., Pittsburgh, Pennsylvania, October 1975.

Lesser, V. R., Fennell, R. D., Erman, L. D., and Reddy, D. R., Organization of the HEARSAY–II speech understanding system. *Proc. IEEE Symp. Speech Recognition, April 1974*, 11–21.

Levin, R., Cohen, E., Corwin, W., Pollack, F., and Wulf, W. A., Policy/mechanism separation in HYDRA. *Operating Systems Review* **9** 5, 122–131 (November 1975).

Newell, A., Barnett, J., Forgie, J., Green, C., Klatt, D., Lickleder, J. C. R., Munson, J., Reddy, R., and Woods, W., *Speech-Understanding Systems: Final Report of a Study Group*. Computer Science Dept., Carnegie-Mellon Univ., Pittsburgh, Pennsylvania, May 1971; reprinted by North–Holland, Amsterdam, 1973.

Newell, A., Freeman, P., McCracken, D., and Robertson, G., The kernel approach to building software systems. *Computer Science Res. Rev.*, Carnegie-Mellon Univ., Pittsburgh, Pennsylvania, 1971.

Newell, A., and Robertson, G., Some issues in programming multi-mini-processors. *Behavior Res. Methods Instrum.* **7** 2, 75–86 (March 1975).

Reddy, D. R., Erman, L. D., Fennell, R. D., and Neely, R.B., The HEARSAY speech understanding system: an example of the recognition process. *Proc. 3rd Intern. Joint Conf. Artificial Intelligence, Stanford, California, August 1973.*

Reddy, D. R., and Newell, A., Multiplicative speedup of a system. In *Perspectives on Computer Science* (A. K. Jones, ed.). Academic Press, New York, 1976.

Reid, B. K. (ed.), HYDRA songbook. Computer Science Dept. Rep., Carnegie-Mellon Univ., Pittsburgh, Pennsylvania, September 1975.

van Lehn, K. A. (ed.), SAIL user manual. Stanford AI Lab. Memo., Stanford Univ., Stanford, California, 1973.

Wulf, W. A., ALPHARD: toward a language to support structured programs. Computer Science Dept. Rep., Carnegie-Mellon Univ., Pittsburgh, Pennsylvania, 1974.

Wulf, W. A., and Bell, C. G., C.mmp—a multi-mini-processor. *Proc. FJCC* **41**, 765–777 (1972).

Wulf, W. A., Russell, D. B., and Habermann, A. N., BLISS: a language for systems programming. *Comm. ACM* **14** 12, 780–790 (December 1971).

Wulf, W. A., Johnsson, R. K., Weinstock, C. R., Hobbs, S. O., and Geschke, C. M., *The Design of an Optimizing Compiler*. American Elsevier, New York, 1975.

Wulf, W. A., Pierson, C., Pollack, F., Levin, R., Corwin, W., Jones, A., and Cohen, E., HYDRA: the kernel of a multiprocessor operating system. *Comm. ACM* **17** 6, 337–345 (June 1974).

Multiplicative Speedup of Systems

R. Reddy and Allen Newell

Department of Computer Science
Carnegie-Mellon University
Pittsburgh, Pennsylvania

This paper attempts to show that speedups of several orders of magnitude are possible in systems where a hierarchy of levels exists. Typical of these are large complex computer systems such as speech- and image-understanding systems. There are many levels of potential improvement in such systems. The levels range from device technology, computer architecture, and software architecture at the lower levels to system organization, algorithmic analysis, knowledge sources, and heuristics at the higher. Potential speedups at each of these levels can be estimated through a careful study of several specific examples that have resulted in speedup. Speedup of components combines additively in systems which are the usual assemblage of components. However, in hierarchical structures where the levels are relatively independent, improvements at various levels combine multiplicatively, resulting in very large total speedup.

1. INTRODUCTION

The problem of speedup of programs and systems is of interest to most of us. At Carnegie-Mellon University we have been attempting to characterize the nature of potential speedup in systems for some time. While we are all aware of some of the common tricks of the trade, such as reprogramming in assembly language, it appears that most of us are unwilling or unable to examine the total range of options that are available to us. In this chapter we will (re)introduce the notion of a hierarchy of levels where improvements at various levels combine multiplicatively. We propose a hypothesis that speedup of several orders of magnitude is possible in systems with many levels of hierarchy.

Our speedup hypothesis is based on several assumptions:

(1) The system has a hierarchy of levels amenable to optimization.

183

(2)   The levels are independent in that optimization at one level does not preclude optimization at the other levels.

(3)   The system has not already been optimized at some of the levels.

(4)   The problem is important, i.e., many people are working on it and instant speedup is not expected (several years of effort may be required to achieve the potential speedup).

The viewpoint presented here is obviously speculative. However, we hope to present evidence from some current experiments, illustrating the type of speedup that has been achieved at various levels, in support of our hypothesis. We will use examples mostly from local work, where we understand the numbers. Equivalent examples and numbers could no doubt be drawn from many other sources. Indeed, our hypothesis suggests that the evidence for it should be widespread.

The problem of estimating potential system speedup is motivated by our efforts to develop speech- and image-understanding systems. These systems tend to be complex, computationally expensive, and run very slowly on present-day computer systems. Thus it becomes essential to study and understand the expected performance of eventual systems. Tables I and II attempt to illustrate the magnitude of the problem. Table I gives the processing requirements (in millions of instructions executed to process a second of speech) of several connected-speech recognition systems [Reddy 76]. Typically these systems tend to have less than 250 word vocabularies with an average branching factor of less than 10 words at each choice point. As the size of vocabulary increases to a few thousand words, it is expected that processing power on the order of 100 million instructions per second (mips) may be required for real-time recognition unless better

TABLE I

Computational Power Required by Various
Systems to Process a Second of Speech[a]

System	No. of instructions/sec of speech (in millions)	
HEARSAY-I	3–10	
DRAGON	15–60	
LINCOLN	45	Avg. branching factor < 10
IBM-Raleigh	35	
HARPY	10	

[a]From Reddy [76].

TABLE II

Processor Speed Required for an Image Understanding
System for Different Size Pictures Assuming 1000 Operations
per Picture Element

Desired response time (sec)	Picture $1024 \times 1024 \times 3$ high-resolution TV (mips)[a]	Size $2500 \times 3300 \times 4$ satellite photo (mips)
1	1000	10000
10	100	1000
100	10 ~ C.mmp)	100

[a]mips, millions of instructions per second.

heuristics and algorithms are devised to reduce search. This implies that 2 to 3 orders of magnitude speedup over a PDP–10 (KA–10) will be necessary if we are ever to have real-time response from the system.

Table II gives the processing requirements for an image-understanding system. Different systems seem to require anywhere from 500 to 5000 operations per pixel (picture element) for processes such as smoothing, differencing, histogram calculation, correlation, color mapping, or distortion calculation. The Table shows that processing power of 10 to 10,000 mips is needed, depending on the size of the picture and the response time desired. Given that a PDP–10 (KA–10) is about a 0.4 mips processor, we can see that it will be impossible to undertake a major effort in image understanding research on KA–10 class machines. We have noted that the minimal point in the table corresponds approximately to C.mmp (equivalently, a CDC–7600).

The hierarchical structure we see in speech- and image-understanding systems starts at the bottom with the technology, and proceeds upward through architecture, system software, program organization, algorithm analysis, program implementation, knowledge sources, and heuristics. We will first take up each of these levels, working bottom up, identifying the potential for speedup and, where we have numbers, trying to estimate increases in speed that might be obtained. After this, we will return to a discussion of the several assumptions of our speedup hypothesis.

2. TECHNOLOGY

Several significant improvements are expected in the areas of device technology and memory technology in the near future. However, when it comes to estimating potential speedup factors, there are interdependencies

TABLE III

Speed Factors Associated with Different Logic Families

	Gate delay (nsec)	Register times (nsec)	Clock times (nsec)
TTL	10	30	120
Schottley-TTL	3	25	100
MECL 10k	2	10	30
MECL 100k	0.7	3 (?)	10 (?)
Josephson J.	0.15		

among device technologies, memory technologies, and the memory bandwidth; i.e., even if we could make an infinitely fast processor, it cannot run faster than the rate at which data are available from memory. This in turn depends on the architectural decisions about the processor-memory-switch structure. Assuming that these decisions are compatible with overall throughput objectives, we can estimate potential speedup factors that can be expected from technology.

Table III presents some typical speeds of different logic families. Present commercially available systems run at about 100 nsec clock speeds. Systems being designed at present (and expected on the market in a year or two) will run between 10 and 30 nsec clock speeds. The present push to increase the component densities is expected to lead to devices capable of running at about 0.15 to 0.2 nsec gate delays and at about 2 to 5 nsec clock time. This implies about 20 to 50 times speedup over technologies used in present systems or about 5 to 10 over the next generation systems.

The high-speed random-access memories will be based on the same technologies as the processor, with many levels of memory hierarchy. Electron beam memories and video disks will probably satisfy most of the bulk memory requirements. Capacities of 10^9 to 10^{12} with 20 to 500 megabit bandwidths can be achieved using these bulk memory technologies. What is important is the interconnection of these levels in the memory hierarchy so that none of them becomes a bottleneck. This in turn is dependent on the task, the algorithms, and the data migration strategies adopted.

3. ARCHITECTURE

Unlike the case of technology, it is much more difficult to estimate the speedup factors that can be achieved through functional specialization of a processor architecture. If one system exhibits significant speedup over another, and we wish to compare their architectures, we must first normalize for the differences in the relative speed of technologies and for relative costs (as a measure of complexity and/or number of components used in each architecture). Finally, we can compute the total system speedup knowing the speedup factor for the part that is specialized.

We have several functionally specialized systems in the CMU environment. The graphics processor [Rosen 73, Kriz 73] is designed to interpret tree-structured display lists, and most of the control is embedded in the display list representation. The Xerox Graphic Printer [Reddy *et al.* 72] provides real-time generation of 1600 bit scan line data from characters and vectors through a combination of specialized hardware and software. The SPS–41, a processor designed by Signal Processing Systems Co. for performing fast Fourier transforms, performs a "butterfly multiply" (4 multiplications and 6 additions) in 1 μsec.

The HARP, a 30 nsec programmable processor element currently under development at CMU [Kriz *et al.* 76], indicates speedup factors of 35 to 70 over a PDP–11/40 in executing some expensive speech and vision algorithms. It has a 64 register instruction memory, 64 register data memory, and an 8K × 16–bit 30 nsec buffer memory; it is attached to the PDP–11 UNIBUS. Using a 3 instruction pipeline execution, and independent paths to instruction and register memories, it achieves a microinstruction execution rate of 30 million/sec.

TABLE IV

Architectural Features of Three Processors
Used in Speech and Vision Research[a]

	PDP-11/40	SPS-41	HARP
Gate delay (nsec)	10	5	2
Clock times (nsec)	140	100	30
Instruction time (nsec)	> 2000	200	30
Number of registers	8	256 +	128
Pipeline execution	No	Yes	Yes
Cost	$10K	$30K	$20K
Production volume	large	small	few
Technology normalization factor	1.0	0.5	0.2

[a]In spite of the cost differences, these systems are of the same order of complexity. Thus, the technology normalization factor is based purely on gate delay.

Table IV gives the architectural features of three systems used in the CMU environment for speech and vision research: PDP–11/40, SPS–41, and HARP. Table V gives the comparative performance of these three systems in the execution of some basic procedures used often in speech and vision. The instruction density shows the relative power of SPS–41 and HARP instruction sets when compared with the PDP–11 instruction set. Note that these microprogrammable processors require only 2 to 3 instructions on the average to equal the power of a PDP–11 instruction. The code density, measured by the total number of bits required to represent the same algorithm, is another measure of the power of an instruction set. The time of execution is given in part C. Finally, in part D we normalize the execution time first with respect to the PDP–11/40 as unity, and then by a factor based on technology. The PDP–11/40 uses TTL logic (gate delay of 10 nsec). The SPS–41, using mixed TTL and Schottky-TTL (gate delay 5 nsec), has a technology advantage factor (TAF) of 2. HARP, using MECL 10k (clock time 30 nsec), has a TAF of 5. With a speedup 45 to 55 (except in data-limited cases such as the histogram program given as the third example of Table V), the HARP architecture seems to provide a normalized speedup factor of about 10 over a general-purpose computer architecture,

TABLE V

Comparison of Three Architectures: Speedup Resulting
from Functionally Specialized Architecture

Program	PDP-11/40	SPS-41	HARP
A. Code size: number of instructions/program			
1. Autocorrelation	36	78	55
2. Dragon loop	35	65	64
3. Histogram	10	21	42
B. Code density: number of bits/program			
4. Autocorrelation	832	1954	880
2. Dragon loop	976	1495	1024
3. Histogram	240	483	672
C. Execution time/program in microseconds			
1. Autocorrelation	90.4	15.6	1.65
2. Dragon loop	89.5	13.0	1.92
3. Histogram	20.9	4.2	1.26
D. Speedup from functional specialization[a]			
1. Autocorrelation	1	5.8 (2.9)	54.8 (11.0)
2. Dragon loop	1	6.9 (3.5)	46.6 (9.3)
3. Histogram	1	5.0 (2.5)	16.6 (8.3)

[a]Technology normalized speedup in parentheses.

with the SPS–41 lying between. The architectural features that provide the speedup are pipeline execution, the use of large number of registers, and the choice of instruction sets and instruction formats.

However, as indicated by the histogram example, the potential speedup factors from technology and architecture may not be realized if much of the program is data limited. This, of course, indicates an architectural mismatch, in that the memory bandwidth provided by the UNIBUS is not adequate for high-speed processors. The HARP–UNIBUS connection would have to be replaced by a wide data path interface to the main memory to correct for this imbalance (at least a 256-bit wide data path). But this is precisely the price of specialization—the advantage is realized only for the right tasks in the right environments.

4. SYSTEM SOFTWARE

Since most present systems are built using higher level languages in general-purpose operating system environments, analysis of inefficiencies and delays introduced by system software could lead to significant speed-up relative to present speed of execution. The techniques involved in functional specialization of system software need not necessarily imply loss of generality or flexibility in programming and use of the system. There are three areas of potential improvement: microprogramming of system primitives, program-dependent operator design, and flexible data and program migration strategies through a hierarchy of memories.

Several programming language and system primitives are being implemented in microcode at CMU. An experiment to code the kernel primitives of an implementation system (L*) in PDP–11/40 microcode has led to a speedup factor of 3 over executing the kernel in PDP–11 assembly language. Clark and Green [76] have studied the problem of memory architectures for LISP language. They find that use of special coding techniques for different types of pointers (adjacent, relative, and so on) reduces the storage requirement by about a factor of 2 to 3. If the pointer decoding can be microcoded efficiently, then one can reduce the space required without a corresponding increase in execution time.

Program-dependent operator design is a term used to indicate that non-standard operators based on program structure can be placed in microcode just as one would a set of vector or matrix operators. If a language subsystem (or a programmer) can discover commonly used inner loops from the execution behavior of a program, then these could be made into primitive operators resident in microcode for the duration of execution of that program. Multiple caches that are large enough to hold inner loops of programs would have essentially the same effect.

We saw in the previous section the importance of making sure that the data are available when the processor needs them. Otherwise the program becomes data limited and the speed of the processor becomes irrelevant. This in turn depends on the data migration strategies and file structures provided in general-purpose operating systems. Often these become a major bottleneck in program execution. Even though a disk may provide 4 mbps bandwidth, the overheads associated with disk access often make it impossible to get more than 100 kbps. This problem is likely to become more difficult in the future. Instead of primary memory and secondary memory we are likely to have about six levels in the memory hierarchy with cycle times ranging from 3 nsec to 15 μsec and widely varying seek–access times. Careful attention is needed in the operating system design to obtain program-specific information and use it in the data and program migration strategies to ensure best throughput. But precisely because the structure is intricate, general-purpose systems will be relatively inefficient and specialization will yield large gains.

For the programs given in Table V, we found that HARP runs 100 to 300 times faster than the same programs written in SAIL (a sophisticated, but not highly optimizing ALGOL-like language) executing on a PDP–10. Given a good *optimizing compiler*, it should be possible to increase the execution speed of the PDP–10 program by a factor of 3 to 6, to a level where the differences in the speed of execution are explainable purely in terms of technology and architecture. Additional speedup can be expected through the use of techniques such as microprogramming of system primitives, program-dependent operator design, and improved data migration strategies.

5. PROGRAM ORGANIZATION

As the programs become more and more complex, many of the functions provided by the operating system and language are taken over by the user program itself. Typical of the operations provided are (1) representation of data structures and facilities for their manipulation; (2) data- and event-directed activation of processes; and (3) goal-directed scheduling. In speech- and image-understanding systems, which are organized as independent, cooperating, asynchronous knowledge processes, many of these issues become even more crucial with the possibility of using multiprocessor systems such as C.mmp, CMU's symmetric multiprocessor.

We do not have much experience in these types of systems and cannot yet propose potential sources of speedup. The only example we have is our experience with programming the HEARSAY–II system in the SAIL language. SAIL has facilities for symbol manipulation, associative data retrieval, and multiple process instantiation. These were important data and process structures needed in HEARSAY–II. Programming this system, which is both large and complex, using SAIL led to a system that was so slow (over a 1000 times real time) that it was impossible to experiment with the system. Redesign (within SAIL) of the program organization with carefully tailored data structures and process instantiation mechanisms led to a speedup of over a factor of 20.

As in the case of system software, much of the speedup is likely to be achieved by the removal of unused generality. The need for generality comes from many sources: not knowing how and when knowledge processes will be activated; not knowing when to use locking structures to prevent process interference; requiring continuous monitoring for events to enable data directed invocation; and inability to choose the correct focus of attention strategies to provide goal-directed scheduling. If we put to one side the improvements that may be achieved through simple reprogramming, truly innovative concepts for speedup at this level will only come from increased use and understanding of these new program organizations.

6. ALGORITHM ANALYSIS

With the advent of algorithmic analysis as a special field in computer science, some remarkable gains have been obtained (factors of 10^3) from deep mathematical analysis of an algorithm central to some task, e.g., sorting or testing for nearest neighbor. The classic example is the fast Fourier transform (FFT), which has revolutionized the field of digital signal processing. Gains from this level are quite independent of the standard gains usually derived from reimplementation of the same basic algorithm. That is, there have been both efficient and inefficient FFT programs.

There are two recent examples of speedup achieved at CMU through reformulation of algorithms. Knudsen [75], in a microcode implementation of the computation of autocorrelation components for linear predictive analysis of speech, reformulated the algorithm to reduce the accesses to the main memory by a factor of 14, thereby speeding up the process by about a factor of 10. Price [75] reformulated a picture-smoothing operator so that the number of operations required were reduced from order n^2 to a constant k which was independent of the size n of the input to the operator. Reformulating the representation and/or control through careful algorithm analyses seems to yield factors of 10 to 1000 in specific algorithms, leading to factors of 2 to 20 in overall program performance.

7. PROGRAM IMPLEMENTATION

If we take an existing system, conduct simple performance analyses to see where the time is being spent within the system, and reimplement parts of the system, it is possible to get a factor of 2 to 10 improvement in a previously unoptimized system. Further improvements to the system will usually require careful redesign at one or more levels of the system.

The paper by Knuth [72] on the optimization of FORTRAN programs represents an important step toward performance analysis and optimization at this level. In this effort, a preprocessor is used to introduce meters into the programs automatically at all the choice points. After a typical execution run of this metered program one gets a listing of the program indicating the number of times each statement, in the original unmetered program, was executed in this run. Typically 10% of the program takes 90% of the time. Careful examination and reprogramming of this 10% of the code, eliminating the common inefficiencies, often results in program speedup factors of 2 to 10.

8. KNOWLEDGE SOURCES

In speech-understanding systems (and analogously for image-understanding systems), there are several task-specific sources of knowledge that help to restrict and reduce the combinatorial search resulting from the nondeterministic nature of choices at the phonetic level. Errors occur at the phonetic level because of the variability due to noise, speaker, dialect, and heuristics. The problem of error can be transformed into a problem of uncertainty by considering several plausible alternative hypotheses for the phones. Now the problem becomes one of nondeterministic search of the phonetic-string space to find the best sequence of phones that are consistent with the sources of knowledge. The knowledge sources include the *vocabulary* to be used, the grammatical structure of legal or acceptable sentences (*syntax*), the meaning and interrelationships of words within a sentence (*semantics*), and the representation and use of context depending on the conversation (*pragmatics*).

In order to speed up a complex system, we can attempt to rewrite it (or add to it), using more knowledge about the task, i.e., more sources of knowledge relevant to problem solution. The potential speedup that can be expected through the addition of a significant knowledge source can be illustrated with examples from syntactic knowledge. The grammatical structure of a language can be viewed as a mechanism that principally reduces search by restricting the number of acceptable alternatives. If any word could follow any other, then we would have word sequences such as "sleep roses dangerously young colorless". Given a vocabulary of 1000 words, one would have to match and verify which one of the thousand words is most likely at any given point in the utterance. Grammar permits us to predict which of the words are acceptable at a given choice point. The constraint provided by the grammar can be measured by the average branching factor of the network.

For restricted grammars with about a 1000 word vocabulary, the average branching factor tends to be less than 50. Thus it is necessary to match only 50 out of the possible 1000 words on the average and this results in a speedup factor of 20 in the match procedure. Given the signal processing and other overhead costs associated with speech understanding, this speed-up appears as only a factor of 2 to 5 in the execution time of the total system. Lowerre [76] shows that, for the same accuracy, the HARPY speech understanding system (see the following section) runs about 4 times faster when using syntactic knowledge for the voice-programming task. The amount of speedup that can be realized through the use of all the knowledge sources is highly task specific and appears to range from around 10 to 100.

9. HEURISTICS

We will illustrate the speedup factors achievable through the use of heuristics by considering the DRAGON speech-understanding system developed at CMU by Baker [75]. Baker constructs an integrated network representing all the valid sentences in the language. This network is regarded as a probabalistic function of a Markov process. The problem of recognizing an utterance is treated as a problem of dynamic programming, i.e., of finding an optimal path through the network that best explains the acoustic evidence. This involves calculating for each time unit t the conditional probability of being in state s_j given the probability p_k that the acoustic evidence at time t represents phone k.

DRAGON evaluates all the possible paths through the network, but exponential growth is constrained through the use of a Markov assumption, which limits the relevant context and collapses many alternative sequences to a single state. With this technique, search time is linear in the number of states in the network and in the length of the utterance. Although the system was slower than HEARSAY–I (a heuristic-search based system also being explored at the time) by 5 to 10 times, it was more accurate, i.e., it increased the accuracy at the sentence level by about 18%. Thus, it was of interest to us to see which of the heuristics used in HEARSAY–I could be used effectively within this new framework.

HEARSAY–I did not search all the paths; it used best first search. It did not evaluate probabilities for each 10 msec time unit; it used segmentation and labeling.

Lowerre [76] generated a new system, HARPY, which uses DRAGON's representational framework and heuristics based on HEARSAY–I experience. The principal heuristics used are the following:

(1)   Do not search all the paths through the network; extend only the best few paths.

(2)   Do not evaluate the conditional probabilities for each 10 msec time unit; instead segment the speech signal into larger acoustically invariant parts and update the conditional probabilities for each state once per segment.

(3)   Do not compute the probabilities for all the phones p_k. Do so only for those which are needed at that stage.

These heuristics have resulted in a total system speedup factor of 25 without any loss of accuracy. In general, it is not uncommon to achieve factors of 10 to 100 in system speedup using heuristics, though this depends on the complexity of the problem.

10.   DISCUSSION

We have sketched a system with some eight levels and made some estimates for each level of what speedups might be expected. These projections are summarized in Table VI. Though they vary widely in their reliability, they will serve to let us discuss the speedup hypothesis more concretely.

The arithmetic of speedup is worth noting explicitly. In a hierarchy of n levels, in which each level is built with components of the next lower level, the speedups combine multiplicatively:

$$\text{total speedup} = S = S_1 \times S_2 \times \cdots \times S_n$$

where S_i is the speedup of the ith level. The relationship is multiplicative because a speedup at one level affects uniformly all processes at the next level. Since the logarithms of the speedups add, in Table VI we have also provided the logarithms (base 2), rounded to the nearest integer as befits the accuracy of the data.

Within a level, the outputs of one component provide the inputs to others. How the total time depends on the components is determined by the type of processing structure at a level. If only one component at a time is active (as in the usual programming system), then the total execution time is the sum of the times spent in each of the components, weighted by

TABLE VI

Range of Speedup Observed in Various Experiments

	Possible speedup factors	Log of two speedup factors
Technology	20 to 50	4 to 6
Architecture	2 to 0	1 to 3
System software	2 to 10	1 to 3
Program organization	2 to 20	1 to 4
Algorithms	2 to 20	1 to 4
Reimplementation	2 to 10	1 to 3
Knowledge sources	10 to 100	3 to 7
Heuristics	10 to 100	3 to 7

the expected number of times that component is to be activated. Then speedup in one component is limited in its effect; as it becomes greater, all of the time is being spent in other components which are not being affected by the speedup. At the other extreme, in a pipeline of simultaneously active components, the speed of the total depends on the speed of the slowest component; speedup in a component is only effective if it is the slowest one, and then only until it loses that dubious distinction. Many variations of processing interconnection and structure are possible. The exact form of their speedup combination is less important than their general feature that speedups in components produce only limited gains in the total speedup and in the end these gains are self-limiting.

Our treatment of potential speedup within the various levels has reflected this additive structure. Several times we have computed a relatively high speedup for the component under consideration and then diminished it by a substantial fraction to take into account its limited contribution to speeding up the system at that level. An example was the work on picture smoothing at the algorithm analysis level, where component speedup factors of 10 to 1000 underwent attrition to factors of 2 to 20 for the total system.

The central question then, corresponds to assumption 2 of our speedup hypothesis: "When do we have a hierarchy such that the multiplicative speedup principle holds?" Notice that a hierarchy need not be limited to the gross levels of computer structure, such as the technology, logic, and programming level. When inner loops in programs are discovered that take 90% of the time, they reveal in essence a level of hierarchy in the processing structure that occurs entirely within the program level.

When two levels are totally independent, as when the same exact architecture is realized with two different technologies, then the multiplicative relationship is clear. But such complete independence is not necessary.

It is only required that whatever speedups occur at one level do not diminish the impact of possible speedups at another. For example, our experience with implementing algorithms in programs says they can be done efficiently or inefficiently, independent of the algorithm. The potential for inefficiency does depend on the size and structural complexity of the algorithm, but not on its specific mathematical content. Thus the potential for speedup at the program implementation level is not diminished by a shift from a relatively weak algorithm for computing a result to a relative powerful one. Similarly, the use of a relatively specialized architecture may preclude some of the tricks used to organize a computation at the program level, but it does not preclude all such—optimizers must simply look in different places.

There are limits to the degree of independence of the levels we have described here, and as yet we have neither the data nor the right simple models to provide a quantitative analysis. When the architecture becomes so specialized that it dictates the algorithm, clearly two levels have coalesced into one. At the knowledge source level, when a system is utilizing very little knowledge, then each type of knowledge (e.g., syntax) contributes across the board to every solution attempt, thus supporting a multiplicative relationship. But at a more advanced stage, when all types of knowledge are incorporated to some extent in the system, new knowledge tends to become only conditionally useful, i.e., only if certain problem situations arise (e.g., knowledge of a rare grammatical construct only helps occasionally). Then the inclusion of new knowledge contributes only additively (i.e., according to its expected occurrence), and the knowledge source level no longer serves as an independent level.

The third assumption in our speedup hypothesis is that the system has not already been optimized. At issue here is not just the notion of saturation—that there is an actual optimal system for a specific computational task, so that one can run out of optimizations to do. The latter may not even be true, given a sufficiently extended task, as the speedup theorems in computational complexity indicate. Rather, we humans, as beings with quite limited cognitive powers, always create extremely inefficient and imperfect systems to begin with, so that there is an immense scope for optimization, available throughout the entire structure of the system. Optimizations will be easy to make initially and become increasingly harder to find as time goes on—not because they are not there, but because the obvious ones have been discovered.

Moreover, for complex tasks, our only view of a task is through the systems we have built to solve it. Thus, our initial estimates of the time and space required to solve tasks, if responsibly made, will strongly reflect the inefficiencies of our systems. Much of our optimization will take on the appearance of removing inefficiencies from our existing systems. We have already seen this in our discussion of programming reimplementations.

The last assumption in our speedup hypothesis is that sufficient time be available for the total speedup to occur. The only way in which complex systems can be optimized is through a social hill-climbing procedure in which many people work on various aspects over several years. This is especially true given that the optimization extends over many different hierachical levels, so that there are very few scientists and technologists who work over the entire range. Reinforcing this assumption is the way speedups at upper levels in a hierarchy depend on lower levels. A radically different solution adopted at some lower level may reset several higher levels to relative inefficiency, so that optimization must begin all over again. This is not inevitable, as the invariance of the instruction set over technology changes indicates, but will still happen over and over again in the course of obtaining large amounts of improvement. Conversely, a new algorithm or a new way of representing some type of knowledge, may open opportunities for functional specialization that require brand new structures at some lower levels.

Given all these assumptions, the preliminary and incomplete estimates of the within-level speedups, and the missing quantitative estimates of the amount of coupling for optimization between levels, it is still useful to carry out the final arithmetic on Table VI. If all the levels were truly independent, then the logarithm of the total gain available for speedup for the total system would lie between 15 and 37, which is to say, gains between 10^4 and 10^{10}. One way to probe these numbers is to assume that the levels are coupled together strongly enough so that the effective height of the hierarchy was halved—to only 4 levels instead of 8. Then, since the average log speedup per level is 2 to 4, the total log speedup would be 8 to 16, which translates to a speedup of 10^2 to 10^5. The large reduction shows the strong influence of the independence assumption. The fact that the speedup still rises above 10,000 shows the potent effect of a deep hierarchy.

Even if a system does not have many levels of potential optimization, one can still assume that improvements in technology, architecture, and system software will permit many programs to run at two to three orders of magnitude faster than at present for about the same cost. Thus, one might not want to reject a solution just because it is too slow today if it has other compensating attributes such as being more accurate, more flexible, or improves programmer productivity. Also, improvements to algorithms that speed up a process by only 10% will be lost in the wake of faster newer technologies and architectures for some years to come.

11. CONCLUSIONS

In this paper we have proposed a speedup hypothesis, i.e., that speedup of several orders of magnitude is possible in systems with many levels of hierarchy and that improvements at various levels combine multiplicatively, provided certain assumptions of independence are satisfied. We have presented evidence from some current experiments, to indicate the amount of speedup that seems possible on various levels. While the viewpoint presented is clearly speculative, it appears possible to us that several orders of magnitude of speedup can be realized, even under the most pessimistic assumptions, in systems with many levels of hierarchy.

ACKNOWLEDGMENTS

We would like to thank Anita Jones and David Jefferson for their helpful comments on this paper. This study was supported in part by the Defense Advanced Research Projects Agency and in part by the John Simon Guggenheim Memorial Foundation.

REFERENCES

Baker, J. K., Stochastic modeling as a means of automatic speech recognition. Ph.D. thesis, Computer Science Dept., Carnegie-Mellon Univ., Pittsburgh, Pennsylvania, 1975.

Clark, D. W., and Green, C. C., An empirical study of list structure in LISP, *Comm. ACM* **20** 2, 78–87 (February 1977).

Knudsen, M. J., Real-time linear-predictive coding of speech on the SPS–41 triple-micro-processor machine. *IEEE Trans. Acoustic Speech and Signal Processing* **ASSP-23**, 140–145 (February 1975).

Knuth, D. E., An empirical study of FORTRAN programs. Computer Science Dept. Rep., Stanford Univ., Stanford, California, 1972.

Kriz, S. J., Hardware for high-speed digital vector drawing. *Digest SID Intern. Symp., New York, May 1973*.

Kriz, S. J., Reddy, D. R., Rosen, B., Rubin, S., Saunders, S., HARP, a 30 MHz processor. Computer Science Dept. Rep., Carnegie-Mellon Univ., Pittsburgh, Pennsylvania, 1976.

Lowerre, B., The HARPY speech recognition system. Ph.D. thesis, Computer Science Dept., Carnegie-Mellon Univ., Pittsburgh, Pennsylvania, 1976.

Price, K., Personal communication, 1975.

Reddy, D. R., Speech recognition by machine: a review. *Proc. IEEE* **64** 4, 501–531 (April 1976).

Reddy, D. R., Broadley, W., Erman, L., Johnsson, R., Newcomer, J., Robertson, G., and Wright, J., XCRIBL—A hardcopy scan line graphics system for document generation. *Inform. Proc. Lett.* **1**, 246–251 (1972).

Rosen, B., The architecture of a high-performance graphic display terminal. *Digest SID Intern. Symp., New York, May 1973*, 50–51.

On the Nature of Understanding

Herbert A. Simon[†]

Departments of Computer Science and Psychology
Carnegie-Mellon University
Pittsburgh, Pennsylvania

The term "understanding" is one of those words—along with "intelligence", "problem solving", "meaning", and the like—that we have borrowed from the vocabulary of everyday life, and that we apply in the field of artificial intelligence without assigning technical definitions to them. There is no harm in this provided that we do not imagine that because a word "understanding" exists, there must also exist some unitary aspect of human intellectual behavior to which the term refers.

Indeed, in artificial intelligence, the very vagueness of the notion of understanding has been of some use. Investigators have tried to penetrate its meaning by constructing programs that would behave like a person who understands in some class of situations. Different investigators have chosen different areas of behavior in which to test their systems; the last decade has seen a substantial number of interesting varieties of intelligent behavior, with a consequent enlargement of our grasp of what information processes and what organizations of those processes are required for understanding. As is typical of this kind of artificial intelligence research, at first we gradually accumulate empirical examples—running programs—that exhibit the phenomena of interest; then we analyze these programs for common mechanisms and common structures; and finally, we try to construct generalizations about what kinds of mechanisms are essential to produce the phenomena, and how these mechanisms produce their effects.

1. EARLY UNDERSTANDING PROGRAMS

The beginnings of artificial intelligence (AI) research on understanding can be found at the beginning of the decade we are celebrating in this symposium. This chapter reviews some of this decade's research on the topic to see what commonalities appear and what generalizations can be made to emerge. The review will have to limit itself to a small number of samples drawn from the rather large body of work in this area; and the

[†]This research was supported in part by Research Grant MH–07722 from the National Institute of Mental Health and in part by the Advanced Research Projects Agency of the Office of the Secretary of Defense (F44620–73–C–0074), which is monitored by the Air Force Office of Scientific Research.

199

particular examples referred to are drawn very nonrandomly, on the basis
of my own familiarity with them, from the whole body of investigations.

To the best of my knowledge, the first title of an AI paper in which the
word "understand" appears was Robert Lindsay's "Inferential Memory as
the Basis of Machines Which Understand Natural Language", published
in 1963 in the Feigenbaum–Feldman collection, and based on Lindsay's
1961 dissertation. A second title was Bert Raphael's [64] "A Computer
Program Which Understands". A third effort that typifies research on
understanding during this period (although the word does not appear in it)
was my own work on the Heuristic Compiler [72], first issued as a RAND
Technical Report in 1963, and published as part of the Simon–Siklossy
collection in 1972.

These three efforts appear to have two main things in common: (1) they
are concerned with the understanding of natural language, but intend by
this something more than parsing; and (2) by "understanding", they mean
extracting from the input message meanings that go beyond the information given explicitly in that message. Inferences were to be drawn from
successive input sentences, or input language transformed until it could be
combined with internally stored information.

Thus, Lindsay's system accepts sentences that describe family relationships—e.g., "John is the father of Fred". The system stores this
information in semantic memory in the form of a genealogical tree, so that
when it learns that A is the brother of B, and B the father of C, it can infer
that A is the uncle of C. Similarly, from "A man has two hands", and "A
hand has five fingers", Raphael's system can infer that a man has ten
fingers. In both systems inference depends upon combining the information contained in two or more input sentences with stored semantic
information about the definitions of common terms (e.g., "uncle" or
"has").

The understanding tasks of the Heuristic Compiler are somewhat different. One of them is to supply from semantic memory missing information about an object mentioned in the input instructions, described incom-
pletely but known to belong to a particular class of objects. In common
with the other systems, understanding in the Heuristic Compiler requires
combining pieces of information acquired at different times and from
different sources.

Although the three programs are quite different in surface appearance,
there is considerable commonality in the mechanisms they employ to
achieve understanding. All three begin by parsing the incoming natural
language string in order to extract the underlying relational structures from
the linear arrays of words. All three store the parsed sentences in common
formats to facilitate the discovery of relations among them. (I will call such

common formats "canonical representations".) All three possess inferential capabilities, although these are rather dissimilar in nature in the three cases.

Inference in Lindsay's system takes place in two steps. First, a relation is established between each new sentence and the preceding ones by attaching the information extracted from the sentence to the genealogical chart. Second, implicit relations among the terms (as in the example given above) can be read directly from the chart. In Raphael's system, inference derives from specified properties of particular relations like "have" (that it is "multiplicative", so to speak, and transitive).

Inference in the Heuristic Compiler rests on the assumption that structures belonging to the same class have common substructures, at least down to some level of detail. Thus, if a house and its door are mentioned in the input sentence, it can be inferred that the house also has a roof and windows. This inference is accomplished by attempting to map the parsed input description onto a list structure stored in semantic memory that describes an archtypical house—complete with all its parts. The matching routine that attempts this mapping is a relatively complex piece of machinery.

Thus, from these initial attempts a decade ago to construct programs that understand natural language, we extract four types of processing mechanisms that appear to be important for the functioning of such programs: (1) a natural language parser, (2) a process for mapping the input information into some canonical representation and storing this in semantic memory, (3) some inferential capabilities for extracting implied meanings by exploiting the relations among several input sentences, and (4) a matching mechanism for accessing in semantic memory stored information that supplements information provided explicitly in input strings.

2. UNDERSTANDING PROGRAMS: THE SECOND HALF-DECADE

When we look at the focus of research on understanding just before 1970, we find that the emphasis has shifted somewhat. Now the extraction of meanings from natural language is taken for granted, and the main question is how to combine these meanings with information obtained through other channels—in particular, information in the form of visual pictures of some sort. I will mention three programs of this general kind, and a fourth that belongs to a different variety.

In the first three schemes to be discussed, the system is not limited in its knowledge of the world to natural language inputs. It can also "look" at the real world, for it has access to some kind of spatial or pictorial model of it. However, the understanding tasks performed by the three systems are quite different.

Coles [72] was concerned with parsing syntactically ambiguous sentences. He reasoned that if information were available about the scene the sentences purported to describe, the ambiguities could be resolved by testing which parsing matched the scene. The picture was input to the computer on a graphic display console by means of a light pen, and the input automatically reduced to a set of relations represented as list structures. By successive transformations, both picture representations and sentence representations were translated into a predicate calculus format, which served as the common canonical representation that permitted them to be compared.

Siklossy [72] was concerned with the learning of language—with the induction of a grammar and vocabulary from a sequence of sentences. With each sentence in the input there was paired a list structure describing a scene that captured the meaning of the sentence. By mapping the known words of the sentence on the list structure, the remaining, unknown words could be matched with the remaining elements of the list structure. In this way, the system could acquire an understanding of new sentences containing one or more previously unknown elements, and could gradually build up its vocabulary and knowledge of syntax.

For Winograd's [72] system, understanding meant being able to answer natural language questions about a canonical representation of a scene, and to obey commands to rearrange the scene.

Thus the behaviors that gave evidence of understanding in these three programs were very diverse: resolving syntactic ambiguities, learning the grammar and vocabulary of a natural language, and answering questions and obeying orders. What was common to all of these tasks was the need to bring together and compare information that was presented initially in two different modalities—in language and in "pictures", respectively. What mechanisms did the programs employ, and how do these mechanisms compare with those that evolved during the previous half-decade of research on understanding systems?

All three systems, obviously, needed a parser to carry out the initial processing of the natural language input. The first two made essential use of a canonical representation into which both language and pictures were translated in order to permit comparison. All three systems incorporated some kind of inferential mechanism. For ambiguity resolution, a relatively straightforward scheme for matching pairs of propositions sufficed. The grammar induction scheme called for a much more complex matching routine, somewhat comparable to that used in the Heuristic Compiler. The inferential mechanism in Winograd's program was a full-fledged problem solver, Microplanner. Thus, at the level of major components, these new understanding programs used much the same kind of machinery as their predecessors.

The tasks undertaken by Winograd's system required several pieces of mechanism beyond those mentioned so far. In order to answer questions about a scene, the program had to be able to recognize objects in that scene and their relations. To obey orders, it had to be able to produce changes in the relations among objects. These capabilities are also part of what we call "understanding" in humans: to be able to recognize an object when it is named, and to be able to point to it, grasp it, or move it. These kinds of meanings are incorporated in the program as test procedures and action procedures, respectively.

A rather similar notion of understanding had been proposed several years earlier by Pople [72], who constructed a goal-seeking system capable of handling nonnumerical goals expressed as relations. Pople proposed explicitly that a program should be regarded as understanding the intention of a relation if (1) it is able to recognize instances of the concept denoted by the relation and classify objects as either belonging to it or not; (2) it can generate objects that satisfy the relation. His system had capabilities for understanding in both of these senses.

Finally, Winograd's system had the capability of answering questions about the reasons for its own actions. Its problem solver was based on the use of means–ends analysis, hence, upon the generation and execution of hierarchically organized goals. By retaining its goal tree in memory, the system could reconstruct and report the sequence of goals and subgoals whose pursuit led to any particular action. In this sense it understood why it performed its actions.

We have now brought the story almost up to the present. The work of the second half-decade extended considerably the range of tasks in which understanding was exhibited, but extended only a little the list of mechanisms required to perform them. Before turning to understanding programs that are under development at the present time, or looking toward prospects for the future, let us pause to see whether we have any clearer picture of the general meaning of "understanding" than we had at the outset.

3. A DEFINITION OF UNDERSTANDING

Moore and Newell [74] have essayed a general definition of what it means to understand:

S understands knowledge K if S uses K whenever appropriate.

Exactly what does this definition mean, and how well does it encompass the forms of understanding incorporated in the programs we have examined? There are three aspects of the definition that call for some explication: first, the fact that it refers explicitly to understanding *knowledge*; second, that it does not make explicit what knowledge it has reference to; and third, the apparent vagueness of the phrase "whenever appropriate".

In everyday speech, we sometimes refer to a person understanding a subject or topic, that is, understanding knowledge. But we refer even more frequently to a person understanding language that is addressed to him, or understanding a situation in which he finds himself. If the definition of Moore and Newell is to be sufficiently broad to cover all or most instances of understanding, we must interpret the last two categories as well as the first as implying the understanding of some kind of knowledge. It is not too hard to see what that knowledge might be. Understanding language means understanding the information the language potentially conveys. Understanding a situation means understanding the information that is implicit in the situation and would be explicit in an adequate description of it. Hence, without too much departure from ordinary usage, the idea of "understanding knowledge" can be interpreted to embrace understanding language and understanding a situation.

With this clarification of the definition, it is easy to see what knowledge "K" denotes. Table I provides a conception of the kinds of knowledge that have been present in the systems we have examined thus far, and to which understanding might extend. First, there are the various forms of "sensory" knowledge derived through input channels. In our examples, this has consisted of natural language input and pictorial knowledge. Second, there is the knowledge, whether derived from input or elsewhere, stored in semantic memory in some form of canonical representation that makes it available to the storage, accessing, and inferential processes. Third, there

TABLE I

Sources of Knowledge for an Understanding System

Knowledge from input
Natural language input
Pictorial input
Semantic memory ("Canonical representation")
Knowledge-containing processes
Parsing processes
Tests of relations, and actions
Recognizers and matching processes
Inferential processes and problem solvers

is the knowledge that is embedded in the processes themselves: the parsers, the tests and actions, the recognizers and matching processes, and the inferential processes and problem solvers. The general definition, then, asserts that the system understands any particular one of these sources of knowledge if it uses that source whenever appropriate.

That brings us to the question of what is meant by "appropriate". Moore and Newell point out that this term becomes definite as soon as the system's tasks or goals are specified. "Whenever appropriate" means whenever using the knowledge in question would facilitate performance of the task or attainment of the system's goals. Thus, in Lindsay's system it is appropriate to use knowledge to infer new facts about family relationships, while in Winograd's, it is appropriate to use it to answer questions about a scene. Thus elucidated, the definition of Moore and Newell would seem to provide a useful framework within which to arrange the many specific meanings that "understanding" takes on in particular contexts.

In addition to providing a general definition of understanding, Moore and Newell have also provided a list of design issues, which must be faced in the construction of an understanding system. The design issues cannot be discussed in detail here, but it will be instructive to see how they are related to what we have been describing as major mechanisms embodied in understanding systems. Briefly labeled, the eight design issues of Moore and Newell are (1) *representation*, (2) *conversion* of knowledge into behavior, (3) *assimilation*, (4) *accommodation*, (5) *directionality*, (6) *efficiency*, (7) *error*, and (8) *depth* of understanding.

The first design issue, *representation*, is concerned with the forms of storage of knowledge, and with the specification of the lingua franca that permits bodies of knowledge originating from different sources and in different formats to be related to each other. It coincides closely with what I have been calling the design of the canonical representation.

The second design issue, *conversion*, has to do with the way in which information causes and determines action. The observation that knowledge incorporated in programs already has a direct potential for producing action suggests that the way to resolve the issue is to embody all meanings in procedures—a general philosophy that is followed in Winograd's program. But it is by no means settled today that this is the best solution of the design problem. For much knowledge originates as sensory information,that is, as data descriptive of an external reality. Hence the location of the boundary where data are transformed into program can be moved, but the task of transforming them cannot be avoided. Where to locate the boundary is an issue that has been decided very differently by different understanding programs.

Of the understanding mechanisms we have considered, all except the inferential mechanisms are involved in the third design issue *assimilation*. The parser, the processes that produce the canonical representation of information from the parsed text, and the match processes all are basically concerned with providing an interface between information as it is received by the system from outside and the formats expected by internal processes, or are concerned with matching information derived from internal and external sources, respectively.

The remaining design issues listed by Moore and Newell do not map as neatly onto the understanding mechanisms we have identified as do these first three. *Accommodation* has to do with those long-term adaptive changes of the system that we call learning. Of the systems we have considered, only Siklossy's grammar induction program takes learning as a central task, and in that system learning and understanding are maximally confounded—it is hardly possible to disentangle processes of accommodation from processes of assimilation. The *directionality* of understanding systems derives from the fact that they can represent goals, and especially in their problem-solving mechanisms can generate goal and subgoal structures in response to what they know and discover. *Efficiency* and the control of *error* are endemic problems that must be solved for all systems. There seems to be nothing special about understanding systems that calls for new or different mechanisms for dealing with them. The matching mechanisms perhaps represent a partial exception, for if the structures to be matched are at all complex, matching attempts are likely to lead to combinatorial explosions with all the complications of computing cost and difficulties in error-free backup that that implies. About "*depth* of understanding", I will have a little more to say later.

4. THE UNDERSTAND PROGRAM

I now want to turn to an ongoing research project that enlarges further the range of tasks for which understanding is requisite. Understanding a problem is different from solving a problem, or even being able to solve it. There are many problems that no one has been able to solve, but that are easy to understand. A well-known example is Goldbach's conjecture: Every even number can be expressed as a sum of two primes. Other examples are Fermat's last theorem and the four-color problem.

What does it mean that one understands Goldbach's conjecture without being able to prove or disprove it? One thing it means is that, for any given even number, it is easy to test whether any two given primes sum up to that number. Another thing it means is that it is easy to test the conjecture for any particular even number by trying all pairs of primes smaller than that number. Hence, if Goldbach's conjecture is false, there must exist some even number for which no such pair can be found. Understanding the conjecture, then, means knowing a good deal about how one would recognize a proof or disproof (or at least a constructive proof or disproof). It does not mean necessarily that one has any good ideas about how to construct a proof or disproof.

John R. Hayes and I [74] have constructed a system that we rather pretentiously call UNDERSTAND, which endeavors to understand problems presented through written instructions, but which has no capabilities for solving those problems. UNDERSTAND takes the written instructions in natural language as its input, and produces as output the information that would be needed, in turn, as input to the General Problem Solver (GPS) so that the latter program could go to work on the problem. Thus, problem understanding is clearly marked off in this system from problem solving:

> *Natural Language Problem Instructions* →
> *UNDERSTAND* → *Input for GPS* →
> *GENERAL PROBLEM SOLVER* → *Problem Solution*

The input for GPS that UNDERSTAND produces consists of a representation for problem states, which permits a description of the objects appearing in the problem and their relations, and routines for legal move operators that can transform one problem state into another. We claim that the program understands because it uses its knowledge appropriately to construct the representation and the routines.

What knowledge does UNDERSTAND call upon in its performance? Its only external source is the set of written problem instructions. Its internal sources, embodied in the program, include (1) a natural language parser, (2) capabilities for transforming the parsed text into an internal list structure representation of objects and relations, (3) stored programs capable of modifying list structures in a variety of ways, and of making tests on list structures, (4) capabilities for mapping the legal move descriptions in the instructions upon appropriate moves and tests selected from among these stored programs, and (5) capabilities for executing the stored programs and tests interpretively so that they operate correctly on the particular representations constructed by (2).

Hence, although the task of UNDERSTAND is different from the tasks of any of the programs we have discussed previously, the same basic mechanisms can be found in its structure that we have already found in the structures of the others: a parser, processes for constructing a canonical representation from the parsed text, a repertory of stored procedures usable in composing tests and actions, and a matching process that uses the parsed input information to select appropriate procedures from this repertory. Finally, the program turns over its output to a problem solver—GPS.

If we compare UNDERSTAND with Winograd's program, we see that, in spite of this common machinery, there are two dimensions along which they differ greatly, as a consequence of the differences in the understanding tasks posed to them. First, Winograd's program already has available to it an internal canonical representation of the scene on which it operates, while part of UNDERSTAND's task is to create that representation from the natural language text. Second, the present version of UNDERSTAND makes use of considerably less stored semantic information than does Winograd's program, especially information about the objects under discussion. The UNDERSTAND program operates largely by abstraction, the written problem description being nearly self-contained. What semantics it employs is largely the semantics of list structures rather than the semantics of the real-world objects these structures represent. This, of course, is a neat trick when it can be carried off, for it greatly increases the generality and flexibility of the program without burdening it with a great store of particularistic knowledge and procedures. The price paid for this economy of semantic memory is that the missing information must be provided by the problem instructions, so that UNDERSTAND appears to be best suited to problems of a rather abstract sort—which most puzzles are.

5. UNDERSTANDING THE TOWER OF HANOI PROBLEM

We have by no means exhausted the meanings of "understanding"—the range of tasks to which knowledge can be applied. Consider, for example, the HEARSAY speech recognition system [Reddy and Newell 74]. Its task is to produce a translation of a sound stream into written language, a task that would not appear to require understanding of the meaning of the sound stream at all. Attempts to build speech-understanding systems have taught us, however, that it is very difficult to decode a sound stream without bringing to bear upon it all of the syntactic and semantic information we can marshal. No one has been able to show how simple phonemic encoding and word recognition, without the use of rich syntactic and semantic information, can be made to work. As a consequence, although understanding meanings is not one of the direct goals of HEARSAY, the program makes extensive use of semantics, and indeed requires virtually all the kinds of mechanisms we have described as constituting an understanding system.

Chess-playing programs illustrate a rather different point. Here, depth of understanding might be measured by quality of play. Yet existing programs achieve a given quality of play by a whole continuum of means ranging from large-scale brute-force search of all legal moves to some depth, to highly selective search making use of feature recognition and other knowledge-interpreting devices. Looking at these programs, we might decide that strength of play does not capture what we usually mean by "understanding", and that the programs that play more selectively somehow understand the situations in which they find themselves more deeply than do the programs that rely on brute-force search. Perhaps all we mean by this is that we place our faith for the long-run future of chess programs in those that are selective rather than in the brute-force searchers.

Every experienced teacher makes a similar distinction between a student's depth of understanding and his ability to perform on particular tests. The teacher knows that some students learn by rote while others learn with understanding, and that this is an important difference even if it does not show up in the grades on the Friday quiz. How can we characterize the distinction, and what is its significance?

Returning from humans to computers, there is a temptation to say that everything a computer knows it knows by rote, for "it can only do what it is programmed to do". The vast differences among chess programs noted above should warn us, however, against equating "doing what the program says" with "doing by rote". In any event, the question deserves a deeper examination.

In order to have a simpler environment than chess in which to explore the issue, let us consider the Tower of Hanoi puzzle [Simon 1975]. This puzzle employs three vertical pegs or posts, and a number of doughnut-like disks of graduated sizes that fit on the pegs. At the outset, all the disks are arranged pyramidally on one of the pegs, say A, with the largest disk on the bottom. The task is to move all of the disks to another peg, C, say, under the constraints that (a) only one disk may be moved at a time, and (b) a disk may never be placed on top of another smaller than itself. The minimum number of moves for a solution of the n-disk problem is $2^n - 1$.

I have chosen three examples to illustrate the wide variety of relatively simple computer programs that will solve the Tower of Hanoi problem. I will show how these different programs exhibit different kinds of understanding of the problem. The first of these examples, illustrated by Table II, is a "rote" solution.

This simple system consists of just three productions. The part of each production to the left of the right-arrow is the *condition* part, the part to the right is the *action* part. At each step, the productions are scanned sequentially until one is found whose conditions are satisfied; then the action part of that production is executed. This sequence is simply repeated until a

"Halt" is reached. In this example, the conditions depend on a symbol labeled "Last-move". If this symbol is absent, only the condition of the third production is satisfied, so that the action of that production is executed. This action consists of retrieving the first move on the list "Hanoi", making that move, and assigning its name to "Last-move". At the next step, the condition of the second production is satisfied, the next move in sequence is retrieved from the list, executed, and assigned to "Last-move". When the final move in the list has been executed, and the value "end" has been assigned to "Last-move", the condition of the first production is satisfied, and the system halts.

With the strategy of Table II, the correct moves for solving the problem are stored in memory on a simple list whose successive members are linked by the relation "next", and which is terminated with the symbol, "end". The symbols that are used as tests for the conditions of the productions are stored in a special part of memory (short-term memory (STM)). In fact, STM holds only the name of the move that has been made most recently, called "last-move".

The first production says that if STM contains the symbol "end", the problem is solved and the program should halt. The second production says that if STM contains any symbol, X, labeled as "last-move", then the move that is next to X in the list of moves in memory should be retrieved and called Y. The move, Y, should then be executed and its name stored in STM as last-move. The third production says that, unconditionally, the first move on the list "Hanoi" should be retrieved from memory, executed, and stored as last-move in STM.

To execute the rote strategy, only a single place-keeping symbol need be retained in STM, and no perceptual tests need be made in order to determine what move to make next. The reasons for regarding this as a rote strategy are obvious: no analysis is involved, but simply recall of a list of items in order; the solution only works for a specified number of disks; and it only works for a specified initial problem situation (all disks on a particular peg) and a particular goal situation. Hence, the system has no capability for transferring what it knows about the problem to variants involving a different number of disks or different (even trivially different) starting and goal points.

TABLE II

Production System for Rote Strategy

Last-move = end	$\rightarrow$	Halt [problem solved]
Last-move = X	$\rightarrow$	Y = Retrieve (next (X)), Move (Y), last-move $\leftarrow Y$
else	$\rightarrow$	Y = Retrieve (first (Hanoi)), Move (Y), last-move $\leftarrow Y$

TABLE III

Production System for Goal-Recursion Strategy

P1. Goal = Move(k, $P(k)$, A) → Move(k, $P(k)$, A), Pop(Goal)
P2. Goal = Move(Pyramid(1), A) → Move(1, $P(1)$, A), Pop(Goal)
P3. Goal = Move(Pyramid(k), A)   → Pop(Goal),   Push[Goal = Move(Pyramid(k − 1), A)],   Push[Goal = Move(k, $P(k)$, A)],   Push[Goal = Move(Pyramid(k − 1), $O(P(k)$, A))]
P4. else → Push[Goal = Move(Pyramid(n), Goal-peg)]

In contrast to the rote program is a program incorporating the usual recursive solution for the Tower of Hanoi problem (Table III). In this production system, the condition depends on the value of "Goal", the top of a pushdown stack. The actions consist of making moves and adding or subtracting goals from the goal stack.

This solution rests on the observation that in order to move a pyramid of n disks from Peg S to Peg G, one need only (1) move a pyramid of $(n − 1)$ disks from S to Peg O, (2) move the remaining, largest, disk from S to G, and (3) move the pyramid of $(n − 1)$ disks from O to G. Notice that the production system of Table III assumes that STM operates as a pushdown stack and has sufficient capacity to hold simultaneously as many uncompleted subgoals as have been generated at any time during solution of the problem. The capacity required is $(2n − 1)$ goals for an n-disk problem.

The obvious difference between the rote and recursive solutions of the problem is that the latter, but not the former, has implicit knowledge of, and makes use of, important aspects of the problem structure. It is not that the one program uses the knowledge it possesses more effectively, or appropriately, than the other, but rather that it possesses more knowledge. (Notice that "possession" of knowledge here means that it is built into the program, not that it is available in explicit declarative form.)

The Moore–Newell definition of understanding emphasizes the use of the knowledge that is available. The example suggests that the definition should be amended and expanded to read:

> System S understands task T to the extent that it possesses knowledge K about T and uses that knowledge wherever appropriate to perform T.

With this modified definition (see also Klahr [74, pp. 295–296]), depth of understanding increases both with the extent of knowledge possessed and the adequacy of use of that knowledge.

The goal-recursion strategy of Table III is knowledgeable about the Tower of Hanoi problem, but is also very introverted. It pays no attention to the current arrangement of disks on pegs, but decides what to do next on the basis of which goal lies uppermost in its goal stack in STM. It could easily be fooled by an outside intervention that changed the disk arrangement between two of its moves, and it would then not be able to continue. Table IV shows a very different strategy, which makes considerable use of its knowledge of the current problem situation ("State") in order to decide upon its next move.

The perceptual strategy requires twelve productions. The first seven of these, the general productions, take as their conditions the information that is held in STM, and act by changing that information, by making moves, or by acquiring new information from the problem display. The latter actions are accomplished by executing (in response to the action "test") the subsidiary system of five perceptual productions. The perceptual produc-

TABLE IV

Production System for Perceptual Strategy

P1'.	State = Problem-solved $\rightarrow$ Halt
P2'.	State = Done, Goal = Move(k, $P(k)$, A) $\rightarrow$ Delete(State), Delete(Goal)
P3'.	State = Can, Goal = Move(k, $P(k)$, A) $\rightarrow$ Delete(State), Move(k, $P(k)$, A)
P4'.	State = Can't(J), Goal = Move(k, $P(k)$, A) $\rightarrow$ Delete(STM), Goal $\leftarrow$ Move(J, $P(J)$, $O(P(k)$, $A)$)
P5'.	Goal = Move(k, $P(k)$, A) $\rightarrow$ Test(Move(k, $P(k)$, A))
P6'.	State = Biggest(J) $\rightarrow$ Goal $\leftarrow$ Move(J, $P(J)$, Goal-peg)
P7'.	else $\rightarrow$ Test(Biggest-remaining)

Test(Move(X), $P(X)$, A)

T1.	(Y)On(Y, Goal-Peg) $\rightarrow$ State $\leftarrow$ Problem-solved, Exit
T2.	On(X, A) $\rightarrow$ State $\leftarrow$ Done, Exit
T3.	(X = Top($P(X)$)) & Free(X, A) $\rightarrow$ State $\leftarrow$ Can, Exit
T4.	else $\rightarrow$ State $\leftarrow$ Can't(J), $J \leftarrow$ Bigger-of[Next-smaller(k, $P(k)$), Next-smaller(k, A)]

Test(Biggest-remaining)

T5.	$\rightarrow J \leftarrow$ Biggest(Not-on-goal-peg), State $\leftarrow$ Biggest(J)

tions take as their conditions the current state of the problem display and act by providing information to STM. In the recursive method, the successive moves are governed by the goal structure in STM; in the perceptual method, they are governed by the current state of the stimulus.

The perceptual strategy will solve not only the problem of moving an n-disk pyramid from one of the pegs to another, but it will accomplish this starting from any arbitrary (legal) arrangement of the disks. Moreover, it will need to retain only two symbols in STM while doing this, instead of the entire goal stack required by the recursive strategy. This difference in performance capabilities derives from differences among the means the various strategies have available for conceptualizing the problem. The rote strategy knows only of individual legal moves. The recursive strategy employs the concept of a macromove: moving a subpyramid of disks. The perceptual strategy lacks this latter concept, but it has the notion of "the largest disk blocking the move of disk X", is able to determine perceptually which disk this is, and can use this knowledge to progress toward its goal.

Our brief exploration of strategies for the solution of the Tower of Hanoi problem has revealed additional dimensions to the meaning of understanding, although, again, these strategies employ no basic mechanisms that go beyond those incorporated in the other programs. We are still not in a position to decide whether we have exhausted the meanings of understanding, or whether there are still other dimensions to be revealed by new programs. My final remarks will be directed to that question.

6. UNDERSTANDING AND AWARENESS

Let us return for a moment from computer programs to human behavior. How would we test a student's understanding of the Tower of Hanoi problem?

(1) We could test the speed with which he learned a solution strategy, how well he retained it over time, and to what range of similar tasks he could transfer it. Research by Katona [40] has shown that "meaningful" solutions of problems are learned faster, retained better, and transferred more effectively than rote solutions.

(2) We could infer the nature of the strategy he was using to solve the problems, and evaluate it with respect to its parsimony and generality, just as we have been evaluating the computer programs.

(3) We could measure his ability to evoke the strategy when it was appropriate for solving a problem. (This is the criterion that comes closest to fitting the original Moore-Newell definition.)

(4)   We could test his ability to paraphrase or describe his strategy in alternative expressions.

(5)   We could test his ability to explain or prove how or why the strategy works.

The final two tests in this list raise entirely new issues beyond those discussed up to this point—issues of what might be called "awareness". But why are we interested in a student's ability to paraphrase, explain, or prove? And what would be involved in a computer program's being aware in these latter senses? We take up the second question first.

Since the three strategies that are described formally in the tables have already been paraphrased in the text, we can take those paraphrases as examples. Note that they are expressed in natural language; they omit much of the detail of the formal programs; and they are in a form that a program having the general characteristics of UNDERSTAND might use as input for generating the programs themselves. Stated otherwise, a paraphrase of a program corresponds closely to an informal description of the top levels of that program. Hence, it might serve as input to a system capable of automatic top-down programming. A system that could paraphrase programs and create programs from paraphrases would have ways of understanding its knowledge that go beyond those previously described. It is not hard to think of tasks for which that knowledge would be useful.

Explaining a program, or proving its efficacy, is similar to paraphrasing, but goes a step further in paying attention to the performability of each program step and to the effectiveness of the procedure in attaining its goal. Knowledge in the forms of paraphrases, explanations, or proofs of strategies is knowledge about knowledge, which is what I take awareness to be. To the extent that a system can examine its own programs, analyze them, and modify them it has additional forms of knowledge that have their own appropriate uses. It appears plausible that these uses are especially closely related to the system's capacity for learning, for acquiring new forms of understanding.

7. CONCLUSION

There appears to be no end of "understanding" problems. Research in AI has identified and attacked at least a half-dozen such problems during the past decade. Understanding was initially viewed as the ability to extract meanings from natural language inputs, and to make explicit by inference information contained implicitly in those inputs. At a later stage, emphasis shifted to capabilities for combining information derived from multiple sources (two or more input sources, or input information with information already available in semantic memory). Just appearing on the horizon, and likely candidates for the next decade's research, are questions about the form of understanding called "awareness".

In our inquiry we have been guided by Moore and Newell's definition of understanding as ability to use knowledge to accomplish tasks. But we found it convenient to extend that definition to encompass not only differences in ability to use knowledge but differences in the knowledge being used.

We have surveyed a considerable range of tasks calling for understanding, but have found a much smaller variety of basic mechanisms for performing those tasks. That is encouraging and comforting when we confront the prospect of extending understanding to new task domains. However, it should not make us complacent in thinking that we have indeed already discovered the main mechanisms required for all forms and types of understanding.

The design and investigation of systems that understand should, therefore, continue to be as exciting and rewarding an area of AI research over the next decade as it has been over the past one. We need to extend our inventory of understanding mechanisms. We need to generalize these mechanisms—many of which are still in a quite primitive state—and enhance their powers. We need much more effective parsing processes, matching processes, inferential processes than we now have as components of our understanding systems. We need to explore the domain of awareness, which has hardly been touched up to the present time. In that exploration, we need to consider how to avoid an infinite regression of programs that have knowledge of programs that understand. We must see if we can learn to use a common set of mechanisms at all levels, constructing programs that have self-awareness—bootstrapping themselves to some kind of ultimate enlightment.

I hope that we will all have an opportunity to come together again at the end of another decade to see what answers we have obtained to these exciting and important questions of computer science.

REFERENCES

Coles, L. S., Syntax directed interpretation of natural language. In *Representation and Meaning* (H. A. Simon and L. Siklossy, eds.), Chapter 5. Prentice-Hall, Englewood Cliffs, New Jersey, 1972.

Hayes, J. R., and Simon, H. A., Understanding written problem instructions. In *Knowledge and Cognition* (Lee W. Gregg, ed.), Chapter 8. Erlbaum Associates, Potomac, Maryland, 1974.

Katona, G., *Organizing and Memorizing*. Columbia Univ. Press, New York, 1940.

Klahr, D., Understanding understanding systems. In *Knowledge and Cognition* (Lee W. Gregg, ed.), Chapter 12. Erlbaum Associates, Potomac, Maryland, 1974.

Lindsay, R. K., Inferential memory as the basis of machines which understand natural language. In *Computers and Thought* (E. A. Feigenbaum and J. Feldman, eds.), 217–233. McGraw-Hill, New York, 1963.

Moore, J., and Newell, A., How can Merlin understand? In *Knowledge and Cognition* (Lee W. Gregg, ed.), Chapter 9. Erlbaum Associates, Potomac, Maryland, 1974.

Pople, H. E., Jr., A goal-oriented language for the computer. In *Representation and Meaning* (H. A. Simon and L. Siklossy, eds.), Chapter 7. Prentice-Hall, Englewood Cliffs, New Jersey, 1972.

Raphael, B., SIR: a computer program which understands. *Proc. FJCC* **26**, 577–590 (1964).

Reddy, R., and Newell, A., Knowledge and its representation in a speech understanding system. In *Knowledge and Cognition* (Lee W. Gregg, ed.), Chapter 10. Erlbaum Associates, Potomac, Maryland, 1974.

Siklossy, L, Natural language learning by computer. In *Representation and Meaning* (H. A. Simon & L. Siklossy, eds.), Chapter 6. Prentice-Hall, Englewood Cliffs, New Jersey, 1972.

Simon, H. A., The heuristic compiler. In *Representation and Meaning* (H. A. Simon & L. Siklossy, eds.), Chapter 1. Prentice-Hall, Englewood Cliffs, New Jersey, 1972.

Simon, H. A., The functional equivalence of problem solving skills. *Cognitive Psychology* **7**, 268–288 (1975).

Winograd, T., Understanding natural language. *Cognitive Psychology* **3**, 1–191 (1972).

Some Thoughts on the Next Generation of Programming Languages

William A. Wulf

Department of Computer Science
Carnegie-Mellon University
Pittsburgh, Pennsylvania

This paper discusses some of the major influences on contemporary programming language design—namely, programming methodology, formal semantic definition techniques, program specification and verification. This discussion is first in general terms and then tries to illustrate how these issues have influenced the design of a specific language, ALPHARD, which has been under development at CMU for about two years.

1. INTRODUCTION

A group at CMU has been working on a new programming language for the last two years. It is called ALPHARD and some aspects of it will be discussed later. However, ALPHARD is not the major point of the paper. Rather I would like to discuss the more global issues of language design in the recent past and for the near future. As one might expect, this will be a somewhat personal view of these issues and not unrelated to the design considerations for ALPHARD.

Not very many years ago quite a number of influential people were declaring that language design was dead as a legitimate research topic in computer science. Some people suggest that the "ultimate" programming language is just around the corner. The most recent, widely circulated statement to this effect appeared in Knuth's "Structured programming with **goto** statements" [Knuth 74], in which he called for "Utopia 84".

Such a view seems fundamentally unrealistic. Programming languages are one of the notational vehicles by which the central concepts of our science are carried. So long as the science lives, the set of "central" concepts will expand and change, and the notations in which they are best expressed will also expand and change. Moreover, it is not simply that expression of new concepts is slightly more convenient in one notation

217

than another, but rather that the notations we use both limit and mold the things we are able to think about effectively. Both natural language and other sciences provide us with ample examples of the symbiotic relation of notation and idea.

We might expect that the rate of change in languages will slow down. Even though the rate of production of new ideas may remain constant, or even increase, the base set to which they are added is now much larger than it was 15 or 20 years ago. Hence the net change in the whole is substantially smaller, and this will be reflected in the rate of change. Moreover, a reasonable set of expectations for any programming language has evolved, and we may expect that new concepts will first be expressed via adaptations of existing notations.

Occasionally, however, we should expect more radical changes. New ideas will inevitably arise whose best expression, and possibly whose only reasonable one, will not fit into the accepted linguistic framework. APL is one example from the recent past; it seems that the fundamental innovation in APL is the incorporation of known sequencing and control patterns into the operators of the language—and the most reasonable expression of this innovation does not fit nicely into the FORTRAN/ALGOL language model.

My intuitions tell me that explicit (programmed) parallelism is a topic that will spawn a significant notational change in the next few years. Our present notations, synchronizing primitives, *fork*, *join*, and the like, are relatively trivial extensions of languages whose structure is predicated on sequentiality. I conjecture that one of these days we will discover a better, more natural way to think about parallelism and that it will involve a quite different notational structure than that which we currently use.

It is interesting to trace the emphasis in language design as a reflection of the emphasis in and maturation of the field as a whole. The early sixties, for example, were a time of general exuberance with the almost limitless potential of computers. Exaggerated claims were made for time-sharing, chess programs, natural language translation, management information systems, and so on. In language design the whole emphasis was on convenience to the programmer—if only we could make it more convenient for the programmer, all sorts of marvelous programs would be written. In this euphoric atmosphere the notion of conversational languages flourished and "features" were piled onto languages like gargoyles.

In the later sixties, as one after another the initial promise of these projects failed to materialize, we began to appreciate the difficulty of the tasks. More than that, we began to appreciate the complexity of programming itself. People began to speak of the "software crisis" and to recognize that, in many cases, we were trying to build programs that were more complex than those with which their human constructors were capable of coping.

These realizations have caused somewhat of a retrenchment and a search for sounder, more precise foundations on which to build. This may be seen in many ways, both within and without the programming language field:

1. the evolution of programming methodology as an intellectual discipline for managing the complexity of programs;

2. the development of various techniques for defining precisely the semantics of programming languages;

3. the development of formalisms and techniques for specifying (precisely) the intended meaning of a program;

4. the development of techniques for the formal "verification" of programs, that is, proving consistency between a specification and a program that purports to implement that specification;

5. the identification of certain language mechanisms, notably the **goto**, global variables, and references (pointers), which if used capriciously may result in intellectually unmanageable programs (there is a corresponding search for more manageable replacements for these mechanisms);

6. a general trend, which is perhaps an overreaction, to simplify both the nature of the tasks we attempt and the languages we use to express their realization.

Of course this list is not complete, nor is all contemporary research on languages and software production involved with or motivated by these concerns. They have, however, motivated our recent language work at CMU and are sure to have a significant impact on other language efforts for quite a few years.

In the following sections I will trace some of the considerations that were involved in the design of ALPHARD and that contributed to its present shape. As mentioned earlier, ALPHARD itself is not really the subject of this paper; yet, it represents a concrete example of the issues I would like to discuss. Thus, the reader should interpret any following ALPHARD-specific remarks in their intended, broader context. I will start with a personal analysis of the issues of programming methodology, then consider the related issues of verification and semantic definition, and finally exhibit how some of these issues have manifested themselves in our design.

2. A PERSONAL VIEW OF PROGRAMS AND STRUCTURE

By now it is almost a cliché to say that there is a "software crisis". Nearly everyone recognizes that software costs more than hardware, and that the imbalance is projected to increase. Nearly everyone recognizes that software is seldom produced on schedule—and worse, that the typical software product, costing more and delivered later than originally planned, seldom meets its performance goals; it is bigger, slower, and vastly more error prone than was originally anticipated. The aggregated cost of a failure to meet performance goals, measured in additional resources, time, and reconstruction of data lost due to an error, may vastly outweigh the initial development cost.

Another component of the software crisis is less commonly recognized, but, in fact, is often more costly than any of those listed above—namely, the extreme difficulty encountered in attempting to modify an existing program. Even though we frequently believe that we know what we will want a piece of software to do and will be able to specify it precisely, it seems to be invariably true that after we have it we know better and would like to change it. Examination of the history of almost every major software system shows that so long as it is used it is being modified! Evolution stops only when the system is dead. The cost of such evolution is almost never measured, but, in at least one case, it exceeded the original development cost by a factor of 100 [Boehm 73].

Assuming we all agree that there is a software crisis, then what is the cause of the problem and what are we to do about it? One can find many answers to both questions in the published literature, but to this author the answer to the first, at least, is clear: *complexity*. Large programs are among the most complex creations of the human intellect; I know of few other artificial objects as complex as, for example, a modern operating system.

Complexity per se is not the culprit, of course; rather, it is our human limitations in dealing with complexity. Dijkstra said it extremely well when he spoke of "our human inability to do much".

It is our human limitation, our inability to deal simultaneously with all the relations and ramifications of a complex situation, that lie at the root of our software problems. Perhaps it is too obvious to say, but if we really understood a program, we would understand why it is correct or incorrect; we would know why it runs as long as it does, and how it must be modified to improve its performance or incorporate a desirable feature.

Many suggestions have been made to "solve" the software crisis. The most recent of these, and the most promising, are the various programming methodologies: **goto**less programming, top-down design, stepwise refinement, modular decomposition, and so on. This collection of methodologies is generally referred to as "structured programming".

Although these methodologies are different, they each have in common the fact that they place restrictions on programs or on the process of creating them. The purpose of these restrictions is the same for all methodologies—to achieve a match between the apparent complexity of the program and our human ability to deal with that complexity.

The phrase "apparent complexity" in the previous paragraph is a key one. It is intended to suggest that the real complexity of a program might be greater than is apparent. For example, there might be ways of expressing the computation to be performed by a program that hide some of its "grubby details", while simultaneously highlighting its essential, major ideas. By ignoring the details and focusing only on the major ideas, the "apparent complexity" of the program is reduced, and hence should be more amenable to human comprehension. Moreover, once the major ideas of the program are appreciated and the intent of the "grubby details" established, understanding those details becomes a subproblem of exactly the same kind.

Before proceeding, I must state another basic premise, namely, that the property of understandability *must be a property of the program text itself*!

I do not believe that (large) programs are designed and written. I believe that the initial development of the program is merely the first step in an evolutionary process that will persist until the program is no longer useful. I do not believe that this situation, which is certainly true now, is the result of an imperfect design methodology. Rather, I believe it to be inevitable; the same human limitations that prevent us from dealing with the full complexity of a system also prevent us from anticipating all the ways in which it will be used—and hence the features it should have.

Given my strong belief in the inevitability of evolutionary modification, I am forced to the conclusion that it is paramount that whatever property of a program makes it understandable must be a property of the program text itself. Programs are read more often than written! Of course, there is not much argument over the assertion that we ought to make the text of our programs understandable, but the implications of the assertion are often not fully appreciated.

Consider, for example, the proposals for "top-down-design" or "stepwise refinement". These are both names for a methodology for writing programs; the methodology involves starting with a high-level, abstract program to perform some task. By definition, the level of abstraction is chosen such that the program is short, understandable, and "obviously correct". Usually this level will be such that the resulting program cannot be expressed directly in one of the extant programming languages. Hence the methodology advocates a deliberate expansion of the program's primitive concepts into "lower-level" ones; in general this process may involve several levels of abstraction, but finally results in something that can be expressed in executable form.

The strength of the methodology, of course, is that, if done properly, the degree of complexity at each step of the process will be within our human ability to cope with it. In effect, it is a technique for decomposing a complex task into subtasks, each of which is manageable in isolation. Unfortunately, practiced *in isolation*, the methodology has two weaknesses.

First, and most important in the present context, the various abstraction and refinement steps are not necessarily present in the final program. Thus the methodology serves well during initial development, but fails to help the future program modifier. This is *not* to say that programs developed in this way are as hard to understand as those developed in a more ad hoc fashion. On the contrary, they are usually much more understandable. It is a matter of degree, and this author believes that the methodology alone is insufficient.

Second, blindly practiced, a top-down methodology ignores an essential aspect of the engineering component of program design, namely, the search for commonality. A pure top-down methodology results in a tree of design decisions, of abstractions, and of their realizations. In such a design each line of code would be traceable through a unique set of decisions to the root program. In almost all cases this is undesirable. If, for example, abstractions exist for queues and sets, and both are implemented in terms of linked lists, it is probably preferable to use a common package of list manipulation routines. We shall examine the issue of commonality in greater detail later.

Let me briefly recap the discussion to this point. It has two essential components:

> The "software crisis" is the result of our human limitations in dealing with complexity.
> To "solve" the problem we must reduce the "apparent complexity" of programs, and this reduction *must* occur in the program text.

Under this view it is the nature of the program, rather than the methodology used to create it, that is central. A methodology is useful precisely to the extent that it leads to understandable programs, but if a program is understandable, the methodology used to create it is irrelevant. For this reason, I much prefer the term "structured program*s*" to "structured programm*ing*".

The next natural question is, "What makes a program understandable?" Unfortunately, the question is similar to "What makes a mathematical proof elegant?" or "What makes a painting aesthetically pleasing?" The properties that make something understandable, or elegant, or beautiful are related to psychological factors, as well as to the training, intelligence, and perhaps even taste of the beholder. It is unlikely that we will find a precise answer.

On the other hand, we do know some things that are hard to understand, e.g., "bowl-of-spaghetti" flow of control, and we can avoid these. More important, we know some properties [Wulf 72] that seem to be common to understandable programs, and we can strive to incorporate these. These latter properties include minimizing the assumptions between portions of a program [Parnas 72], and keeping each portion (reasonably) small.

Finally, and most important of all, we know something about the way humans have traditionally dealt with understanding complex problems—in fact, the way we are trained to deal with them—and we can try to mold the expression of a program so that it facilitates these techniques. Among the most powerful techniques are those of abstraction and structuring [Dijkstra 65, 68; Wirth 71]. In practice these two notions are often intertwined, but by abstraction we mean the process of ignoring detail and dealing instead with a generalized, idealized model of a complex entity; by structure we mean the relations among the parts of a whole.

Focus on the word "structure" for a moment: the relations among the parts of a whole. Both the notion of *parts* and that of the *relations* among them are important. Every program has some sort of structure—some parts and some relations among them—even if it is the vacuous structure consisting of a single part and the empty relation. If, however, each of the parts of the program is conceptually simple in isolation and the relations among them are also simple, then the whole program will be easy to comprehend.

But notice that if either the parts or the relations are difficult to understand, the whole will also be incomprehensible. Thus the process of constructing a well-structured program involves the choice of both of these, and neither can be considered less important than the other. This is the reason that simplistic rules such as "avoid **goto**'s" or "subroutinize" do not necessarily lead to well-structured, understandable programs.

Abstraction may play a role in making either the parts or the relations among them simpler, but the more common case is probably related to the "parts". Functional abstraction via procedures and data abstractions via type or mode definitions are both examples of the use of abstraction to reduce the apparent complexity of some portion of a program.

3. A PERSONAL VIEW OF VERIFICATION

There is a key relation between the notion of abstraction, verification and the modification of programs. To date most of the work on program verification has focused on treating (small) programs as monolithic entities and showing that a given property, the specification, holds between the input and output states of the program. There are several potential problems with this approach:

1.   The complexity of a proof grows rapidly with the size of a program. Relatively small programs tax the limits of contemporary theorem provers; thus proofs of large programs by these means seem unlikely.

2.   The proofs generally proceed from "first principles" and prove the correctness of both the algorithm and its implementation. In many cases the algorithm itself is well known and its correctness is not in doubt; only the implementation of the algorithm is of concern. This exaggerates the problem of proof size.

3.   The treatment of programs as monolithic entities for proof purposes implies that any change will require reproof. My earlier remarks about the inevitability of evolutionary change then suggest a continual, major reproof activity.

An alternative approach would be the separate proof of the correctness of the implementation of each abstraction—thus factoring the proof process along the same lines as the program decomposition. If the decomposition is a good one, and a proposed modification is not too incompatible with it, we can hope that it will affect very few of the abstractions—and hence very few proofs.

Hoare [72] has neatly formalized the notion of verifying the correctness of the implementation of an abstraction independent of its use in any particular program. In the following paragraphs I shall develop the same basic ideas in a slightly different form; this formulation is due primarily to Ralph London and myself, although many others in the ALPHARD group have also contributed to it.

Suppose that we have an abstract type T, that y is an arbitrary object of this type, and that $A_1, \ldots, A_n$ are abstract operations defined on this type of object. Our first concern will be to define the objects of this type and the operations on them in a manner that permits the verification of a higher level program using these objects. This definition shall consist of three parts. First, we shall define the class of objects belonging to this type by a predicate, which for reasons that become clear later is called the abstract invariant I_a. Second, the abstract type T may only be defined under certain assumptions about the environment in which it is created; these assumptions are captured by a predicate β_{req}. Third, when an abstract object is created we shall presume it has an initial value characterized by a predicate β_{init}. Fourth, the abstract operations are defined by their input–output relation, that is, by a pair of predicates that characterize their effect. We call these β_{pre} and β_{post}; using Hoare's notation [Hoare 69]:

$$\beta_{pre}(y)\{A_i\}\,\beta_{post}(y',y)$$

Where the primed variable (in the postcondition) represents the value of that variable prior to execution of the operation. Thus, the effect of the operation A_i is characterized by asserting that if the predicate β_{pre} holds before the operation is executed, then β_{post} will hold afterward.

Our next concern will be to characterize a concrete implementation of these abstract objects and operations. Suppose that x is the concrete representation of an object of type T, and hence, in general, x will be a collection or *record* of concrete variables. Further, suppose that $C_1, \ldots, C_n$ are the concrete operations that purport to be the implementations of the abstract operations $A_1, \ldots, A_n$. The set of concrete objects is also defined by a predicate, which we shall call the *concrete invariant* I_c. The relation between a concrete object x and the abstract object that x represents may be expressed by a *representation function* (rep):

$$\text{rep}(x) = y$$

Note that the rep function need not be one-to-one, that is, there may be more than one concrete object that represents the same abstract object.

The concrete operations C_i must also be characterized in terms of their input–output relations. To avoid confusion in the sequel we shall refer to these predicates as the input and output conditions, β_{in} and β_{out}, rather than pre- and postconditions. Using Hoare's notation again,

$$\beta_{in}(x)\{C_i\}\,\beta_{out}(x',x)$$

Finally, we shall presume a distinguished concrete operation C_{init}, which is invoked whenever an object is created; this operation is responsible for initializing the concrete representation (this initial value is called x_0 below).

Now, at an intuitive level, we wish to show that the concrete representation and the implementation of the concrete operations are "correct." More specifically, we wish to show that it is safe for the programmer working at the abstract level to prove the correctness of his program using *only* the abstract specifications I_a, β_{req}, β_{init}, β_{pre}, and β_{post}. In the sequel, we often discuss an arbitrary function whose corresponding abstract and concrete operations are denoted by the symbols A and C, respectively; our remarks are therefore implicitly quantified over the set of such operations.

We choose to break the proof of the correctness of the concrete realization into four steps. The first establishes the validity of the concrete representation. The second establishes that the concrete initialization operation is sufficient to ensure that β_{init} holds initially, assuming that β_{req} holds, of course. The third establishes that the code of the concrete operations is in fact characterized by the input–output assertions β_{in} and β_{out}. The last step establishes the relation between the concrete input–output assertions and the abstract pre- and postconditions.

1. Validity of the representation[†]:

$$I_{\mathrm{c}}(x) \supset \exists y \text{ st } y = \mathrm{rep}(x) \wedge I_{\mathrm{a}}(y).$$

2. Initialization of an object:

$$\beta_{\mathrm{req}}\{C_{\mathrm{init}}\}I_{\mathrm{c}}(x_0) \wedge \beta_{\mathrm{init}}(\mathrm{rep}(x_0)).$$

3. Verification of concrete operations:

$$\beta_{\mathrm{in}}(x) \wedge I_{\mathrm{c}}(x)\{C\}\beta_{\mathrm{out}}(x', x) \wedge I_{\mathrm{c}}(x).$$

4. Relation between concrete and abstract specifications:

(a) $\beta_{\mathrm{pre}}(\mathrm{rep}(x)) \supset \beta_{\mathrm{in}}(x),$

(b) $I_{\mathrm{c}}(x) \wedge \beta_{\mathrm{pre}}(\mathrm{rep}(x)) \wedge \beta_{\mathrm{out}}(x', x) \supset \beta_{\mathrm{post}}(\mathrm{rep}(x'), \mathrm{rep}(x)).$

Note that steps 1 and 4 are theorems to be proven, while 2 and 3 are standard verification formulas. Only step 4 should require further explanation. Step 4(a) ensures that whenever in the higher level, abstract program the abstract operation A could legally be applied (that is, whenever β_{pre} holds), the input assertion of the concrete operation β_{in} will also hold. Step 4(b) ensures that if the concrete operation is legally invoked, i.e., $I_{\mathrm{c}}(x) \wedge \beta_{\mathrm{pre}}(\mathrm{rep}(x))$ holds, then the output assertion of the concrete operation β_{out} is strong enough to imply the abstract postcondition β_{post}.

In his paper, Hoare defines a technique similar to that given above for verifying the correctness of the implementation of an abstraction. His result differs in two respects: first, he did not deal with the issue of the validity of the representation, and second, he did not break the proof into several steps. The first of these is a fairly serious omission; the second is largely a matter of methodology and taste—we chose to divide the proof into steps for clarity and, to a lesser extent, for methodology, for modularity, and to facilitate mechanical verification.

[†]This condition is actually slightly stronger than is needed since we only need to ensure that those representations *reachable* by a finite sequence of applications of the concrete operations represent abstract objects; in practice, however, the stated theorem is not restrictive since I_{a} can be made stronger if necessary. Note, by the way, that we need not prove the converse, that $I_{\mathrm{a}}(y)$ implies the existence of an x such that $y = \mathrm{rep}(x) \wedge I_{\mathrm{c}}(x)$, since this is guaranteed for reachable abstract objects by steps 1–4.

Steps 1–4 together imply the hypotheses of a theorem in Hoare's paper. That theorem says that if sufficient properties have been shown to hold for the implementation of some abstraction, then a concrete program using this implementation will produce the (representation of the) same result as an abstract program would have.[†] We shall not reproduce the proof of this theorem here, but simply note that it proceeds by induction on the length of the sequence of applications of operations in the abstract program. Steps 1 and 2 establish the basis step; steps 3 and 4 are used to establish the induction.

In the next section we shall turn to the description of ALPHARD and in particular to how the various pieces of information required by the proof technique are supplied. First, however, we must say a few words about the predicate language—the language in which β_{pre}, and so on, are expressed. The real issue here, of course, is the language used for expressing the abstract predicates I_a, β_{init}, β_{pre}, and β_{post}. (The concrete predicates, e.g., I_c, are stated in terms of whatever predicate language was used in the specification of the next lower level abstractions.)

In the example we shall give below, the definitions are stated in terms of the mathematical notion of a "sequence". We presume the properties of sequences are defined elsewhere, and in particular are known to the verifier. An axiomatic definition of sequences may be found in [Dahl *et al.* 72]; a version adapted to the needs of the example to follow is included below for completeness.

The following defines the notion of a sequence:
1. Let D be a set called the "domain" of elements, of a sequence; then
   (a) $\langle \, \rangle$ is a sequence, the "null" sequence;
   (b) if x is a sequence and $d \in D$, then $x \sim \langle d \rangle$ is a sequence;
   (c) the only sequences are as specified in (a) and (b).
2. The notation $\langle d1, d2, \ldots, dn \rangle$ is an abbreviation for $\langle d1 \rangle \sim \langle d2 \rangle \sim \cdots \sim \langle dn \rangle$.
3. The following functions and relations are defined:
   (a) $\text{last}(x \sim \langle d \rangle) = d$,
   (b) $\text{leader}(x \sim \langle d \rangle) = x$,
   (c) $x \sim (y \sim z) = (x \sim y) \sim z$,
   (d) $\text{first}(\langle d \rangle) = d \wedge (x \neq \langle \, \rangle \Rightarrow \text{first}(x \sim \langle d \rangle) = \text{first}(x))$,
   (e) $\text{trailer}(\langle d \rangle) = \langle \, \rangle \wedge (x \neq \langle \, \rangle \Rightarrow \text{trailer}(x \sim \langle d \rangle) = \text{trailer}(x) \sim \langle d \rangle)$
   (Note: first, last, leader, and trailer are undefined for the null sequence $\langle \, \rangle$),
   (f) $\text{length}(\langle \, \rangle) = 0 \wedge \text{length}(x \sim \langle d \rangle) = 1 + \text{length}(x)$.

[†]Assuming, of course, that both the abstract and concrete programs terminate.

4. If V is a vector whose elements are in D and n and m are integers, then seq(V, n, m) is an abbreviation defined by:

$$n > m \Rightarrow \text{seq}(V, n, m) = \langle\ \rangle$$
$$n \leqslant m \Rightarrow \text{seq}(V, n, m) = \langle V[n], V[n+1], \ldots, V[m]\rangle.$$

It appears that a relatively small set of such notions, e.g., the integers, sets, and sequences should be adequate for defining a large and useful collection of abstractions. At the moment it also appears to be easier for the programmer to use such specifications rather than to axiomatize each new abstraction. We also see this approach as relatively easy to automate. Thus, for the moment at least, we envision using this type of specification. Note, however, that this is not a language issue and we are prepared to reverse our field if the situation warrants.

4. ALPHARD

In this section I would like to illustrate how the issues of structure and verification manifest themselves in the ALPHARD design. Please keep in mind, however, that my intent is primarily to expose general language design considerations, not to talk about ALPHARD. Thus I won't discuss all of ALPHARD, and in fact I'll gloss over or grossly simplify many of the most important features of ALPHARD.

First, consider the structural issues raised earlier. Obviously the notion of abstraction played a central role in that discussion, as did the premise that understandability must be a property of the program text. The notion of an abstraction is closely related to that of "type" as it appears in many contemporary languages. In particular, Simula [Dahl and Nygaard 66] introduced the notion of a "class" to tie together the notion of the representation of a type and the implementation of operations on it. This encapsulation mechanism is taken as much of the basis for ALPHARD. In particular, we adopt the syntax

> **form** $A =$
> **beginform**
> $\vdots$
> **endform**;

to define a new abstract concept A. (Note that here, as throughout the sequel, ellipses are used to denote further detail that I wish to ignore for the moment.)

The purpose of such a definition is to introduce a new abstract concept, to give it a name, A in this case, to define its properties, and to define how it is to be implemented. The latter two issues, the properties and implementation, are those we prefer to defer for the moment; however, both are defined by the text that appears between the **beginform** and **endform**. Note that the notion of a form as used here is essentially identical to that of "type" in the discussion of verification; the ALPHARD form is used for more than type definitions, hence the change in terminology.

We must carefully distinguish between an abstract concept and an *instance* of it. Thus, for example, "computer" is an abstract concept; the particular computer on which this text is being prepared is an instance of the abstraction. Our language must contain the ability to create instances of an abstraction; it will often be the case that we have several instances of an abstraction and we shall want to name them so that we may talk about the distinct instances. One way to do this (but not the only way) is in a declaration:

> **local** $x:A$;

Such a declaration has the effect of creating an instance of the abstract notion A (instantiating A) and giving the name x to this particular instance. In the jargon of programming language, we "bind" the name x to an instantiation of A.

As another example, one that we shall follow through the sequel in some detail, we might wish to introduce the abstract concept of a (finite depth) stack of integers. Such an abstraction would be introduced by a declaration such as

> **form** $i$stack(n:integer) =
>   **beginform**
>   ⋮
>   **endform**;

where n is the permissible depth of the stack. Subsequent to this declaration, specific stacks might be declared as

> **local** S1:$i$stack(42);
>   ⋮
> **local** S2:$i$stack(13);
>   ⋮

The abstract program which uses the notion of an *istack* will apply stack operations to the instances of this abstraction. The **form** *istack* must specify how the stack is to be represented and how the abstract operations are implemented in terms of this representation. To permit the verification of the abstract program and the implementation of the abstraction to be independent, the body of the **form** must also supply a precise specification of the abstraction. Thus, in general a **form** is composed of three parts:

> **form** $i$stack(n:integer) =
>   **beginform**
>   **specifications** . . . ;
>   **representation** . . . ;
>   **implementation** . . . ;
>   **endform**;

At the very least, the **specifications** must provide the names of the operations supplied by the form together with the types of their arguments and results. To permit verification, however, we must add (1) the initial value of the abstract entity, and (2) the pre- and postconditions. Using the mathematical notion of a sequence, defined earlier, we can write

> **form** $i$stack(n:integer) =
>   **beginform**
>   **specifications**
>   **requires** $n > 0$;
>   **invariant** $i$sseq($i$stack) $\wedge$ 0 $\leqslant$ length($i$stack) $\leqslant$ n;
>   **initially** $i$stack = nullseq;
>   **function**
>   push(s:$i$stack, x:integer)
>   **pre**   0 $\leqslant$ length(s) $< n$ **post** $s = s' \sim x$
>   pop(s:$i$stack)
>   **pre**   0 $<$ length(s) $\leqslant$ n **post** $s = $ leader(s'),
>   top(s:$i$stack)   **returns**(x:integer)
>   **pre**   0 $<$ length(s) $\leqslant$ n **post** $x = $ last(s');
>   **representation** . . . ;
>   **implementation** . . . ;
>   **endform**;

Note how the various pieces of information needed about the abstraction implemented by the **form** are introduced; the **requires** clause specifies β_{req}, the **invariant** clause specifies I_a, the **initially** clause specifies β_{init}, and each of the **function** clauses specifies β_{pre} and β_{post} for that function.

In this case, then, the notion of an $i$stack is defined in terms of the mathematical notion of a sequence of bounded length. The operation pop, for example, is defined to produce a new sequence that is just like the old one except that its last element has been deleted. (In the postconditions the primed symbols, e.g., s', refer to the value of the symbol prior to execution of the operation.)

This particular example allows us to illustrate something that was awkward to introduce in the more abstract discussion in the previous section. Because the **form** may be parametrized, it is more properly a *type* *generator* (that is, it defines a set of *types*) than a simple type definition. Note that not all values of the parameters may make sense. In this case, for example, a stack of negative size is senseless. Restrictions on the parameters are conveniently expressed in β_{req}, that is, the **requires** portion of the **specifications**.

The **representation** portion must define the data structure to be used by each instantiation of the **form** to represent the abstraction. It also specifies (1) the initialization to be performed whenever the **form** is instantiated, (2) the rep function, and (3) the concrete invariant. Thus, this section provides the major information relating an abstract entity and its concrete representation.

For this example we have chosen a simple representation for the stack. A vector holds the contents of the stack and an integer variable points to the top of the stack.

```
form istack(n: integer) =
  beginform
    specifications . . . ;
    representation
      unique   v: vector(integer, 1, n), sp: integer init   sp ← 0;
      rep (v, sp) = seq(v, 1, sp);
      invariant   sp ⩾ 0 ∧ sp ⩽ n;
    implementation . . . ;
  endform;
```

The first clause of the **representation** portion describes the data structure(s) to be used concretely to represent the abstraction; the key word **unique** used here indicates that the following data structure(s) are unique to each instantiation (as opposed to being shared by, or **common** to, all instantiations). The **rep** clause specifies the representation function—the mapping from concrete objects to abstract ones. The **invariant** clause specifies I_c. Also, note the init clause attached to the data structure declaration; this is the distinguished operation C_{init} mentioned in the previous section. The initialization operation is automatically invoked whenever an instantiation of the **form** is created, and is responsible for establishing β_{init}.

At this point we would also like to point out the use of the names "vector" and "integer" in this example. These are *not* primitive *types* of the language, they are simply **form** names. They happen to be the names of **forms** that are automatically provided along with the compiler, but they are not special in any other way.

From experience in writing **forms,** we have found that it is convenient to add another piece of information to the **representation**—a set of **state** definitions. These states are merely a shorthand for a set of boolean conditions, but, as we shall see below, they help to accent certain interesting situations. So, a more complete version of the **representation** portion of the **form** is

```
form   istack(n: integer) =
  beginform
    specifications . . . ;
    representation
      unique   v: vector(integer, 1, n),
               sp: integer   init   sp ← 0;
      rep(v, sp) = seq(v, 1, sp);
      invariant   sp ⩾ 0 ∧ sp ⩽ n;
      states
        mt              when   sp = 0,
        normal          when   sp ⩾ 0 ∧ sp < n,
        full            when   sp = n,
        err             otherwise;
    implementation . . . ;
  endform;
```

The **implementation** portion of the **form** contains the bodies of the functions listed in the **specifications**, together with their concrete input and output assertions (β_{in} and β_{out}). In defining these function bodies we make use of the states defined in the **representation** part. The **state** of the representation is determined when any function in the **form** is invoked, but is not reevaluated as changes to the representation are made within a function body. Thus the state may be used, as in this example, to select one of several possible bodies for a function when it is called. In this particular example the ability to select alternate bodies is used only for error detection, but it is certainly not limited to this use.

```
form istack(n: integer) =
  beginform
    specifications . . . ;
    representation . . . ;
    implementation
      body   push   out (s.sp = s.sp′ + 1 ∧ s.v = α(s.v′, s.sp′, x)) =
             mt, normal::   (s.sp ← s.sp + 1; s.v[s.sp] ← x);
             otherwise:: FAIL;
      body   pop   out   (s.sp = s.sp′ − 1) =
             normal, full:: s.sp ← s.sp − 1;
             otherwise:: FAIL;
      body   top   out   (x = s.v[s.sp]) =
             normal, full:: x ← s.v[s.sp];
             otherwise:: FAIL;
  endform;
```

Note that in this example the input assertions for the concrete operations were omitted. When this happens, the input assertion for each alternative body is assumed to be the **state** condition for that body, or *true* if no **state** selection is being used. Thus the **state** definitions provide a standard set of input assertions for function bodies; these **state** assertions are *and*ed as appropriate with the explicit assertions on function bodies to produce the complete input assertion. The notation $\alpha(V, n, x)$, used in the output assertion of *push*, denotes a vector identical to V except that $V_n = x$. Finally, the symbol FAIL used above is intended to connote failure—we prefer to avoid a detailed discussion of the exception mechanism and hence will avoid further elaboration of this symbol here.

The purpose of this example, of course, was to illustrate how the issues of structure, modification, and verification might impact the design of a programming language. It also illustrates, in a more indirect way, the consideration of precise semantic definition. I have not illustrated enough of the language to make the following point completely, but let me try.

Note that, for example, the identifiers *vector* and *integer* were not boldface in the example. By inference these familiar data types and constructors do not have a special role in ALPHARD—they are merely **forms** similar to ones that a user may define for himself. (Their only claim to uniqueness is that they are predefined by the compiler.) In particular, each of the operations provided by these forms is defined in terms of abstract pre-and postconditions Thus, the semantics of at least the data operators of a complete program are axiomatically defined. This is true of control as well, but we have not exhibited the machinery to illustrate this. The real point is that axiomatic definitions of semantics appear more useful for verification than operational ones.

5. CONCLUSION AND ACKNOWLEDGMENTS

The next generation of programming languages must come to grips with the fact that human writers and readers of programs can deal with only limited complexity. They must facilitate and encourage programs each of whose components as well as the relations among these components lies safely within these limits. Further, to permit the next increment in the complexity of the programs we write, the foundations on which these programs are built must be more secure; in short, verification is essential. The next generation of programming languages must facilitate verification.

These are not new ideas; they have been said many times by many people. In particular, the ALPHARD group has been invaluable in sharpening my own thoughts on these issues: Mary Shaw, Anita Jones, Mario Barbacci, Paul Hilfinger, Karla Perdue, and Kamesh Ramakrishna. I also owe a great debt to Ralph London, particularly with relation to verification.

REFERENCES

Boehm, B., The high cost of software. *Proc. Symp. High Cost of Software, Naval Postgraduate School, Monterey, California, September 1973.*

Dahl, O. J., and Nygaard, K., Simula—an ALGOL-based simulation language. *Comm. ACM* **9** 9, 671–678 (September 1966).

Dahl, O. J., Dijkstra, E. W., and Hoare, C. A. R., *Structured Programming.* Academic Press, New York, 1972.

Dijkstra, E. W., Programming considered as a human activity. *Proc. IFIP Cong. 1965,* 213–217.

Dijkstra, E. W., A constructive approach to the problem of program correctness. *BIT* **8,** 174–186 (1968).

Hoare, C. A. R., An axiomatic basis for computer programming. *Comm. ACM* **12** 10, 576–580, 583 (October 1969).

Hoare, C. A. R., Proof of correctness of data representations. *Acta Informat.* **1,** 271–281 (1972).

Knuth, D. E., Structured programming with **goto** statements. *Computing Surveys* **6** 4, 261–301 (December 1974).

Parnas, D., On the criteria to be used in decomposing systems into modules. *Comm. ACM* **15** 12, 1053–1058 (December 1972).

Wirth, N., Program development by stepwise refinement. *Comm. ACM* **14** 4, 221–227 (April 1971).

Wulf, W. A., A case against the **goto**. *Proc. ACM Conf., Boston, Massachusetts, August 1972,* 791–797.

Excerpts from the Symposium Panel Discussions

THE LITTLE ENGINES THAT COULD! We Think We Can . . . We Think We Can . . . We Think We Can . . . (Experiences with C.mmp)

Ed McCreight (Moderator), Bill Broadley, Sam Fuller, Philip Karlton, Victor Lesser, Roy Levin, and Allen Newell

> C.mmp was the first multiprocessor in the CMU environment. Many research groups (hardware designers, operating system developers, application developers), each with their own objectives, share this hardware. The "little engines" panel discussed the symbiosis and the tensions that resulted. Though some could build on the completed work of others, many researchers were confronted with what Ed McCreight dubbed "error 33".

MCCREIGHT: One commits error 33 if the ability to do one's research is based on the not-yet-complete results of somebody else's research. For example, users complained that they were forced to live with an incomplete, developing software environment. One aspect of this issue is the problem of developing software that does not contribute to anyone's research, but that is necessary to make the system a tolerably comfortable environment in which to compute.

NEWELL: Suppose I have a new system; it is thus by definition a system that does not have enough software. I have a bunch of users who are waiting to use it. I assert, then, that it is simply not possible to get enough manpower to produce software that makes the system look comfortable to the users. Users go right through to the software boundary; they are ready to exploit what's there and are always going to be operating against the boundary of things that are not yet there.

FULLER: When in developing benchmarks we come up against the sharp edges we are rather sympathetic for the following reason: Hydra-C.mmp is the first operational multiprocessor in this department, and we're putting these benchmarks on

---

Selected, slightly edited, and assembled by the Editor.

it for exactly that reason. So, the fact that we might come up against some rough edges is the very reason it is researched.

NEWELL: So your proposition is that if you're cut and bleeding, you know it's research.

McCREIGHT: I wonder if the learning curve for people first encountering Hydra-C.mmp is just another penalty that one pays for exploring the world of multiprocessors. How do you debug a process that is in 17 states in 17 processors. You can't just shout, "Stop."

One paradigm for doing research is what Newell defined in his invited talk as the "Reddy Principle" namely, "When in doubt, sprout." A researcher can choose to develop several approaches in parallel to his problem, hoping that one thread among them will be fruitful.

WULF: It seems to me that there is something slightly different about an operating system that is intended to be used, and the speech system that is a demonstration of a concept. We face the issue of to what extent it is reasonable to rig up quick and dirty solutions to problems. In the multiple-thread approach, every thread is going to have a set of incompatible assumptions and every user gets seduced into using one of those threads. When he has to change, he loses by definition; at best, he has to make massive changes.

NEWELL: The answer is that if you can move fast enough, you can scrap the iterations on applications.

LESSER: We talked about a multiple strategy with respect to Hydra or with respect to C.mmp. I would have liked a simpler version of an operating system that you could have gotten enough applications earlier in the game, explored what are the crucial parameters of problem decomposition, for instance process communication ports.

NEWELL: With regard to the small address problem, I'm not sure there was a better decision to be made about processor selection. There was a fair amount of flap about why we did not do anything really sexy in the implementation of the switch. I do believe the worst decision was not bringing up multiple operating systems in order to let a set of users get experience a year earlier than they could have otherwise, to begin to produce that feedback that would have helped in the adjustments all along the way.

LESSER: When I first came here and worked on the multiprocessor, I said we didn't have to worry about hardware architecture; that we had something, and to just get on with some applications. And that the 16-bit address space issue won't be a major problem. But it has turned into a major problem for the Hearsay-II effort on C.mmp—defining an overlay structure in a modular fashion in the face of expanding data structures is difficult.

NEWELL: What one has to ask is the question, If you look at the rate at which things actually move, not the dissatisfaction of the users while they're in the process of helping it move, then what is being stymied and what is moving too slow? But you can't use the sensation of the users who will, by their very adaptive nature, find all the things that are not ready in the system, no matter how many things are ready.

METHODS FOR PROGRAM PRODUCTION

Ralph London (Moderator), Robert Floyd, Jim King, Jim Mitchell, George Robertson, and Mary Shaw

> The panel focused on the tools that assist the programmer in developing quality software, that is, software that is reliable, maintainable, modifiable, understandable, verifiable, and (optimistically) low in cost. The spectrum of issues includes language design, programming methodologies and strategies, programming environments, team organization, and program testing and verification.

KING: I think that during the last ten years there appeared to be a genuine crisis brewing in producing software. There were a lot of facts and figures to show that we've done a fairly bad job of producing large software systems. But, I'd like to propose that the last ten years were a historical coincidence of several factors that are no longer in play. I think the schools are training people to approach computer programming in a much more rational way, and they do have training; the people building these systems have built them before and they are beginning to have experience.

MITCHELL: I think we could solve a lot of problems if we simply had a press conference today, and declared the software crisis to be over.

FLOYD: I don't very often write programs any more and decided that I should make a virtue of necessity. I decided to come here and say that at least sometime, not too far in the future, none of us should write programs. I see the possibility of the guy who used to be a programmer becoming in some sense a policymaker. He comes to the computer and defines objects. Basically, he gives definitions that may not be direct, but may be recursive definitions or be definitions by property. He gives definitions that can be made operational in some way or other, and he expects the computer to have a reasonable amount of facility in expanding those definitions into something that can be computed. The mode of action will probably be interactive and if he hasn't specified enough, the computer can come back to get advice from him on an exception basis. We take this for granted already in our organizational behavior. Somebody managing an office doesn't tell people how to do their jobs; he tells them what policies he wants carried out, what goals he wants to reach, and insofar as those goals lie within the reach of standard techniques, he doesn't have to say how.

SHAW: A program is like a growing, changing, living, breathing object. We develop it; we change it. The things that we do to it need to be assimilated in a single information structure. A program can be thought of as a data base that is capable of accepting information, that has functions capable of massaging that information to derive new information and to spread the new information around, possibly updating old information that has been outdated by the changes that have been made.

FLOYD: It is worthwhile to program in such a way to avoid putting into the program many different representations of the same thing.

SHAW: I think that it's not so much important to have only a singular representation as it is to have it possible to mechanically update all the others that we want changed, so that only one thing has to be maintained.

MITCHELL: I have a feeling that unless we change our genetic makeup that documentation is forever going to be a problem. When I program, I'm highly motivated and excited; a lot of things are flying through my mind that ultimately I will regard as design decisions. And I'm not interested in writing them down. If there were some easy way to capture them, like voice protocols, that would be a help.

MITCHELL: Mary said that she thought that programs were growing, living, changing, breathing objects; I think that the word "breathing" should be changed to "breeding". Aside from the initial production of the program, adapting systems during their useful lifetimes seems to be an even greater problem.

KING: If I had to spend my money on something, I think I'd spend it on data abstraction languages. I believe strongly in what I read into those languages—that we're trying to get the documentation into the program and to show the hierarchy. On the other hand, I'd probably spend even more of my money on training people and getting the right people.

KING: If you look at the big factors in reliability and productivity of programmers, I think you'll find it's in the guy who wrote it, and not in the tools he uses.

ROBERTSON: Given the high variability of programmer talent, we may have to have different sets of tools for the best programmers and the worst programmers.

ROBERTSON: One way you can increase the ability of an average programmer is to make him do some of the maintenance on some average program. Let him see how bad it is and what he has to do to fix it up.

BOB BALZER: One of the traps that we've fallen into is to say, "Well we have to do better what we're doing now." I think it's the root of that problem that we attempt during maintenance to deal with an optimized object and that's what's terrible, because optimization spreads related pieces of knowledge far apart. To deal with an object in that state is absolutely ridiculous. What we need, therefore, is a technology that allows us to perform our modifications before that optimization occurs, saving immense energy.

MITCHELL: Changes to any system increase its complexity and decrease its capacity for future change. The cost of a change to a system tends to be much more a function of the size of the system than of the complexity of the change. The side effects of proposed changes are often more surprising and devastating than the intended alteration. Every housekeeper knows to clean up after every change. Put some energy back into the system to decrease its entropy again, rather than putting in the change. Throw it away after n changes, no matter what. I remember a quote in Knuth, about some of the best systems resulting from dropping the source deck.

WHAT CAN COMPUTATIONAL COMPLEXITY AND ARTIFICIAL INTELLIGENCE LEARN FROM EACH OTHER?

Joe Traub (Moderator), Jerry Feldman, John Gaschnig, Don Loveland, Albert Meyer, and Herbert Simon

The main concern of this discussion is whether there is some common meeting ground between those interested in computational complexity and those interested in artificial intelligence. Computational complexity results show that combinatorial explosions occur in many problems and, in general, are not avoidable. Heuristics have been successfully used to solve artificial intelligence problems at less than exponential cost.

MEYER: I want to talk mainly about the results of complexity theory that have to do with theorem proving, which is one problem that has been of concern to people in artificial intelligence, although certainly not the only one. But it is one area in which we have a lot of theoretical results. But what are those results? Well, to begin with, when we look at this problem of theorem proving, there is a well-established historical notation for describing mathematical sentences, the language of logic—first-, second-, and higher-order logic. The meaning of a statement in that language is mathematically well-understood and rigorously defined. We also have had a notion of what a proof of such a formal statement in this language would consist of. Both the notion of an algorithm and of a computable function have been well-understood for some time. And these notions play a critical role, even in this discussion about proofs, because part of the definition of a proof is that it should be something that can be seen to be correct by an algorithm. You don't have to understand it, you just check it.

So all these words do have solid precise definitions. As soon as this happens, precise definitions, one can start proving negative results about them. There are two major kinds of negative results. The first is the blow to the great Hilbert program of capturing all of mathematics in a mechanical system. Godel's incompleteness theorem says that that can't be done—there is no way to embody in a finite set of axioms and a finite set of effective rules of proof, a system that would enable you to prove all of the true statements about numbers. One can rigorously prove theorems that say roughly that if you have a formal system that is capable of enabling you to do true statements, then there will be statements that will be true and that cannot be proven in this system. And the statements are of the size that they contain a few more bits of characters in length than the number of bits used to build your defining system. The second major theoretical obstacle is that you can't even tell of an assertion, written in pure logical language, whether or not it's logically tautologous, whether or not it's valid. That's the undecidability of the predicate calculus.

Now I've filled you in on the classical background; that will give you a way to understand the complexity results, which are very much the same kind of results. Here we take a class of more restricted notations, usually a logical calculus of some kind, which in theory is decidable; this means that, in theory, there is an algorithm with the property that if you drop in any sentence in this language, there is a calculational procedure to prove it and to deduce whether or not it's true. However, the complexity results say that any algorithm that carries out this process, and that always gives a correct answer, must take an inconceivably large amount of time compared to the size of the sentences to which it is applied. And when one looks carefully at the proofs one can get out hard numbers that are depressingly small: they indicate that this phenomenon occurs quite early.

SIMON: Artificial intelligence has always been concerned with computational complexity, although perhaps not always in a very formal way. We know that artificial intelligence is very often concerned with tree search, and that tree searches tend to be exponential. While exponential searches cause a lot of our everyday difficulties in building programs, they hold no deep terror for us. We've lived with them for many years now. Now, the kinds of complexity problems that one has found in the artificial intelligence literature (where there have been some attempts at formalization) have not been attempts to show that a particular algorithm solves all problems of a given class in a reasonable time, but rather have gone to the question of how one should design an algorithm so that it does less search than some other algorithms. These formalisms address different questions than the formalisms that AI has been talking about, and I think that one thing we might try to clarify is whether there is any way of going from one end of this road to the other.

One idea that is stolen from human practice, an awfully good place to get ideas, is that maybe the reason we have the illusion that large numbers of things are computable is that we only notice the ones that we've computed. So what we may have is the illusion that most problems can be solved. Perhaps human beings working forward from what they already know, working forward from the theorems that they already have, prove other theorems. And that there are a large number of theorems that you can prove in reasonable computing time. So if you really want to have success in life proving theorems, what you should not do is start with Fermat's Last Theorem, or the four-color problem. Instead, you ought to start with a nice axiom system and see what you can get in the way of new theorems out of that axiom system.

Now another possibility is that if we are interested in a class of problems, say, tree searches, we're interested in a class of problems that don't have unique solutions, but where there are many potential solutions. Then we can talk about something called solution density in that tree, and at least in some probabilistic sense, we ought to be able to talk about expected length of search as a function of solution density. We ought to formulate our AI problems as far as we can, as problems of satisficing, of searching for "good enough" solutions.

Consider the mutilated-checkerboard problem. Approached as a combinatorial problem, to be solved by trying all possible ways of laying down the dominoes, it is a very big problem. Yet, we all know that there is a shift in the problem space that makes it a trivial problem, that can be solved by almost anybody who searches for a solution. This suggests that if we go to richer domains, with more powerful predicates, that the complexity of problems may decrease a great deal. I'm struck by the fact that some of the complexity results hold for very impoverished arithmetic systems; maybe one reason for the lengths of proofs of some simple results in such a system is the impoverished character of the system, impoverished in that you don't have any very powerful inference methods in it. Many things that are complicated in that system can become uncomplicated if you move into a metalanguage that allows you a richer set

MEYER: What can we deduce from the theoretical results? I'm making a judgment, but I feel it is a fair judgment on what one can read out of the mathematics. Consider the basically naive notion: "If we just truncate the problem, we will be able to cope with it even though, in general, it's either hopelessly complex or undecidable." I don't believe it. What the technical results do say is, you can put an upper bound on everything. The AI community says, "We want our systems to be smart. We're going to build knowledge in that's going to guide the search in some heuristic fashion." My response to that is, "Great! Let's do it." The only thing that bothers me now is where is the theoretical basis for thinking it's going to work? It's worth trying, probably. The payoff seems to be very high. But it seems to me that the burden of proof that this strategy can work lies more with the AI community.

SIMON: There's a very simple argument that should appeal to the theorists; it's a theoretical argument. Why do we think we can imitate people? Because people imitate people; people are machines, and all of the theorems of uncomputability, undecidability you prove about Turing machines are just as applicable to systems made out of organic molecules as they are to systems made out of inorganic molecules. Or, if that's not true, we know no reason for thinking that is not true. So, what you've proved is either that AI programs are possible, or that people are impossible and I'll let you choose the alternative.

Contributed Talks

PETER B. ANDREWS, Theorem-Proving Using Matings

ROBERT M. BALZER, An Automatically Generated Program for Message Distribution

MICHAEL L. COLEMAN, System Modification in an Operational Environment

L. ERMAN, F. HAYES-ROTH, V. LESSER, D. R. REDDY, L. SHOCKEY and CSD Speech Group, Overview of the HEARSAY Speech Understanding Research

NICHOLAS V. FINDLER, Studies in Machine Cognition Using the Game of Poker

DAVID A. FISHER, A Common High-Order Programming Language for the Department of Defense

S. H. FULLER, D. P. SIEWIOREK and R. J. SWAN, The Design of a Multi-Micro-Computer System

JOHN GASCHNIG, An Analytic Measure of the Power of Heuristics in A*

CHARLES M. GESCHKE, Designing an Instruction Set for Executing Mesa Programs

JAMES J. GILLOGLY, Applied AI at Rand

FREDERICK HAYES-ROTH and DAVID J. MOSTOW, Syntax and Semantics Knowledge in the HEARSAY-II Speech Understanding System

FREDERICK HAYES-ROTH, J. BURGE and J. McDERMOTT, Computer Based Approaches to Learning

RUDOLPH A. KRUTAR, A Pocket Language for a Pocket Computer

H. T. KUNG, Searching on C.mmp

GORDON LILLY, Ultrahigh-Performance Computing for Weather Modeling

NELSON L. MAX, A Computer Animation of Sphere Eversion

JOSEPH RINDE, Centralized Network Routing

GEORGE ROBERTSON, Software Experiments: A Progress Report

MICHAEL IAN SHAMOS, Surprises in Computational Geometry

MARK STICKEL, Mechanical Theorem Proving and Artificial Intelligence Languages

ROBERT W. TAYLOR, Human Communication—The Social Relevance of University and Industry Computer Science

Demonstrations

DRAGON on C.mmp
  Multiprocessor PDP-11 version of the DRAGON speech system

Segmentation in Vision
  A film showing the picture segmentation process of CMU's vision system

HEARSAY-I
  A film showing the operation and principles of CMU's HEARSAY-I speech system

Sphere Eversion
  A computer-animation film showing the topological process of turning a sphere inside out

HEARSAY-II
  A demonstration of the HEARSAY-II speech system in its current state of development

HEARSAY-I
  A live demonstration of HEARSAY-I understanding spoken chess commands

Graphics Display Processor
  A demonstration of the capabilities of CMU's graphics displays

Color Video Display
  A demonstration of CMU's system for producing color pictures

Production Systems
  A demonstration of some classical AI programs (Tic-Tac-Toe and GPS)

C.mmp Benchmarks
  Demonstration of multiprocessor algorithms implemented on C.mmp

Symbolic Manipulation of Computer Descriptions
  Demonstration of programs to help mechanize the computer design process

Chess Programs
  Demonstration and comparison of chess programs

Chess Endgames
  Demonstration of a chess endgame program

HYDRA
  Demonstration of the performance–evaluation features of the HYDRA
  operating system running on C.mmp

T HIS BOOK was produced almost entirely by computer. Like so many other projects, it probably would have been easier to do it by hand, but we didn't, and in the long process of interfacing an academic computer with commercial typesetting, we think that both parties have benefited. With only a couple of exceptions authors entered their text into a local computer. This digitized text was shipped to CMU's PDP-10 computer, and the many document-formatting dialects were standardized. Once the text was online, a mockup of the finished book was made at CMU on a Xerox Graphics Printer, using the PUB document compiler. Geographically local authors, or alternatively Brian Reid, Anita Jones, Guy Almes, and David Lamb, worked with chapter mockups, editing their text online and producing new mockup chapters as needed, until they were happy with their appearance. The final mockups were sent to Academic Press, whose editors copymarked them for uniformity of spelling, typography, and style, then returned the copymarked pages to CMU, where the changes were made online. The finished text was then processed, using a special variant version of PUB developed for this purpose, to produce input to a commercial typesetter's computer-driven system. Alas, the operation of getting the text out of our PDP-10 computer and into the typesetter's CDC-6600 computer was fraught with problems. Many many unreadable magnetic tapes later, we finally resorted to shipping boxes of punched cards from CMU to the typesetter. Page proof corrections were entered manually. The result of this venture is more than a book: we have a system for producing more books by the same mechanism, and have learned enough to be able to build a better system.